T4-AJR-763

SONG OF SONGS RABBAH
An Analytical Translation
Volume Two

Program in Judaic Studies
Brown University
BROWN JUDAIC STUDIES
Edited by
Jacob Neusner
Wendell S. Dietrich, Ernest S. Frerichs, William Scott Green,
Calvin Goldscheider, David Hirsch, Alan Zuckerman

Project Editors (Projects)

David Blumenthal, Emory University (Approaches to Medieval Judaism)
William Brinner (Studies in Judaism and Islam)
Ernest S. Frerichs, Brown University (Dissertations and Monographs)
Lenn Evan Goodman, University of Hawaii (Studies in Medieval Judaism)
William Scott Green, University of Rochester (Approaches to Ancient Judaism)
Norbert Samuelson, Temple University (Jewish Philosophy)
Jonathan Z. Smith, University of Chicago (Studia Philonica)

Number 198
SONG OF SONGS RABBAH
An Analytical Translation
Volume Two
by
Jacob Neusner

SONG OF SONGS RABBAH
An Analytical Translation
Volume Two

SONG OF SONGS RABBAH TO SONG
CHAPTERS FOUR THROUGH EIGHT

by

Jacob Neusner

Scholars Press
Atlanta, Georgia

BM
517
.M72
A3
1989
v.2

SONG OF SONGS RABBAH
An Analytical Translation

© 1989
Brown University

Library of Congress Cataloging in Publication Data

Midrash rabbah. Song of Solomon. English.
   Song of Songs rabbah : an analytical translation / by Jacob
Neusner.
   p.   cm. -- (Brown Judaic studies ; no. 197-198)
   Translation of: Midrash rabbah, Song of Solomon.
   ISBN 1-55540-418-9 (v. 1. : alk. paper). -- ISBN 1-55540-419-7 (v.
2 : alk. paper)
   1. Bible. O.T. Song of Solomon--Commentaries--Early works to
1800. I. Neusner, Jacob, 1932-   . II. Title. II. Series.
BM517.M72A3   1989
296.1'4--dc20
                                    89-24055
                                    CIP

Printed in the United States of America
on acid-free paper

For

HERBERT BASSER
QUEENS UNIVERSITY

Principal exegete of Midrash texts in our time,
possessed of the union of erudition and wit,
strengthened by that love for the documents and their truths
that in the end brings to those who study diligently and appreciatively
the satisfactions
an indifferent world may deny.

Torah is its own reward.

Table of Contents

Part Six
PARASHAH SIX

Part Seven
PARASHAH SEVEN

Part Eight
PARASHAH EIGHT

Preface

Now concluding my sustained project of translating or retranslating every document of the canon of the Judaism of the Dual Torah that reached closure by the seventh century, I proceed to the second half of Song of Songs Rabbah, one of the Midrash compilations of the sixth century. This Midrash compilation forms part of a group assigned to the late fifth or early sixth centuries, the others being Lamentations Rabbah, Esther Rabbah I, and Song of Songs Rabbah I. In many ways, I think Song of Songs Rabbah is the greatest intellectual achievement of our sages of blessed memory,[1] because it surmounts the most formidable challenge of all of Scripture: understanding the Song of Songs as a metaphor. So far as our sages work out the meanings of the *is* in response to the messages of the *as-if*, in these pages we see with great clarity the outer limits of their labor. For here the *is* is the love of man for woman and woman for man, and the *as-if* is the love of God for Israel and Israel for God. But that is leaping from metaphor to metaphor, and that is precisely what our sages have done: like a hart, like a gazelle. In my language, they attain here that level of abstraction that fully exposes the deepest layers of sensibility within.

So real and concrete is that poetry that understanding its implicit meanings, identifying its hidden messages as an account of the lovers,

---

[1]Admittedly, I have reached the same judgment of every rabbinic document I have studied, in order and in sequence, falling in love with each in its day, then finding the next still more engaging. Still, now that I have completed my translation of all or large parts of every document produced by the Judaism of the Dual Torah – that is, the entire canon, from the Mishnah through the Bavli – I see this last one as in many ways the climax of the whole. From the laconic philosophy of the Mishnah through the erotic sensibility of Song of Songs Rabbah a single path moves always upward, from the concrete to the most abstract. And the road from the Mishnah down there to Song of Songs Rabbah up here surely is from this world and the everyday to the transcendent height attained in the pages of the document before us. So my profession of admiration for the compilers and authors whose work is before us is not merely the enthusiasm of the commited moment.

xii Song of Songs Rabbah: An Analytical Translation

God and Israel, and the urgency of their love for one another – these represent a triumph of the *as-if*-mentality over the mentality of the merely *is*. But, we rapidly realize, the poem is the metaphor, and the reality, the tangible and physical and material love of Israel for God and of God for Israel: the urgent, the never-fully satisfied desire of each for the other. The relationship so obsessive, pressing, immediate, finds its metaphor in the love of woman for man and man for woman. Given the character of the Song of Songs, our sages' power to grasp its wholly other meanings and plausibly to state them attests to the full givenness of their affirmations of God and Israel as the principal figures in contention – as the lover and the beloved must always contend – in this world. No wonder that, from most ancient times, the Song of Songs was understood as the holiest of Israel's sacred scriptures. And it is not surprising that a narrow and physical reading of the poem was dismissed with contempt by all those who insisted upon an honored place in the canon for the lyrics of love. Indeed, if we wish to measure how far the understanding of Scripture has traveled from the real meanings intended by Scripture's makers, we have only to consider how it is possible to read the Song of Songs in any other way but the one deemed implicit and self-evident by not only our sages of blessed memory but all those masters of Judaisms and Christianities that understood, as some contemporaries do not seem to, the reality of the love of God for us and of us for God. I am only last and least among those to fall in love with this Song – but solely through the mediation of our sages of blessed memory, theirs alone.

For the text, I follow the standard printed edition, there being no alternative so far as I know. For the date I am guided, as always, by what seems to me the established consensus of the moment, which I find in Moses D. Herr, "Midrash," *Encyclopaedia Judaica* 11:1511. Herr places Ruth Rabbah in the fifth century, along with Genesis Rabbah, Leviticus Rabbah, and Lamentations Rabbah; he lists as sixth-century compilations Pesiqta deRab Kahana, Esther Rabbah I, and Song of Songs Rabbah. In due course in this sequence of translations I shall turn to the last-named item. If the consensus shifts, all hypotheses of interpretation deriving from context will of course fall away. But nothing in my work of exposition and analysis will change, since I concentrate on the intrinsic traits of form and logic, rather than on extrinsic pieces of evidence, such as contents. The indicative characteristics of a document will not be altered by the assignment of a different date from the present one; they only will be seen in a different context.

Herr describes the whole group of later fifth and sixth century compilations of scriptural exegeses as follows: "These Midrashim all consist of a collection of homilies, sayings, and aggadot of the amoraim (and also of the tannaim) in Galilean Aramaic and rabbinical Hebrew, but they also include many Greek words. It seems that all these Midrashim, which are not mentioned in the Babylonian Talmud, were edited in Erez Israel in the fifth and sixth centuries C.E. Two types can be distinguished: exegetical and homiletical. The exegetical Midrash (Genesis Rabbah, Lamentations Rabbah, et al.) is a Midrash to one of the books of the Bible, containing comments on the whole book – on each chapter, on every verse, and at times on every word in the verse. The homiletical Midrash is either a Midrash to a book of the Pentateuch in which only the first verse...of the weekly portion is expounded...(e.g. Leviticus Rabbah), or a Midrash that is based only on the biblical and prophetic reading of special Sabbaths....in which, also, only the first verses are expounded (e.g., Pirkei deRav Kahana). In both cases in contrast to the exegetical Midrashim, the homiletical Midrashim contain almost no short homilies or dicta on variegated topics, but each chapter...constitutes a collection of homilies and sayings on one topic that seem to combine into one long homily on the specific topic" ("Midrash," p. 1510). While Herr's somewhat murky prose and imprecise categories (with "Midrash" used in a variety of distinct senses) are not always easy to follow, the main points as to the identification and dating of the documents seem to me to serve for the moment, absent any more rigorous rethinking of matters.

It remains to explain why I have done this large-scale project of Midrash translation, since my interests have moved far beyond the literary problems that engaged me when I originally turned to the earlier Midrash compilations. The place of this work in my larger program of present inquiry requires explanation. I am in process of exploring the requirements of the social description of a religion, with special interest in the philosophy, politics, and economics that a religious system lays out (or, may lay out) as its statement of the social order. That program, of course, carries forward the inquiry of Max Weber, founder of social science in the study of religion. In the preface of my *Ecology of Religion* (Nashville, 1989: Abingdon), I explain in some detail my reframing of the program of Max Weber. My aim is to set forth religion as an independent variable and so a primary component in the study of society.

Within the sequence of my own researches, now completing my third reading of the entire canon of formative Judaism, the work is readily situated. Since I have already demonstrated that documents are to be read as autonomous statements, not only in connection with other documents, and also as part of a continuity of all canonical writings, I determined to describe the politics, philosophy, and economics of the Mishnah and its associated writings, then to turn to what I have already shown is an autonomous, but connected, corpus, the Yerushalmi and its friends, particularly Genesis Rabbah and Leviticus Rabbah, and finally, at the third phase, to take up the Bavli and its colleagues. These, by all accounts, are Lamentations Rabbah, Esther Rabbah I, Ruth Rabbah, and Song of Songs Rabbah. In preparation for the third phase of my inquiry, therefore, I addressed these documents. As I have provided introductions to all of the earlier documents in the canon of formative Judaism, so I plan to introduce these in the proper way, following the model of my *Sifré to Deuteronomy. An Introduction* (Atlanta, 1987: Scholars Press for Brown Judaic Studies).

A further factor explains the particular timing of this work. Planning to begin the second phase – the economics, politics, and philosophy of the Yerushalmi and associated writings – at The Institute for Advanced Study in 1989-1990, I found that I had come to an end of the work on the first phase when, in 1988-1989, I had closed and sent to press *The Philosophy of Judaism: The First Principles.* The interval between the conclusion of the one stage and the commencement of the next seemed a good time to turn to the initial work, and thought, concerning the third stage, the one that is to come only beyond the description of what served for philosophy, politics, and economics in the second stage in the formation of Judaism, and that explains the occasion for studying the late Rabbah compilations. I have always wanted to reread and retranslate these final compilations of the formative age, and now I had the opportunity while planning the execution of the study of the second phase in the unfolding of the politics, philosophy, and economics of that same Judaism. That these writings are best associated with the Bavli will become clear in due course. I see no doubt whatsoever that in rhetoric and logic, these Rabbah compilations fall within the circle of the Bavli, and in my introductions, I shall explain why.

My thanks go to Oxford University Press for permission to reprint the Revised Standard Version translation of the Song of Songs (© 1962 by Oxford University Press), and to Professor Andrew M. Greeley for permission to reprint his rendition of the same poetry (© 1988 by Andrew M. Greeley Enterprises). In the Introduction to Volume I of this translation, which serves the present Volume as well, I explain why I think both responses to the poetry should be read side by side.

It is appropriate, also, to call attention to the generous support for my research provided by Brown University, which has paid the costs of formatting this book for the preparation of camera-ready copy; and to the conscientious and elegant presentation of the work by Mr. Joshua Bell, Verbatim Inc., Providence, Rhode Island, and his staff. The constant improvement in the aesthetic quality and accuracy of my books is owing to him and his proofreaders and formatters.

I acknowledge with real thanks the everyday help of Rabbi and Professor Bernard Mandelbaum, who was kind enough to read every line of my translation and criticize it. I have always benefited from his comments. This work could not go forward without the generous gift of his great learning. He is an ornament to The Jewish Theological Seminary of America, where he received his rabbinical education and served for decades in successive posts of great responsibility, including the Chancellorship. I greatly value his criticism and appreciate his friendship.

I have now translated or retranslated every document of the Judaism of the Dual Torah, whole or in large part: the Mishnah, Tosefta, the Talmud of the Land of Israel (twenty-nine out of thirty-nine tractates), the Talmud of Babylonia (six out of thirty-seven tractates), tractate Avot and The Fathers According to Rabbi Nathan, Sifra, Sifré to Numbers, Sifré to Deuteronomy, Mekhilta Attributed to R. Ishmael, Pesiqta deR. Kahana, Pesiqta Rabbati (five chapters), Genesis Rabbah, Leviticus Rabbah, Lamentations Rabbah, Esther Rabbah I, Ruth Rabbah, and Song of Songs Rabbah. I expect to translate some more Bavli-tractates in due course, when the need arises, and perhaps all those my former students and I have not already (re)translated. But most of the work is done; in fact, I have made three complete trips through the canon of the Judaism of the Dual Torah, with the passports, successively, of historian, literary critic, and historian of religion. This, the end of the third and beginning of my fourth trip, it is self-evident, will find my passport marked, historian of culture and of civilization, and the fifth, perhaps, even "theologian," to which honor I scarcely have aspired.

The Bible text is from the Revised Standard Version Bible, copyright 1946, 1952, 1971 by the Division of Christian Education of the National Council of the Churches of Christ in the USA, and is used by permission.

To have spent thirty-five years, from when I came to study at The Jewish Theological Seminary of America, every day, to this very day, in this work is to have spent life in a museum filled with compelling beauty, or to have spent life within an orchestra, or on a stage; it is to live out one's years amid the greatest creations of which humanity is capable – but among the greatest of them all. For in these always-compelling, always-engaging, always-insistent, urgent writings is to live surrounded by souls reaching out to God, searching into the depths of being for the image and likeness that make us metaphors, here on earth, for God in all being and beyond all time and space, forming the outer limits of all that was and is and will ever be. Who can compare! To what is comparison to be made! Here, within imagination, sentiment, and intellect, I have made my life among our sages of blessed memory, who in soul and mind have transcended all limits in their quest, through the Torah, for God. *Lekhakh nosarti.*

JACOB NEUSNER

September 1, 1989

The Institute for Advanced Study
Princeton, New Jersey 08540 USA

The Song of Songs
in the Revised Standard Version

[Translation: *The Oxford Annotated Bible with the Apocrypha. Revised Standard Version.* Edited by Herbert G. May and Bruce M. Metzger (New York, 1965: Oxford University Press), pp. 815-821. © 1962 by Oxford University Press. Reprinted by permission.]

The Song of Songs Chapter One

1:1   *The Song of Songs, which is Solomon's.*

1:2   *O that you would kiss me with the kisses of your mouth!*
For your love is better than wine.

1:3   *Your anointing oils are fragrant,*
your name is oil poured out;
therefore the maidens love you.

1:4   *Draw me after you, let us make haste.*
The king has brought me into his chambers.
We will exult and rejoice in you;
we will extol your love more than wine;
rightly do they love you.

1:5   *I am very dark, but comely,*
O daughters of Jerusalem,
like the tents of Kedar,
like the curtains of Solomon.

1:6   *Do not gaze at me because I am swarthy,*
because the sun has scorched me.
My mother's sons were angry with me,
they made me keeper of the vineyards;
but my own vineyard I have not kept!

1:7   *Tell me, you whom my soul loves,*
where you pasture your flock,
where you make it lie down at noon;
for why should I be like one who wanders
beside the flocks of your companions?

1:8   *If you do not know,*
O fairest among women,
follow in the tracks of the flock,
and pasture your kids

1

    beside the shepherds' tents.

1:9   I compare you, my love,
    to a mare of Pharaoh's chariots.

1:10   Your cheeks are comely with ornaments,
    your neck with strings of jewels.

1:11   We will make you ornaments of gold,
    studded with silver.

1:12   While the king was on his couch,
    my nard gave forth its fragrance.

1:13   My beloved is to me a bag of myrrh,
    that lies between my breasts.

1:14   My beloved is to me a cluster of
    henna blossoms,
    in the vineyards of En-gedi.

1:15   Behold, you are beautiful, my love;
    behold, you are beautiful;
    your eyes are doves.

1:16   Behold, you are beautiful, my beloved,
    truly lovely.
    Our couch is green;

1:17   the beams of our house are cedar,
    our rafters are pine.

The Song of Songs Chapter Two

2:1   I am a rose of Sharon,
    a lily of the valleys.

2:2   As a lily among brambles,
    so is my love among maidens.

2:3   As an apple tree among the trees of the wood,
    so is my beloved among young men.
    With great delight I sat in his shadow,
    and his fruit was sweet to my taste.

2:4   He brought me to the wine cellar,
    and his banner over me was love.

2:5   Sustain me with raisins,
    refresh me with apples;
    for I am sick with love.

2:6   O that his left hand were under my head,
    and that his right hand embraced me!

2:7   I adjure you, O daughters of Jerusalem,
    by the gazelles or the hinds of the field,
    that you not stir up nor awaken love
    until it please.

2:8   The voice of my beloved!
    Behold he comes,
    leaping upon the mountains,
    bounding over the hills.

2:9   My beloved is like a gazelle,
    or a young stag.
    Behold, there he stands
    behind our wall,

gazing in at the windows,
looking through the lattice.

2:10   *My beloved speaks and says to me,*
"Arise, my love, my fair one,
and come away;

2:11   *"for lo, the winter is past,*
the rain is over and gone.

2:12   *"The flowers appear on the earth,*
the time of singing has come,
and the voice of the turtledove is heard in our land.

2:13   *"The fig tree puts forth its figs,*
and the vines are in blossom;
they give forth fragrance.
"Arise, my love, my fair one,
and come away.

2:14   *"O my dove, in the clefts of the rock,*
in the covert of the cliff,
"let me see your face,
let me hear your voice,
"for your voice is sweet,
and your face is comely.

2:15   *"Catch us the foxes,*
the little foxes,
that spoil the vineyards,
for our vineyards are in blossom."

2:16   *My beloved is mine and I am his,*
he pastures his flock among the lilies.

2:17   *Until the day breathes*
and the shadows flee,
turn my beloved, be like a gazelle,
or a young stag upon rugged mountains.

The Song of Songs Chapter Three

3:1   *Upon my bed by night*
I sought him whom my soul loves;
I sought him, but found him not;
I called him, but he gave no answer.

3:2   *"I will rise now and go about the city,*
in the streets and in the squares;
I will seek him whom my soul loves."
I sought him but found him not.

3:3   *The watchmen found me,*
as they went about in the city.
"Have you seen him whom my soul loves?"

3:4   *Scarcely had I passed them,*
when I found him whom my soul loves.
I held him and would not let him go
until I had brought him into my mother's house,
and into the chamber of her that conceived me.

3:5   *I adjure you, O daughters of Jerusalem,*
by the gazelles or the hinds of the field,

that you not stir up nor awaken love
until it please.

3:6   What is that coming up from the wilderness,
like a column of smoke,
perfumed with myrrh and frankincense,
with all the fragrant powders of the merchant?

3:7   Behold it is the litter of Solomon!
About it are sixty mighty men
of the might men of Israel,

3:8   all girt with swords
and expert in war,
each with his sword at his thigh,
against alarms by night.

3:9   King Solomon made himself a palanquin,
from the wood of Lebanon.

3:10   He made its posts of silver,
its back of gold, its seat of purple;
it was lovingly wrought within
by the daughters of Jerusalem.

3:11   Go forth, O daughters of Zion,
and behold King Solomon,
with the crown with which his mother crowned him
on the day of his wedding,
on the day of the gladness of his heart.

The Song of Songs Chapter Four

4:1   Behold, you are beautiful, my love,
behold you are beautiful!
Your eyes are doves
behind your veil.
Your hair is like a flock of goats
moving down the slopes of Gilead.

4:2   Your teeth are like a flock of shorn ewes
that have come up from the washing,
all of which bear twins,
and not one among them is bereaved.

4:3   Your lips are like a scarlet thread,
and your mouth is lovely.
Your cheeks are like halves of a pomegranate
behind your veil.

4:4   Your neck is like the tower of David,
built for an arsenal,
whereon hang a thousand bucklers,
all of them shields of warriors.

4:5   Your two breasts are like two fawns,
twins of a gazelle,
that feed among the lilies.

4:6   Until the day breathes
and the shadows flee,
I will hie me to the mountain of myrrh
and the hill of frankincense.

4:7   *You are all fair, my love;*
         there is no flaw in you.

4:8   *Come with me from Lebanon, my bride;*
         come with me from Lebanon.
         Depart from the peak of Amana,
         from the peak of Senir and Hermon,
         from the dens of lions,
         from the mountains of leopards.

4:9   *You have ravished my heart, my sister, my bride,*
         you have ravished my heart with a glance of your eyes,
         with one jewel of your necklace.

4:10   *How sweet is your love, my sister, my bride!*
         how much better is your love than wine,
         and the fragrance of your oils than any spice!

4:11   *Your lips distill nectar, my bride;*
         honey and milk are under your tongue;
         the scent of your garments is like the scent of Lebanon.

4:12   *A garden locked is my sister, my bride,*
         a garden locked, a fountain sealed.

4:13   *Your shoots are an orchard of pomegranates*
         with all choicest fruits,
         henna with nard,

4:14   *nard and saffron, calamus and cinnamon,*
         with all trees of frankincense,
         myrrh and aloes,
         with all chief spices —

4:15   *a garden fountain, a well of living water*
         and flowing streams from Lebanon.

4:16   *Awake, O north wind,*
         and come, O south wind!
         Blow upon my garden,
         let its fragrance by wafted abroad.
         Let my beloved come to his garden,
         and eat its choicest fruits.

The Song of Songs Chapter Five

5:1   *I come to my garden, my sister, my bride,*
         I gather my myrrh with my spice,
         I eat my honeycomb with my honey,
         I drink my wine with my milk.
         Eat, O friends, and drink;
         drink deeply, O lovers!

5:2   *I slept, but my heart was awake.*
         Hark! my beloved is knocking.
         "Open to me, my sister, my love,
         my dove, my perfect one;
         for my head is wet with dew,
         my locks with the drops of the night."

5:3   *I had put off my garment,*
         how could I put it on?
         I had bathed my feet,

how could I soil them?

5:4   *My beloved put his hand to the latch,*
       and my heart was thrilled within me.

5:5   *I arose to open to my beloved,*
       and my hands dripped with myrrh,
       my fingers with liquid myrrh,
       upon the handles of the bolt.

5:6   *I opened to my beloved,*
       but my beloved had turned and gone.
       My soul failed me when he spoke.
       I sought him, but found him not;
       I called him, but he gave no answer.

5:7   *The watchmen found me,*
       as they went about in the city;
       they beat me, they wounded me,
       they took away my mantle,
       those watchmen of the walls.

5:8   *I adjure you, O daughters of Jerusalem,*
       if you find my beloved,
       that you tell him
       I am sick with love.

5:9   *What is your beloved more than another beloved,*
       O fairest among women!
       What is your beloved more than another beloved,
       that you thus adjure us?

5:10   *My beloved is all radiant and ruddy,*
       distinguished among ten thousand.

5:11   *His head is the finest gold;*
       his locks are wavy,
       black as a raven.

5:12   *His eyes are like doves,*
       beside springs of water,
       bathed in milk,
       fitly set.

5:13   *His cheeks are like beds of spices,*
       yielding fragrance.
       His lips are lilies,
       distilling liquid myrrh.

5:14   *His arms are rounded gold,*
       set with jewels.
       His body is ivory work,
       encrusted with sapphires.

5:15   *His legs are alabaster columns,*
       set upon bases of gold.
       His appearance is like Lebanon,
       choice as the cedars.

5:16   *His speech is most sweet,*
       and he is altogether desirable.
       This is my beloved, and this is my friend,
       O daughters of Jerusalem.

The Song of Songs Chapter Six

6:1　　Whither has your beloved gone,
　　　O fairest among women?
　　　Whither has your beloved turned, that we may seek him with
　　　　　you?

6:2　　My beloved has gone down to his garden,
　　　to the beds of spices,
　　　to pasture his flock in the gardens,
　　　and to gather lilies.

6:3　　I am my beloved's, and my beloved is mine;
　　　he pastures his flock among the lilies.

6:4　　You are beautiful as Tirzah, my love,
　　　comely as Jerusalem,
　　　terrible as an army with banners.

6:5　　Turn away your eyes from me,
　　　for they disturb me —
　　　Your hair is like a flock of goats,
　　　moving down the slopes of Gilead.

6:6　　Your teeth are like a flock of ewes
　　　that have come up from the washing,
　　　all of them bear twins,
　　　not one among them is bereaved.

6:7　　Your cheeks are like halves of a pomegranate,
　　　behind your veil.

6:8　　There are sixty queens and eighty concubines,
　　　and maidens without number.

6:9　　My dove, my perfect one, is only one,
　　　the darling of her mother,
　　　flawless to her that bore her.
　　　The maidens saw her and called her happy;
　　　the queens and concubines also,
　　　and they praised her.

6:10　"Who is this that looks like the dawn,
　　　fair as the moon, bright as the sun,
　　　terrible as an army with banners?"

6:11　I went down to the nut orchard
　　　to look at the blossoms of the valley,
　　　to see whether the vines had budded,
　　　whether the pomegranates were in bloom.

6:12　Before I was aware, my fancy set me
　　　in a chariot beside my prince.

6:13　Return, return, O Shulammite,
　　　return, return that we may look upon you.
　　　Why should you look upon the Shulammite,
　　　as upon a dance before two armies?

The Song of Songs Chapter Seven

7:1　　How graceful are your feet in sandals,
　　　O queenly maiden!

          Your rounded thighs are like jewels,
          the work of a master hand.

7:2   *Your navel is a rounded bowl,*
          that never lacks mixed wine.
          Your belly is a heap of wheat,
          encircled with lilies.

7:3   *Your two breasts are like two fawns,*
          twins of a gazelle.

7:4   *Your neck is like an ivory tower.*
          Your eyes are pools in Heshbon,
          by the gate of Bath-rabbim.
          Your nose is like a tower of Lebanon,
          overlooking Damascus.

7:5   *Your head crowns you like Carmel,*
          and your flowing locks are like purple;
          a king is held captive in the tresses.

7:6   *How fair and pleasant you are,*
          O loved one, delectable maiden.

7:7   *You are stately as a palm tree,*
          and your breasts are like its clusters.

7:8   *I say I will climb the palm tree*
          and lay hold of its branches.
          O, may your breasts be like clusters of the vine,
          and the scent of your breath like apples,

7:9   *and your kisses like the best wine*
          that goes down smoothly,
          gliding over lips and teeth.

7:10   *I am my beloved's,*
          and his desire is for me.

7:11   *Come my beloved,*
          let us go forth into the fields,
          and lodge in the villages;

7:12   *let us go out early to the vineyards,*
          and see whether the vines have budded,
          whether the grape blossoms have opened
          and the pomegranates are in bloom.
          There I will give you my love.

7:13   *The mandrakes give forth fragrance,*
          and over our doors are all choice fruits,
          new as well as old,
          which I have laid up for you, O my beloved.

The Song of Songs Chapter Eight

8:1   *O that you were like a brother to me,*
          that nursed at my mother's breast!
          If I met you outside, I would kiss you,
          and none would despise me.

8:2   *I would lead you and bring you*
          into the house of my mother,
          and into the chamber of her that conceived me.
          I would give you spiced wine to drink,

the juice of my pomegranates.

8:3   O that his left hand were under my head,
and that his right hand embraced me!

8:4   I adjure you, O daughters of Jerusalem,
that you not stir up nor awaken love
until it please.

8:5   Who is that coming up from the wilderness,
leaning upon her beloved?
Under the apple tree I awakened you.
There your mother was in travail with you,
there she who bore you was in travail.

8:6   Set me as a seal upon your heart,
as a seal upon your arm;
for long is strong as death,
jealousy is cruel as the grave.
Its flashes are flashes of fire,
a most vehement flame.

8:7   Many waters cannot quench love,
neither can floods drown it.
If a man offered for love
all the wealth of his house,
it would be utterly scorned.

8:8   We have a little sister,
and she has no breasts.
What shall we do for our sister,
on the day when she is spoken for?

8:9   If she is a wall,
we will build upon her a battlement of silver;
but if she is a door,
we will enclose her with boards of cedar.

8:10   I was a wall,
and my breasts were like towers;
then I was in his eyes
as one who brings peace.

8:11   Solomon had a vineyard at Baal-hamon;
he let out the vineyard to keepers;
each one was to bring for its fruit a thousand pieces of silver.

8:12   My vineyard, my very own, is for myself;
you, O Solomon, may have the thousand,
and the keepers of the fruit two hundred.

8:13   O you who dwell in the gardens,
my companions are listening for your voice;
let me hear it.

8:14   Make haste, my beloved,
and be like a gazelle
or a young stag
upon the mountains of spices.

The Song of Songs in the Translation of Andrew M. Greeley

The following is Professor Andrew M. Greeley's freehand translation of the same poetry, aiming at sense rather than verbatim rendition. Greeley provides a preface essential to understanding both the Song of Songs and also his response to it.

The Egyptian love songs and the Song of Songs are first of all all songs about love. The poets reveal their views of love not by speaking about love in the abstract, but by portraying people in love, making lovers' words reveal lovers' thoughts, feelings, and deeds. The poets invite us to observe lovers, to smile at them, to empathize with them, to sympathize with them, to recall in their adolescent pains our own, to share their desires, to enjoy in fantasy their pleasures. The poets show us young lovers flush with desire and awash in waves of new and overwhelming emotions. We watch lovers sailing the Nile to a rendezvous, walking hand in hand through gardens, lying together in garden bowers. We come upon them sitting at home aching for the one they love, standing outside the loved one's door and pouting, swimming across rivers, running frantically through the streets at night, kissing, fondling, hugging and snuggling face to face and face to breast, and – no less erotically – telling each other's praises in sensuous similes.
Michael V. Fox

How is one to understand the Song in terms of human and divine love? It is we moderns who have difficulty with this question. But the bible suggests that these loves are united and not to be separated. Israel, it is true, understood that Yahweh was beyond sex. He had no consort; and the fertility rites were not the proper mode of worship for him. Yet the union between man and woman became a primary symbol for the expression of the relationship of the Lord to His People. The covenant between God and His People is consistently portrayed as a marriage.
Roland Murphy O. Carm.

First Song

Beloved:

A captive enslaved by your amorous lips,
A prisoner of your sweet embrace,
Drawn after you in passionate chase,
Helplessly bound by your searing kiss,
Dark is my skin, I know, and slim my waist,
My breasts, dear brothers tell me, inferior.
Yet I undress swiftly when you draw near,
Of my prudish modesty you see no trace.
I am yours, my love, for what I am worth,
Play with me, I beg, however you will,
Fondle me, use me till your pleasure is filled.
I live only for your delight and mirth.

Lover:

But I am the one enraptured as slave,
Captured completely by your form and face.
Chained forever to your numinous grace,
O mistress of love whose favor I crave.
Firm and full your bosom, an exquisite gift,
Your slender legs lead to a perfumed cave.
I am, that I might draw near that sacred nave,
A meek servant to your slightest wish.

Duet:

Lay your head against my breast,
Sooth me with your azure eyes,
Heal me with your gracious thighs,
In my arms forever nest.
You are as soft as raisin cake,
You're as warm, dear, as new baked bread.
You are a blossoming apple grove,
And you a sandalwood treasure trove.
Drink me like expensive wine!
Consume me, I am only thine!
Beneath this star dense sky,
Lay quiet now on my chest.
Then again, after a little rest,
Drown me in your happy sighs.

My wondrous love, softly sleep
Your gift tonight I'll always keep.

Sg. 1/1 to Sg 2/7

Second Song

Beloved:

On my garden path a hint of eager feet,
At the window ardent eyes strive to see,
Then my lover's arms reach out strong for me.
My sick and defeated heart begins to beat!

Lover:

Rise up, dear one, the snow is gone.
We are drenched in lemon scented dew,
The lake again is melted blue,
See, flowers bloom and green the lawn.
Time, I insist, to play and sing and dance,
Let me see once more your laughing face
As together we run our ardent race
And, with darkness gone, we renew romance.

Beloved:

My lover left, quiet with the morning breeze,
Back to the city's busy squares and streets.
On my bed I shivered in icy air,
Unclothed, frightened, alone – what if I freeze?
All day, I pined, I missed him so,
At dusk wanton and wild, I ran to the gate
"Welcome, my darling, I could hardly wait,
I've caught you now, I'll never let you go!"

Lover:

Enough of your running, my darling, my dove,
Ah, off with your dress, and lie at my side,
My woman now I claim you, and my bride,
In triumph I possess you and seal our love!

Sg 2/8-3/5

Third Song

Beloved:

On my bed in the dark of night
I took off my gown for the one I love.
I prayed to God and the saints above
But he did not come, my life, my light.
So I sought him everywhere in town,
In alleys, streets, and decrepit bars.
Recklessly I begged the unfeeling guards,
"Tell me, my love, where is he to be found?"
I lost all I had, freedom, hope, and fame,
Those who were my friends cruelly pulled me down.
I still wait for him, cold and harshly bound,
Stripped, humiliated, and ashamed.

I dream of him:

Lover:

In the silent, windless heat of day,
Wine sparkling in our goblets, you and me,
Two alone under the eucalyptus tree,
Still your lips, listen to what I must say.
While we recline in our aromatic batch,
And my teeth your taut nipples gently bite
Let me sing, dearest, of your blazing lights:
As my fingers roam your fertile garden paths:
Your lips are chocolate, dark for a feast,
Your mouth is as sweet as honey and milk,
Your unblemished skin the finest silk,
Your clear eyes sunrise shining in the east.
Your hair is as smooth as lace,
Your complexion glows like the rising moon,
Irish linen your flesh, and roses in bloom.
An artist's miracle your lovely face.
Your ivory throat, lithe, supple and clean,
Your elegant shoulders shapely and bare,
Invite me to a bed warmed by loving care,
A house of grace where I'll be free to dream.
I take your round breasts, one prize in each hand,
Generous and rich, thick cream in my mouth –
I suckle and drain them, thirsty after drought.
Your hips sweet flowing hills round for my hand,

Your belly a peach sugared to my tongue.
Your flanks burnt cinnamon tart to my teeth
Then a mountain forest, fragrant and neat,
Whose depths I'll explore before I am done.

Beloved:

I am deprived of my sense, dear poet mine,
Swept away by the winds, the song in your voice.
Here are my poor favors, what is your choice?
I am your harvest, darling...reap me and dine!

    Sg 3/6-5/1

Fourth Song

Beloved:

My lover came to unlock the secret door –
Bathed, fragrant, and unveiled I waited on my bed –
"Unfold, O Perfect One," he gently said,
Hand in the keyhole, his forever more!
I was powerless, mere putty to shape,
He opened me up, skilled master of the game,
Filled me with his incandescent flame,
And lighted a fire I'll never escape

Then, my turn to attack, I disrobed my man.
I devoured him, uncovered, full length,
Explored, then reveled in his youthful strength,
And traced his wonders with my eager hand.
I tickled and tormented my poor darling one,
Embarrassed him, aroused him, drove him quite mad.
"Don't squirm, dearest, you're cute when you're nude;
I'll stop teasing you only when I'm done.
You are clever, good, and kind, I admit,
And also, belly, arms, and loins, rock hard,
A tree, a mountain, a fiercely loving guard,
In my body and plans I think you might fit.
Black hair, blue eyes, tawny sunrise skin,
Demanding hands, determined virile legs –
And also an appealing, trustful babe,
Savage chest outside, wounded heart within.
Lie here quietly on my garden couch,
I'll encircle you with affection and love.
My lilies and spices fit you like a glove,
It's fun to torment you with my giddy touch.

On your pleasured smile, I complacently gaze,
Oh!...Stay here, my dear, be with me all my days!"

    Sg. 5/2-6/3

Fifth Song

Lover:

There are many girls, but you're my special one,
Fierce and passionate woman, kindest friend,
Without you my hours never seem to end,
Where have you been, my sun, my moon, my dawn?
There's no escape now, I'm holding you down.
Do not pretend that you want to flee,
Tremble at my touch, you belong to me,
Be still while I slip off your frilly gown!
You were sculpted an elegant work of art,
Dark hair falling on snow white chest,
Honeydew, your high and graceful breasts,
One taste enough to break my heart.
In the curve of your wondrous thighs:
A deep valley flowing with perfumed wine
Around which wheat and blooming lilies twine
Whose sweetness invites my enchanted eyes.
I will seize the fruit, press them to my teeth.
Then, famished, impassioned, and lightly deft,
Explore the valley's tantalizing cleft
And your delicacy savor, drink, and eat!

Beloved:

I will be dry white wine to slake your thirst
And a tasty morsel to tease your mouth.
A trembling prize from the misty south,
A plundered vessel for your nightly feast,
A submissive trophy you can carry off
To a cool treasure house in your magic lands,
A most willing slave to your artful hands,
A total gift, passionate, loving, soft!

Lover:

She sleeps now, my innocent little child,
Wake her not, good winds, adore her radiant smile!

    Sg 6/4-8/4

Sixth Song

Beloved:

Let my breasts be towers for you to scale
Above my belly's captured ivory wall.
Climb them again each day, my love, my all,
As I your victory forever hail.
Let my face be branded on your heart
That you may feel my heat in every breath,
My love, implacable as death,
My passion like a wall of raging fire,
Impervious to the storm and flood
Of deadly friction and foolish strife
And the insidious anxieties of life,
A burning need forever in my blood.

Sg 8/5-8

Whatever answer one may give to the problem...one cannot be unaware
of the fact that even if it is only an anthology, in the vision of the final
redactor (unless he be taken for a simpleton), Canticles does not end:
true love is always a quest of one person for another; it is a constant
straining toward the unity of the one who is preeminently the beloved
with the companion who is the unique one.
Daniel Lys
Le Plus Beau Chant de la Creation

Part Four
PARASHAH FOUR

Song of Songs - Chapter Four

4:1   *Behold, you are beautiful, my love,*
behold you are beautiful!
Your eyes are doves
behind your veil.
Your hair is like a flock of goats
moving down the slopes of Gilead.

4:2   *Your teeth are like a flock of shorn ewes*
that have come up from the washing,
all of which bear twins,
and not one among them is bereaved.

4:3   *Your lips are like a scarlet thread,*
and your mouth is lovely.
Your cheeks are like halves of a pomegranate
behind your veil.

4:4   *Your neck is like the tower of David,*
built for an arsenal,
whereon hang a thousand bucklers,
all of them shields of warriors.

4:5   *Your two breasts are like two fawns,*
twins of a gazelle,
that feed among the lilies.

4:6   *Until the day breathes*
and the shadows flee,
I will hie me to the mountain of myrrh
and the hill of frankincense.

4:7   *You are all fair, my love;*
there is no flaw in you.

4:8   *Come with me from Lebanon, my bride;*
come with me from Lebanon.
Depart from the peak of Amana,
from the peak of Senir and Hermon,
from the dens of lions,

from the mountains of leopards.

4:9   *You have ravished my heart, my sister, my bride,*
        you have ravished my heart with a glance of your eyes,
        with one jewel of your necklace.

4:10   *How sweet is your love, my sister, my bride!*
        How much better is your love than wine,
        and the fragrance of your oils than any spice!

4:11   *Your lips distill nectar, my bride;*
        honey and milk are under your tongue;
        the scent of your garments is like the scent of Lebanon.

4:12   *A garden locked is my sister, my bride,*
        a garden locked, a fountain sealed.

4:13   *Your shoots are an orchard of pomegranates*
        with all choicest fruits,
        henna with nard,

4:14   *nard and saffron, calamus and cinnamon,*
        with all trees of frankincense,
        myrrh and aloes,
        with all chief spices —

4:15   *a garden fountain, a well of living water*
        and flowing streams from Lebanon.

4:16   *Awake, O north wind,*
        and come, O south wind!
        Blow upon my garden,
        let its fragrance be wafted abroad.
        Let my beloved come to his garden,
        and eat its choicest fruits.

Song of Songs Rabbah to
Song of Songs 4:1

4:1   *Behold, you are beautiful, my love, behold you are beautiful! Your*
       eyes are doves behind your veil. Your hair is like a flock of
       goats moving down the slopes of Gilead.

XLV:i
1. A.   "Behold, you are beautiful, my love, behold you are beautiful:"
    B.   "Behold you are beautiful" in religious deeds,
    C.   "Behold you are beautiful" in acts of grace,
    D.   "Behold you are beautiful" in carrying out religious obligations of commission,
    E.   "Behold you are beautiful" in carrying out religious obligations of omission,
    F.   "Behold you are beautiful" in carrying out the religious duties of the home, in separating priestly ration and tithes,
    G.   "Behold you are beautiful" in carrying out the religious duties of the field, gleanings, forgotten sheaves, the corner of the field, poor person's tithe, and declaring the field ownerless.
    H.   "Behold you are beautiful" in observing the taboo against mixed species.
    I.   "Behold you are beautiful" in providing a linen cloak with woolen show-fringes.
    J.   "Behold you are beautiful" in [keeping the rules governing] planting,
    K.   "Behold you are beautiful" in keeping the taboo on uncircumcised produce,
    L.   "Behold you are beautiful" in keeping the laws on produce in the fourth year after the planting of an orchard,
    M.   "Behold you are beautiful" in circumcision,
    N.   "Behold you are beautiful" in trimming the wound,
    O.   "Behold you are beautiful" in reciting the Prayer,
    P.   "Behold you are beautiful" in reciting the *Shema*,
    Q.   "Behold you are beautiful" in putting a *mezuzah* on the doorpost of your house,

R.   "Behold you are beautiful" in wearing phylacteries,

S.   "Behold you are beautiful" in building the tabernacle for the Festival of Tabernacles,

T.   "Behold you are beautiful" in taking the palm branch and etrog on the Festival of Tabernacles,

U.   "Behold you are beautiful" in repentance,

V.   "Behold you are beautiful" in good deeds,

W.   "Behold you are beautiful" in this world,

X.   "Behold you are beautiful" in the world to come.

2. A   "your eyes are doves:"

B.   "your eyes" stand for the Sanhedrin, which is the eyesight of the community.

C.   That is in line with this verse: "If it is hid from the eyes of the community" (Num. 15:24).

D.   There are two hundred forty-eight limbs in a human being, and all of them function only through eyesight.

E.   So the Israelites can function only in line with their Sanhedrin.

3. A   "doves:"

B.   Just as a dove is innocent, so the Israelites are [Simon supplies: innocent; just as the dove is beautiful in its movement, so Israel are] beautiful in their movement, when they go up for the pilgrim festivals.

C.   Just as a dove is distinguished, so the Israelites are distinguished: not shaving, in circumcision, in show-fringes.

D.   Just as the dove is modest, so the Israelites are modest.

E.   Just as the dove puts forth its neck for slaughter, so the Israelites: "For your sake are we killed all day long" (Ps. 44:23).

F.   Just as the dove atones for sin, so the Israelites atone for other nations.

G.   For all those seventy bullocks that they offer on the Festival of Tabernacles correspond to the nations of the world, so that the world should not become desolate on their account: "In return for my love they are my adversaries, but I am all prayer" (Ps. 109:4).

H.   Just as the dove, once it recognizes its mate, never again changes him for another, so the Israelites, once they recognized the Holy One, blessed be He, never exchanged him for another.

I.   Just as the dove, when it enters its nest, recognizes its nest and young, fledglings and apertures, so the three rows of the disciples of the sages, when they take their seats before them, knows each one his place.

J.   Just as the dove, even though you take its fledglings from under it, does not ever abandon its cote, so the Israelites, even though the house of the sanctuary was destroyed, never nullified the three annual pilgrim festivals.

K.   Just as the dove renews its brood month by month, so the Israelites every month renew Torah and good deeds.

L.   Just as the dove [Simon:] goes far afield but returns to her cote, so do the Israelites: "They shall come trembling as a bird out of Egypt" (Hos. 11:11), this speaks of the generation of the wilderness; "and as a dove out of the land of Assyria" (Hos. 11:11), this speaks of the Ten Tribes.

	M.	And in both cases: "And I will make them dwell in their houses, says the Lord" (Hos. 11:11).
4.	A.	Rabbi says, "There is a kind of dove, who, when it is being fed, attracts her fellows, who smell her scent and come to her cote.
	B.	"So when an elder is in session and expounding, many proselytes convert at that time, for example, Jethro, who heard and came, and Rahab, who heard and came.
	C.	"Likewise on account of Hananiah, Mishael, and Azariah, many converted: 'For when he sees his children...sanctify my name...they also that err in spirit shall come to understanding' (Isa. 29:23)."
5.	A.	Rabbi was in session and expounding, but the community's attention wandered, so he wanted to wake them up. He said, "A single woman in Egypt produced six hundred thousand at a single birth."
	B.	Now there was present a disciple, named R. Ishmael b. R. Yosé, who said to him, "Who was this?"
	C.	He said to him, "This was Jochebed, who produced Moses, and he was numbered as the equal to six hundred thousand Israelites: 'Then sang Moses and the children of Israel' (Ex. 15:1); 'And the children of Israel did according to all that the Lord has commanded Moses' (Num. 1:54); 'And there has not arisen a prophet in Israel like Moses' (Dt. 34:10)."
6.	A.	"your eyes are doves:"
	B.	They are like doves.
	C.	Your likeness is similar to that of the dove:
	D.	Just as a dove brought light to the world, so you bring light to the world: "And nations shall walk at your light" (Isa. 60:3).
	E.	When did a dove bring light to the world?
	F.	In the time of Noah: "And the dove came in to him in the evening, and lo, in her mouth was an olive leaf, freshly plucked" (Gen. 8:11).
7.	A.	[Supply: "And the dove came in to him in the evening, and lo, in her mouth was an olive leaf, freshly plucked" (Gen. 8:11).] What is the meaning of "freshly plucked"?
	B.	It was killed: "Joseph is without doubt torn in pieces" (Gen. 37:33).
	C.	Said R. Berekhiah, "Had she not killed it, it would have turned into a great tree."
8.	A.	**[Genesis Rabbah XXX:VI.3]** Whence did the dove bring the olive branch?
	B.	R. Levi [Gen. R.: Abba] said, "She brought it from the young shoots in the Land of Israel."
	C.	[Gen. R.: R. Levi said, "She brought it from the Mount of Olives,] for the Land of Israel had not been submerged in the flood. That is in line with what the Holy One, blessed be He, said to Ezekiel, 'Son of man, say to her: "You are a land that is not cleaned nor rained upon in the day of indignation"' (Ez. 22:24)."
	D.	R. Yohanan said, "Even millstone cases dissolved in the water of the flood."
	E.	R. Tarye [Gen. R.: Birai] said, "The gates of the Garden of Eden opened for the dove, and from there she brought it."

F.   Said to him R. Abbahu, "If she had brought it from the Garden of Eden, should the dove not have brought something of greater value, such as cinnamon or balsam? But in choosing the olive leaf, the dove gave a signal to Noah, saying to him, 'Noah, better is something bitter from this [source, namely,] the Holy One, blessed be He, than something sweet from you.'"

The whole is lifted from Song 1:15. The pattern of No. 1 derives from the hermeneutic that treats our poem as a source of metaphors for Israel's religious reality. No. 2 follows suit. No. 3 reverts to the metaphor of the dove for Israel. No. 4 is attached with good reason, and No. 5 is parachuted down because it was attached to No. 4 before No. 4 entered our document; the principle of agglutination prior to the making of documents clearly was the making of collections in the names of authorities. No. 6 then reverts to our base verse, and it also introduces the inevitable appearance of the dove in the story of Noah. The rest then is attached for thematic reasons.

XLV:ii

1.   A.   "[Your eyes are doves] behind your veil:"
      B.   Said R. Levi, "In the case of a bride whose eyes are ugly, her whole body has to be examined. But in the case of a bride whose eyes are beautiful, her whole body does not have to be examined.
      C.   "When a woman ties up her hair in a pony-tail [the words for tie up and veil use the same consonants], that is an ornament for her.
      D.   "So too the great Sanhedrin went into session behind the house of the sanctuary, and that was an ornament to the sanctuary."
      E.   Said R. Abbuha, "They appeared to be cramped [which uses the same consonants as veil], but in fact they had ample room, like the great [hall] of Sepphoris."
      F.   And R. Levi said, "[The word for behind] is Arabic.
      G.   "If one wants to say, 'Make room for me,' he uses that word."

2.   A.   "Your hair is like a flock of goats moving down the slopes of Gilead:"
      B.   [Simon, verbatim:] "The mountain that I tore away [spoil] I made a standing witness to the other nations."
      C.   And what was this?
      D.   The Red Sea [Simon, p. 179, n. 1:] referred to as a mountain perhaps because the waters stood upright."
      E.   And R. Joshua of Sikhnin in the name of R. Levi said, "It is a mountain from which [Simon, verbatim:] you streamed away. When a woman's hair thickens, she thins it; when pumpkins sprout in profusion, they must be thinned.
      F.   "What did I tear away from it?
      G.   ""Your teeth are like a flock of shorn ewes that have come up from the washing, all of which bear twins, and not one among them is bereaved" (Song 4:2)."

The comments are narrowly exegetical. I follow Simon verbatim for the bulk of No. 2. As we note, in Simon's presentation, G answers F, thus

Song 4:1 flows into 4:2. We follow the remainder of the treatment of Song 4:2 in Chapter Forty-Six.

46

Song of Songs Rabbah to Song of Songs 4:2

4:2   *Your teeth are like a flock of shorn ewes that have come up from the washing, all of which bear twins, and not one among them is bereaved.*

XLVI:I
1. A.   "Your teeth are like a flock of shorn ewes:"
    B.   well-defined things,
    C.   the spoil of Egypt and the spoil of the sea.
2. A.   "that have come up from the washing:"
    B.   R. Abba b. R. Kahana said in the name of R. Judah b. R. Ilai, "Before the song [of Deborah] it is written, 'And the children of Israel did again that which was evil in the sight of the Lord' (Judges 4:1), but afterward, 'And the children of Israel did that which was evil in the sight of the Lord' (Judges 6:1).
    C.   "Was it now the first time?
    D.   "But the Song had bestowed forgiveness for what had been done in the past.
    E.   "Along these same lines: 'Now these are the last words of David' (2 Sam. 23:1).
    F.   "What were the first ones?
    G.   "But the Song had bestowed forgiveness for what had been done in the past."
3. A.   "all of which bear twins:"
    B.   For all of them were situated between the angel and the Presence of God: "And the angel of God who went before the camp of Israel removed" (Ex. 14:19).
4. A.   "and not one among them is bereaved:"
    B.   not one of them was injured.

The episodic amplifications, Nos. 1, 3, take for granted that we deal with Israel at the Sea. Beyond that decision, everything is trivial. No. 2 is a free-standing propositional composition. I take it the reason for including the passage is the reference to coming up from the washing, and the proposition, which should be stated but is not, is that coming up from the Sea and the singing of the Song at the Sea effected forgiveness for the sins that the Israelites had committed in Egypt.

47

Song of Songs Rabbah to Song of Songs 4:3

4:3 *Your lips are like a scarlet thread, and your mouth is lovely. Your cheeks are like halves of a pomegranate behind your veil.*

XLVII:i

1. A. "Your lips are like a scarlet thread:"
   B. When they said the Song at the Sea: "Then sang Moses" (Ex. 15:1).
2. A. "and your mouth is lovely:"
   B. For they pointed in respect with their finger and said, "This is my God and I will glorify him" (Ex. 15:2).
   C. Then Moses began to praise them: "Your cheeks are like halves of a pomegranate behind your veil."
3. A. [Supply: "Your cheeks are like halves of a pomegranate behind your veil:"]
   B. The emptiest in your midst is as full of religious deeds as a pomegranate is with seeds,
   C. and it is not necessary to say, those who are "behind your veil."
   D. That is to say, the modest and self-restrained in your midst [the words for self-restrained and veil sharing the same consonants].

The motif of God's praise for Israel continues, with the occasion, the redemption at the Sea.

48

Song of Songs Rabbah to Song of Songs 4:4

[4:1   *"...behind your veil. Your hair is like a flock of goats moving down the slopes of Gilead. 4:2 Your teeth are like a flock of shorn ewes that have come up from the washing, all of which bear twins, and not one among them is bereaved. 4:3 Your lips are like a scarlet thread, and your mouth is lovely. Your cheeks are like halves of a pomegranate behind your veil.] 4:4 Your neck is like the tower of David, built for an arsenal, whereon hang a thousand bucklers, all of them shields of warriors. [4:5 Your two breasts are like two fawns, twins of a gazelle, that feed among the lilies.]*

XLVIII:i

1.   A.   "Your neck is like the tower of David:"
      B.   This is how David extolled you in his book.
      C.   And how did David extol you in his book? "To him who divided the Red Sea in two...and made Israel pass through the midst" (Ps. 136:13-14).
2.   A.   "built for an arsenal:"
      B.   What is the sense of "arsenal?"
      C.   It is a book that was said by many mouths [the words for mouths and arsenal use the same consonants].
3.   A.   Ten men said the book of Psalms:
      B.   the first Man, Abraham, Moses, David, Solomon, thus five.
      C.   As to these five none differs.
      D.   Who were the other five?
      E.   Rab and R. Yohanan:
      F.   Rab said, "Asaph, Heman, Jeduthun, the three sons of Korach, and Ezra.
      G.   R. Yohanan said, "Asaph, Heman, Jeduthun are one; the three sons of Korach and Ezra."
      H.   In the view of Rab Asaph is not covered by the sons of Korach, and in the view of R. Yohanan, the Asaph here is the same as the

29

Asaph there [the Asaph mentioned in Psalms is the one in 1 Chr. 25:2].

I.   But because he was a master of the Torah, he had the merit of reciting a Psalm with his brothers, and he had the merit also to recite a Psalm entirely on his own.

J.   In the opinion of Rab, it was another Asaph: "Under the hand of Asaph, who prophesied according to the direction of the king" (1 Chr. 25:2).

4. A.   [Supply: Jeduthun:]

B.   Rab and R. Yohanan:

C.   Rab said, "'For Jeduthun' means, for the one who prophesied, and 'upon Jeduthun' means, a psalm concerning the decrees and punishments that happened to him and to Israel."

D.   R. Yohanan said, "'For Jeduthun' means, for the one who prophesied, and 'upon Jeduthun' means, a psalm concerning the decrees and punishments that happened to him and to Israel."

5. A.   [Reverting to No. 3:] R. Huna in the name of R. Aha: "Even though ten men wrote the book of Psalms, among them all, the only one of them in whose name the Psalms are said is David, king of Israel.

B.   "The matter may be compared to the case of a group of men who wanted to recite a hymn to the king. Said the king to them, 'All of you sing pleasantly, all of you are pious, all of you are praiseworthy to say a hymn before me. But Mr. So-and-so is the one who will say it in behalf of all of you.

C.   "'Why so? Because his voice is sweet.

D.   "Thus when the ten righteous men proposed to say the book of Psalms, said the Holy One, blessed be He, to them, all of you are praiseworthy to say a hymn before me. But Mr. So-and-so is the one who will say it in behalf of all of you.

E.   "'Why so? Because his voice is sweet.

F.   "So when the ten righteous men proposed to recite the book of Psalms, said the Holy One, blessed be He, to them, 'All of you are praiseworthy to say a hymn before me. But David is the one who will say it in behalf of all of you.

G.   "'Why so? Because his voice is sweet.'

H.   "That is in line with the following verse of Scripture: 'The sweet one of the songs of Israel' (2 Sam. 23:1)."

6. A.   [Supply: "The sweet one of the songs of Israel" (2 Sam. 23:1)"]

B.   R. Huna in the name of R. Aha said, "It is the one who sweetens the songs of Israel, namely, David son of Jesse."

7. A.   "whereon hang a thousand bucklers:"

B.   All those thousands and myriads who stood at the Sea and whom I protected, I protected only on account of the merit of that one who will come in a thousand generations. [Simon, p. 181, n. 4: Moses, who came to give the Torah, "commanded to a thousand generations" (Ps. 105:8).]

8. A.   "all of them shields of warriors:"

B.   This encompasses the one who stands and rules over his inclination to do evil and overcomes his inclination to do evil,

C.   for instance, Moses in his time,

D.   David in his time,

E.   Ezra in his time.

F.   The entire generation depends on him [the words for shield and depend use the same consonants].

G.   And through whom is the Red Sea opened up for you? It is through your two breasts, Moses and Aaron.

While our exposition deals only with the base verse in hand, as we shall see in a moment, it brings to an end the sustained program that began with Song 4:1; the whole is meant to assign the provenance to Israel at the Sea, as we have already noted. But now we shall proceed to have Israel at Sinai and at other moments as well. To be sure, the bulk of the opening segment is devoted to the exposition of extraneous matters. But the structure – encompassing the prior chapters as well – is crystal clear, even though the main point comes in only at No. 7.

XLVIII:ii

1. A.   [Supply: 4:1 "...behind your veil. Your hair is like a flock of goats moving down the slopes of Gilead. 4:2 Your teeth are like a flock of shorn ewes that have come up from the washing, all of which bear twins, and not one among them is bereaved. 4:3 Your lips are like a scarlet thread, and your mouth is lovely. Your cheeks are like halves of a pomegranate behind your veil. 4:4 Your neck is like the tower of David, built for an arsenal, whereon hang a thousand bucklers, all of them shields of warriors. 4:5 Your two breasts are like two fawns, twins of a gazelle, that feed among the lilies.] R. Yohanan interpreted the passage to speak of Israel at Mount Sinai:

    B.   "The 'flock' that stood at Mount Sinai were not standing in a happy mood.

    C.   "'behind your veil:' for they were shrinking together [a word that uses the same consonants as veil] at every word, and did not stand in a happy mood but in fear, trembling, and agitation."

2. A.   R. Abba b. Kahana in the name of R. Yohanan derives proof of the same proposition from the following verse of Scripture: "For that nation and kingdom that will not serve you shall perish; yes, those nations shall be utterly wasted" (Isa. 60:12).

    B.   "'they were wasted' from Horeb [the words Horeb and utterly wasted use the same consonants].

    C.   "They were then sentenced to death."

3. A.   [Resuming 1:C:] "Your hair is like a flock of goats moving down the slopes of Gilead:"

    B.   R. Joshua in the name of R. Levi said, "[Gilead is] [Simon, verbatim:] the mountain from which you streamed away, the mountain from which you tore away I made into a heap and a witness for the nations of the world.

    C.   "And what is it? It is Mount Sinai.

    D.   "And what did you strip away from it? 'Your teeth are like a flock of shorn ewes.'

E.   "These are things that are counted out in number [the words for
      flock of shorn ewes and counted out in number use the same
      consonants],

F.   "namely, two hundred and forty-eight affirmative religious duties,
      and three hundred and sixty-five negative religious duties.

G.   "'that have come up from the washing:' for all of them were
      cleansed of sins."

4. A.   R. Aha and R. Mesharshia in the name of R. Idi says, "In
          connection with all other additional offerings [of Sabbaths and
          festivals], a sin-offering is included, for example, 'one he goat for a
          sin-offering' (Num. 28:22), 'a goat for a sin-offering.'

    B.   "But as to Pentecost, there is no sin-offering mentioned.

    C.   "This serves to teach you that at that time they were not subject to
          either transgression or sin."

5. A.   "all of which bear twins:"

    B.   Said R. Yohanan, "On the day on which the Holy One, blessed be
          He, came down onto Mount Sinai to give the Torah to Israel, with
          him came down sixty myriads of ministering angels.

    C.   "In the hand of each one of them was a crown with which to adorn
          each Israelite."

    D.   R. Abba b. Kahana in the name of R. Yohanan said, "There were a
          hundred and twenty myriads of ministering angels that came
          down with the Holy One, blessed be He,

    E.   "one to put on a crown on each one, the other to put a girdle on
          him."

6. A.   What is the sense of the word translated as girdle?

    B.   R. Huna the Elder of Sepphoris said, "It is a proper garment, in
          line with this usage: 'He looses the bond of kings and binds their
          loins with a girdle' (Job 12:18)."

7. A.   "and not one among them is bereaved:"

    B.   For not a single one of them was injured.

8. A.   "Your lips are like a scarlet thread:"

    B.   This is the thunder that came before the act of speech [the Ten
          Commandments]:

    C.   "'for your voice is sweet:' this is the voice after the Ten
          Commandments: 'And the Lord heard the voice of your
          words...and said...they have said well all that they have spoken'
          (Dt. 5:25)."

9. A.   [Supply: "And the Lord heard the voice of your words...and
          said...they have said well all that they have spoken" (Dt. 5:25).]

    B.   What is the meaning of "they have said well all that they have
          spoken"?

    C.   R. Hiyya b. R. Ada and Bar Qappara:

    D.   One said, "It was like the act of trimming [which uses the same
          consonants as the word well] in the trimming of the lamps."

    E.   The other said, "It was like the act of preparation in the
          preparation of the incense."

10. A.   At that moment Moses began to praise them, saying, "'Your
          cheeks are like halves of a pomegranate [behind your veil].'

    B.   "The most empty-headed among you is as filled with Torah-
          teachings as a pomegranate,

	C.	"and it is not necessary to say, 'behind your veil,'
	D.	"the most modest among you, the most self-restrained among you [where we find the consonants used in veil]."
11.	A.	"Your neck is like the tower of David:"
	B.	That is how David extolled you in his book. [The words for tower and extol share the same consonants].
	C.	And how did David extol you in his book?
	D.	"God, when you went forth before your people" (Ps. 68:8) – and then? "The earth trembled" (Ps. 68:9).
	E.	Along these same lines, "The mountains quaked at the presence of the Lord" (Judges 5:5), and then, "Even Sinai at the presence of the Lord the God of Israel" (Judges 5:5). This "Even Sinai..." adds nothing. [Simon, p. 184, n. 1: "Sinai is obviously included in 'the earth' already mentioned. Hence Sinai here must be an allusion to the Israelites who stood there to receive the Torah and it is mentioned to their credit. This then is the eulogy.]
12.	A.	"built for an arsenal:"
	B.	It is the book that was said by many mouths.
13.	A.	"whereon hang a thousand bucklers:"
	B.	All those thousands and myriads who stood at the Sea and whom I protected, I protected only on account of the merit of that one who will come in a thousand generations [Simon, p. 181, n. 4: Moses, who came to give the Torah, "commanded to a thousand generations" (Ps. 105:8).]
14.	A.	"all of them shields of warriors:"
	B.	This encompasses the one who stands and rules over his inclination to do evil and overcomes his inclination to do evil,
	C.	for instance, Moses in his time,
	D.	David in his time,
	E.	Ezra in his time.
	F.	The entire generation depends on him [the words for shield and depend use the same consonants].
	G.	And through whom is the Red Sea opened up for you? It is through your two breasts, Moses and Aaron.

The interesting side of the exposition comes at the points of repetition. There we see, once more, that not the intrinsic message of the cited verses, read in some fresh way, provokes the exegesis, but the decision to read the verses in the motif announced by Yohanan makes its appearance prior to any attention paid to the verses themselves.

XLVIII:iii

1.	A.	[Supply: 4:1 "...behind your veil. Your hair is like a flock of goats moving down the slopes of Gilead. 4:2 Your teeth are like a flock of shorn ewes that have come up from the washing, all of which bear twins, and not one among them is bereaved. 4:3 Your lips are like a scarlet thread, and your mouth is lovely. Your cheeks are like halves of a pomegranate behind your veil. 4:4 Your neck is like the tower of David, built for an arsenal, whereon hang a thousand bucklers, all of them shields of warriors. 4:5 Your two breasts are like two fawns, twins of a gazelle, that feed among the

lilies.] R. Isaac interpreted the passage to speak of the war with Midian:

B. "'Your hair is like a flock of goats:'

C. "the platoons that went to war against Midian went only on account of the merit of Moses and Phineas: 'And Moses and Eleazar the priest took the gold' (Num. 31:51).

D. "'moving down the slopes of Gilead:'

E. "[Simon, verbatim:] the mountain from which I tore away [spoil] I made a standing witness to the other nations. And what is that? It is the war against Midian.

F. "And what is the spoil that was torn away?

G. "'Your teeth are like a flock of shorn ewes:' this refers to matters of a fixed number [the word for fixed and shorn ewes use the same consonants],

H. "the twelve thousand volunteers, and the twelve thousand draftees: 'So were delivered out of the thousands of Israel a thousand of a tribe, a thousand of a tribe' (Num. 31:5)."

I. Said R. Hananiah b. R. Isaac, "With twelve thousand they went forth to do battle against Midian [and not the twenty-four thousand just now posited]."

2. A. [Resuming from H:] "that have come up from the washing:"

B. R. Huna said, "The meaning is that not a single one of them put on the phylactery of the head before putting on the phylactery of the hand. For if one of them had put on the phylactery of the head before the phylactery of the arm, Moses would not have praised them, and they would not have gone up from there in peace.

C. "One must therefore conclude that they were the most righteous men."

3. A. "all of which bear twins:"

B. [That is to say, they went about in pairs,] for when they would go in pairs to a [Midianite] woman, one of them would blacken her face, the other would remove her jewelry.

C. But the women would say to them, "Are we not of those that have been created by the Holy One, blessed be He, that you treat us in such a way?"

D. And the Israelites would say to them, "Is it not enough for you that you have taken what is ours on your account: 'And the Lord said to Moses, Take all the chiefs of the people and hang them up' (Num. 25:4)."

4. A. "and not one among them is bereaved:"

B. For not one of them was suspect of transgression.

5. A. "Your lips are like a scarlet thread:"

B. When they said to Moses, "Your servants have taken the sum of the men of war that are under our charge, and not one of us is missing" (Num. 31:49) – on account of transgression or sin.

6. A. "and your mouth is lovely:"

B. For they said to him, "And we have brought the Lord's offering" (Num. 31:50).

7. A.   Said to them Moses, "What you say is contradictory. You have said, 'not one of us is missing' (Num. 31:49) – on account of transgression or sin,

   B.   "and you also have said, 'And we have brought the Lord's offering.'

   C.   "If you have not sinned, then how come this offering?"

   D.   They said to him, "Our lord, Moses, we went about in pairs to each woman, and one of us would blacken her face, the other would remove her jewelry. Is it possible that the impulse to do evil was in no way stirred? On account of that stirring of the impulse to do evil, we want to bring an offering."

   E.   At that moment Moses began to praise them: "'Your cheeks are like halves of a pomegranate:'

   F.   "The emptiest of you are filled with religious duties and good deeds like a pomegranate.

   G.   "For whoever is saved from a transgression that falls within his power and does not do it has carried out an enormous religious duty.

   H.   "And it is not necessary to say, 'behind your veil,' meaning that the same is so of the most modest and self-restrained among you.

   I.   "'Your neck is like the tower of David:' this is how David extolled you in his book.

   J.   "And how did David extoll you in his book? It was in saying, 'Sihon, king of the Amorites and Og king of Bashan...and gave their land for a heritage' (Ps. 135:11-12).

   K.   "'Built for an arsenal:' This refers to a book that many mouths spoke.

8. A.   "Whereon hang a thousand bucklers:" [God says,] "all the thousands and myriads who went out to do battle against Midian and whom I shielded, I shielded only on account of the merit accruing to him who is to come for a thousand generations.

   B.   "Nor do you alone depend upon him, but rather, 'all of them shields of warriors:' whoever stands and shields himself and overcomes his impulse to do evil is called a warrior,

   C.   "for instance, Moses in his time, David in his time, Ezra in his time.

   D.   "And their entire generation depends upon them.

9. A.   "And through whom was the war against Midian carried out?

   B.   "It was through 'Your two breasts,'

   C.   "namely, Moses and Phineas."

The pattern is well established, and where prior materials do not compete with an interpretation more particular to the proposed subject of metaphorization, we simply repeat what is in hand or make minor revisions. The upshot is a well-crafted reading of the whole, in which what is said about one critical event or person is said about another. The uniformities then convey a subterranean message that, through the specific redemptive moments, there are general rules that operate. That seems to me the power of Nos. 7ff.

XLVIII:iv

1. A.   [Supply: 4:1 "...behind your veil. Your hair is like a flock of goats moving down the slopes of Gilead. 4:2 Your teeth are like a flock of shorn ewes that have come up from the washing, all of which bear twins, and not one among them is bereaved. 4:3 Your lips are like a scarlet thread, and your mouth is lovely. Your cheeks are like halves of a pomegranate behind your veil. 4:4 Your neck is like the tower of David, built for an arsenal, whereon hang a thousand bucklers, all of them shields of warriors. 4:5 Your two breasts are like two fawns, twins of a gazelle, that feed among the lilies.] R. Huna interpreted the passage to speak of the Jordan:

    B.   "'Your hair is like a flock of goats moving down the slopes of Gilead:'

    C.   "The flock that crossed the Jordan crossed only on account of the merit accruing to our father, Jacob: 'Then you shall let your children know, saying, Israel came over this Jordan on dry land' (Josh. 4:22)."

2. A.   R. Judah bar Simon in the name of R. Yohanan: "In the Torah, in the Prophets, and in the Writings we find proof that the Israelites were able to cross the Jordan only on account of the merit achieved by Jacob:

    B.   "In the Torah: '...for with only my staff I crossed this Jordan, and now I have become two companies.'

    C.   "In the prophets: 'Then you shall let your children know, saying, "Israel came over this Jordan on dry land"' (Josh. 4:22), meaning our father, Israel.

    D.   "In the Writings: 'What ails you, O you sea, that you flee? You Jordan, that you burn backward? At the presence of the God of Jacob' (Ps. 114:5ff.)."

3. A.   [Reverting to 1.C:] "'moving down the slopes of Gilead:'
    B.   "[Simon, verbatim:] the mountain from which I tore away [spoil] I made a standing witness to the other nations. And what is that? It is the Jordan.
    C.   "And what is the spoil that was torn away?
    D.   "'Your teeth are like a flock of shorn ewes:' this refers to the spoil of Sihon and Og.

4. A.   "that have come up from the washing:"
    B.   Said R. Eleazar, "It was by sixty thousand troops that the land of Canaan was conquered."
    C.   That is consistent with the view of R. Eliezer, who said, "Any war that involves more than sixty thousand troops is a total snafu."

5. A.   R. Judah in the name of R. Hezekiah said, "Any passage in which it is said, 'about ten,' 'about twenty,' 'about thirty,' 'about forty,' may involve more or less than that number.

6. A.   "About forty thousand ready armed for war" (Josh. 4:13) as against "Forty four thousand seven hundred and sixty" (1 Chr. 54:18):
    B.   Said R. Aha, "They were a full thousand and the left fell off on the route-march."
    C.   Then [reverting to 4.B:] where were the other sixty thousand?

D.   He said to them, "They were guarding the baggage, and Scripture did not count them."

7. A. "all of which bear twins:"

    B. For they were [Simon:] enclosed [the words for twins and enclosed using the same consonants] between the vanguard [Simon, p. 187, n. 5: the tribes of Gad, Reuben, and half of Manasseh] and the rearguard [Simon: the tribe of Dan]:

    C. Thus: "And the armed men went before the priests...and the rearward..." (Josh. 6:9).

8. A. "and not one among them is bereaved:"

    B. For not a single one of them was injured.

9. A. "Your lips are like a scarlet thread:"

    B. When they said to Joshua, "All that you have commanded us we will do" (Josh. 1:16).

    C. "and your mouth is lovely:"

    D. When they said, "Whoever he is who will rebel against your commandment" (Josh. 1:18).

10. A. Then Joshua began to extol them: "'Your cheeks are like halves of a pomegranate behind your veil:'

    B. "The emptiest among you is full of Torah-teachings like a pomegranate,

    C. "And it is not necessary to say, 'behind your veil,' meaning that the same is so of the most modest and self-restrained among you.

    D. "'Your neck is like the tower of David:' this is how David extolled you in his book.

    E. "And how did David extoll you in his book? It was in saying, 'To him who smote great kings' (Ps. 136:17).

    F. "'Built for an arsenal:' This refers to a book that many mouths spoke.

11. A. "Whereon hang a thousand bucklers:" [God says,] "all the thousands and myriads who went out to do battle against Midian and whom I shielded, I shielded only on account of the merit accruing to him who is to come for a thousand generations.

    B. "Nor do you alone depend upon him, but rather, 'all of them shields of warriors:' whoever stands and shields himself and overcomes his impulse to do evil is called a warrior,

    C. "for instance, Moses in his time, David in his time, Ezra in his time.

    D. "And their entire generation depends upon them.

12. A. "And through whom did the Israelites cross the Jordan?

    B. "It was through 'Your two breasts,'

    C. "namely, Joshua and Eleazar."

The movement from the war against Midian to the crossing of the Jordan requires only a few revisions in detail, and none in the familiar pattern. The cumulative effect seems to me considerable. Not surprisingly, we now move from the Land to the Temple.

XLVIII:v

1. A. Another interpretation of the verse, "...behind your veil. Your hair is like a flock of goats moving down the slopes of Gilead:"

	B.	[Simon, verbatim:] the mountain from which I tore away [spoil] I made a standing witness to the other nations.
	C.	And what is that?
	D.	It is the house of the sanctuary: "Fearful is God from your holy place" (Ps. 68:36).
	E.	Now whence does fear go forth? Is it not the house of the sanctuary?
2.	A.	That is in line with the following:
	B.	"You shall keep my Sabbaths and fear my sanctuary" (Lev. 26:2).
	C.	This indicates that it is sanctified when it is in ruins just as much as it is sanctified when it is standing intact.
	D.	And that fact yields an argument *a fortiori:*
	E.	if the Holy One, blessed be He, did not show favor to his own sanctuary,
	F.	then, when he comes to exact punishment from those who destroyed it, how much the more so!
3.	A.	And what is that which I tore away [spoil]?
	B.	It is "Your teeth are like a flock of shorn ewes."
	C.	That is to say, things that are subject to a definite and fixed number, specifically, the garments of the high priesthood.
4.	A.	For we have learned in the Mishnah:
	B.	**The high priest serves in eight garments, and an ordinary priest in four:**
	C.	**tunic, underpants, head-covering, and girdle.**
	D.	**The high priest in addition wears the breastplate, apron, upper garment, and frontlet [M. Yoma 7:5A-C].**
	E.	The tunic would atone for bloodshed: "And they dipped the coat in the blood" (Gen. 37:31).
	F.	Some say, "It atoned for those who wear mixed varieties: 'And he made him a coat of many colors' (Gen. 37:3)."
	G.	The underpants atone for fornication: "And you shall make them linen underpants to cover the flesh of their nakedness" (Ex. 27:42).
	H.	The head-covering atones for arrogance: "And he set the head-covering on his head" (Lev. 8:9).
	I.	For what did the girdle atone?
	J.	For [Simon:] the double-dealers.
	K.	Others say, "For thieves."
	L.	The one who says that it was for thieves maintains that view because the garment was hollow, standing for thieves, who work in hiding.
	M.	The one who says that it was for the double-dealers is in accord with that which R. Levi said, "It was thirty-two cubits long, and he would twist it on either side."
	N.	The breastplate would atone for those who pervert justice: "And you shall put in the breastplate of judgment the Urim and the Thummim" (Ex. 28:30).
	O.	The apron [ephod] would atone for idolatry: "And without ephod or teraphim" (Hos. 3:4).
	P.	The upper garment [robe] would atone for slander.

5. A.   R. Simon in the name of R. Jonathan of Bet Gubrin: "For two matters there was no atonement, but the Torah has provided atonement for them, and these are they:

    B.   "Gossip and involuntary manslaughter.

    C.   "For gossip there was no atonement, but the Torah has provided atonement for it, specifically through the bell of the robe: 'And it shall be upon Aaron to minister, and the sound thereof shall be heard' (Ex. 28:35).

    D.   "Let the sound that this makes come and atone for the sound of slander.

    E.   "For involuntary manslaughter there was no atonement, but the Torah has provided atonement for it, specifically through the death of the high priest: 'And he shall dwell therein until the death of the high priest' (Num. 35:25)."

6. A.   [Resuming 4.P:] The frontlet would atone for impudence.

    B.   Some say, "It was for blasphemy."

    C.   The one who says it was for impudence cites the following verse of Scripture: "And it shall be upon Aaron's forehead" (Ex. 28:38), and also, "Yet you had a harlot's forehead" (Jer. 3:3).

    D.   The one who says it was for blasphemy cites the following verse of Scripture: "And it shall always be upon his forehead" (Ex. 28:38) along side, "And the stone sank into his forehead" (1 Sam. 17:49).

7. A.   "And he fell upon his face to the earth" (1 Sam. 17:49):

    B.   Why did he fall upon his face?

    C.   To begin with you interpret as follows: "His height was six cubits and a span" (1 Sam. 17:4).

    D.   It is so that that righteous man [David] should not have to be troubled to walk the entire length [of the giant],

    E.   therefore it is written, "And he fell upon his face to the earth."

    F.   Said R. Huna, "It was because Dagon, his god, was engraved on his heart.

    G.   "Thus was carried out this verse: 'And I will cast your carcasses on the carcasses of your idols' (Lev. 26:30)."

8. A.   Another interpretation of the verse, "And he fell upon his face to the earth" (1 Sam. 17:49):

    B.   [Supply: Why did he fall upon his face?]

    C.   Said Rabbi, "It was so that that foul mouth, which had blasphemed and cursed, might be buried in dirt: 'Hide them in the dust together' (Job 40:13)."

9. A.   Another interpretation of the verse, "And he fell upon his face to the earth" (1 Sam. 17:49):

    B.   [Supply: Why did he fall upon his face?]

    C.   It was so that that that righteous man should not be troubled to go back [his full length].

10. A.   Another interpretation of the verse, "And he fell upon his face to the earth" (1 Sam. 17:49):

    B.   [Supply: Why did he fall upon his face?]

    C.   It was so that that that righteous man should come and tread upon his neck,

    D.   so fulfilling this verse: "And you shall tread upon their high places" (Dt. 33:29).

11. A. [Returning to No. 3's inquiry:] "that have come up from the washing:"
    B. For they atone for Israel.
12. A. "all of which bear twins:"
    B. This speaks of the two [Simon, verbatim:] wreathen chains that issued from the middle of the breastplate and looked like two tassels hanging down from it.
13. A. "and not one among them is bereaved:"
    B. None of them ever wore out.
14. A. Your lips are like a scarlet thread:"
    B. This is the holy crown.
15. A. "and your mouth is lovely:"
    B. This refers to the plate.
16. A. [In the Version of Genesis Rabbah XXXII:X.1:] [Supply:"And the waters prevailed so mightily upon the earth that all the high mountains under the whole heaven were covered, the waters prevailed above the mountains, covering them fifteen cubits deep" (Gen. 7:19):]
    B. R. Jonathan went up to pray in Jerusalem. When he went by the Palatinus, a Samaritan saw him and asked him, "Where are you going?"
    C. He said to him, "To pray in Jerusalem."
    D. He said to him, "Wouldn't it be better for you to pray on this holy mountain and not on that dunghill?"
    E. He said to him, "Why is it regarded as blessed?"
    F. He said to him, "Because it was not submerged by the water of the Flood."
    G. For a moment R. Jonathan lost his learning in the law. His ass driver said to him, "Sir, give me permission and I shall answer him."
    H. He said to him, "Go ahead."
    I. He said to him, "If this place falls into the category of mountains, then it is written, 'And it covered all the high mountains' (Gen. 7:19). And if it does not fall into the category of mountains, then Scripture had no need to make special reference to it [since obviously it was submerged]."
    J. At that moment R. Jonathan got off the ass and mounted the ass-driver on it for a span of three *mils*, and he recited in his regard the following verses of Scripture:
    K. "'There shall not be barren among you, male or female, or among your cattle' (Deut. 7:14), even among your cattle drivers.
    L. "'No weapon that is formed against you shall prosper, and every tongue that shall rise against you in judgment you shall condemn' (Isa. 54:17)."
    M. "'Your empty heads are like pomegranates split open' (Song 4:3), meaning that even the emptiest head among you is as full of good replies as a pomegranate is full of seeds.
    N. "'behind your veil:' needless to say, the modest and self-controlled among you.

The exposition of the verse in terms of the Temple and the priestly garments works quite nicely, though it bears the burden of rather substantial interpolations. These enrich and really do not impede the discourse.

XLVIII:vi

1. A. Another interpretation of the verse, "...behind your veil. Your hair is like a flock of goats moving down the slopes of Gilead:"

    B. [Simon, verbatim:] the mountain from which I tore away [spoil] I made a standing witness to the other nations.

    C. And what is that?

    D. It is the priestly watches.

    E. And what did you strip away?

    F. "Your teeth are like a flock of shorn ewes" – things that are counted out,

    G. this refers to the twenty-four priestly watches, the twenty-four Levitical watches, and the twelve divisions [1 Chr. 27].

    H. "that have come up from the washing:" who guard Israel.

    I. "all of which bear twins:"

    J. For we have learned: At three seasons of the year all of the priestly watches were equivalent to one another.

    K. "and not one among them is bereaved:"

    L. For we have learned in the Mishnah: (1) the first, with the head and a hind-leg, [the head in his right hand, with its muzzle along his arm, and its horns in his fingers, and the place at which it was slaughtered turned upwards, and the fat set on top of it [that place], and the right hind leg in his left hand, and the flayed end outermost; (2) the second, with the two forelegs, that of the right hand in his right hand, and that of the left in his left, with the flayed end outermost; (3) the third, with the rump and the [other] hind leg, the rump in his right hand, and the fat tail hanging down between his fingers, and the lobe of the liver and the two kidneys with it, the left hind leg in his left hand, with the flayed end outermost; (4) the fourth, with the breast and the neck, the breast in his right hand, and the neck in his left, and with its ribs between his fingers; (5) the fifth with the two flanks, that of the right in his right hand, that of the left in his left, with the flayed ends outwards; (6) the sixth, with the innards put in a dish, and the shanks on top of them, above; (7) the seventh, with the fine flour; (8) the eighth, with the baked cakes; (9) the ninth, with the wine] [M. Tamid 4:3].

    M. "Your lips are like a scarlet thread:"

    N. As we have learned in the Mishnah: [They gave him wine to pour out. The prefect stands at the corner, with a flag in his hand, and two priests stand at the table of the fat pieces, with two silver trumpets in their hands. They sounded a prolonged sound, a wavering sound, and a prolonged sound. They came and stood near Ben Arza, one on his right, one on his left.] He stepped down to pour out the wine, and the prefect waved the flag, and Ben Arza dashed the cymbal, and the Levites broke out in song] [M. Tamid 7:4K-O].

O.   "and your mouth is lovely:"

P.   This refers to the song.

Q.   For we have learned in the Mishnah there: The singing which the Levites did sing in the sanctuary: On the first day they did sing, The earth is the Lord's and the fulness thereof, the world and they who live therein (Ps. 24). On the second day they did sing, Great is the Lord and highly to be praised in the city of our God, even upon his holy hill (Ps. 48). On the third day they did sing, God stands in the congregation of God, he is a judge among the gods (Ps. 82). On the fourth day they did sing, O Lord God to whom vengeance belongs, thou God to whom vengeance belongs, show yourself (Ps. 94). On the fifth day they did sing, Sing we happily to God our strength, make a joyful noise to the God of Jacob (Ps. 81). On the sixth day they did sing, The Lord is king and has put on glorious apparel (Ps. 93). On the Sabbath day they did sing, A Psalm, A song for the Sabbath day (Ps. 92) A psalm, a song for the world that is to come, for the day which is wholly Sabbath rest for eternity. [M. Tamid 7:4].

From the Temple we move to the priesthood. The interpolation of sizable passages of Mishnah-tractate Tamid fills space. From the priesthood, predictably, we proceed to the sacrifices.

XLVIII:vii

1.   A.   Another interpretation of the verse, "Your hair is like a flock of goats moving down the slopes of Gilead:"

      B.   [Simon, verbatim:] the mountain from which I tore away [spoil] I made a standing witness to the other nations.

      C.   And what is that?

      D.   It is the offerings.

      E.   And what did you strip away?

      F.   "Your teeth are like a flock of shorn ewes" – things that are counted out,

      G.   "The one lamb you offer in the morning" (Num. 28:4).

      H.   "that have come up from the washing:"

      I.   For they perpetually make atonement for Israel.

      J.   "all of which bear twins:"

      K.   For we have learned: The ram is brought by eleven priests, by fifteen.

      L.   "and not one among them is bereaved:"

      M.   The inwards and the fine flour and wine are brought by three at a time. [Compare M. Tamid 3:1:] The superintendent said to them, "Come and cast lots [to determine] (1) who executes the act of slaughter, (2) who tosses the blood, (3) who removes the ashes of the inner altar, (4) who removes the ashes of the candlestick, (5) who carries up the limbs to the ramp: (1) the head, (2) the [right] hind leg, (3) the two forelegs, (4) the rump, and (5) the [left] hind leg, (6) the breast, (7) the neck, (8) the two flanks, (9) the innards, (10) the fine flour, (11) the cakes, (12) the wine." They drew lots. Whoever won won.]

The movement to the sacrifices presents no surprises and is more important than the details, which are sparse; there is scarcely any fresh exegesis.

XLVIII:viii

1. A. Another interpretation of the verse, "Your hair is like a flock of goats:"

    B. [Simon, verbatim:] the mountain from which I tore away [spoil] I made a standing witness to the other nations.

    C. And what is that?

    D. It is the Sanhedrin.

    E. And what did you strip away?

    F. "Your teeth are like a flock of shorn ewes" – things that are counted out,

    G. these vote to acquit, those vote to condemn.

    H. "that have come up from the washing:"

    I. For they acquit Israel.

    J. "all of which bear twins:"

    K. For we have learned in the Mishnah: If they found him innocent, they sent him away. If not, they postpone judging him till the next day. They would go off in pairs and would not eat very much or drink wine that entire day, and they would discuss the matter all that night. And the next day they would get up and come to court [M. Sanhedrin 5:5A-C].

    L. "and not one among them is bereaved:"

    M. R. Levi said, "For they make connections between one thing and another."

    N. R. Abba said, "For the law is not dim for them."

    O. "Your lips are like a scarlet thread:"

    P. R. Yudan said, "Like the decree of the king is the decree of the court.

    Q. "They give an order at their own authority for death through stoning, burning, decapitation, and strangulation."

    R. R. Hunia said, "The verse, 'Your lips are like a scarlet thread,' refers to blood.

    S. "For we have learned in the Mishnah: And a red line goes around it at the middle, to effect a separation between the drops of blood which are tossed on the top and the drops of blood which are tossed on the bottom. [And the foundation extended all the length of the north side and all the length of the west side, and projects one cubit to the south and one cubit to the east] [M. Middot 3:1Q-S]."

T.   R. Azariah in the name of R. Judah: "Just as the red line divides
            the blood to be tossed above from the blood to be tossed below,
U.   "so the Sanhedrin distinguishes that which is unclean from that
            which is clean, that which is prohibited from that which is
            permitted, that which is exempt from liability from that which is
            liable."

From the sacrifices we proceed to the Sanhedrin, a move that, by
now, we should readily predict. There is a very limited repertoire of
fundamental components that will be subject to metaphorization. We
have, as a matter of fact, now completed our review of that repertoire
and turn to what is an essentially miscellaneous and ad hoc conclusion.
The closely composed sequences that have carried us through the sacred
symbols have now concluded.

XLVIII:ix

1.   A.   Another interpretation of the verse, "Your lips are like a scarlet
            thread:"
      B.   this refers to the crimson strip [of wool, tied to the scapegoat on
            the Day of Atonement].
      C.   "and your mouth is lovely:"
      D.   [Since the word for mouth uses consonants that can yield the word
            for wilderness, we interpret:] This refers to the goat that is sent
            forth.
      E.   Said the Israelites before the Holy One, blessed be He, "Lord of
            the world, we no longer have the crimson strip and the goat that is
            sent forth."
      F.   He said to them, "'Your lips are like a scarlet thread:' the
            utterance of your lips is as precious to me as the strip of crimson."
2.   A.   [Supply: "Your lips are like a scarlet thread:"]
      B.   On this verse R. Abbahu said, "'So shall we render for bullocks the
            offering of our lips' (Hos. 14:3):
      C.   "What shall we pay instead of the bullocks and the goat that is
            sent away?
      D.   "Our lips."
3.   A.   "and your mouth is lovely:"
      B.   [Since the word for mouth uses consonants that can yield the word
            for wilderness, we interpret:] Your wilderness is lovely.
      C.   [Since the word for mouth uses consonants that can yield the word
            for statement, we interpret:] Your statement is lovely.
4.   A.   [Supply: "and your mouth is lovely:" Since the word for mouth uses
            consonants that can yield the word for wilderness,] R. Abba b.
            Kahana said, "Even though [the Temple mount] is a wilderness,
            people are liable for its boundaries [should they walk through the
            sacred space in a condition of cultic uncleanness]
      B.   "even now, when it is a ruin, just as they are liable for its
            boundaries when it is intact."
      C.   Said R. Levi, "Said the Holy One, blessed be He, 'During the time
            that it has lain in ruins, it has raised up for me righteous persons,

		while during the time that it was standing, it produced for me wicked persons.
	D.	"'During the time that it has lain in ruins, it has raised up for me righteous persons, for example, Daniel and his allies, Mordecai and his allies, Ezra and his associates.
	E.	"'while during the time that it was standing, it produced for me wicked persons, for instance, Ahaz and his co-conspirators, Manasseh and his, Amon and his.'"
	F.	R. Abba b. Kahana in the name of R. Yohanan concerning this statement of R. Levi said, "'For more are the children of the desolate than the children of the married wife' (Isa. 54:1): 'During the time that it has lain in ruins, it has raised up for me more righteous persons than during the time that it was standing.'"
5.	A.	"Your cheeks are like halves of a pomegranate:"
	B.	R. Abba b. Kahana and R. Aha:
	C.	One said, "The emptiest head in the three rows [of disciples, sitting before the Sanhedrin] is as full of Torah as a pomegranate is filled with seeds, and one need not say, those who are 'behind your veil,' that is, those who are seated on the Sanhedrin itself."
	D.	The other said, "The emptiest of those who are on the Sanhedrin are as full of Torah as a pomegranate is filled with seeds, and one need not say, those who are 'behind your veil,' that is, those who are seated under the olive, vine, and fig tree and are taken up with words of the Torah."
6.	A.	"Your neck is like the tower of David:"
	B.	This is the house of the Sanctuary.
	C.	And why is it compared to the neck?
	D.	For so long as the house of the sanctuary endured, the neck of Israel was raised proudly among the nations of the world.
	E.	But now that the house of the sanctuary lies in ruins, then it is as though the neck of Israel is bowed down: "And I will break the pride of your power" (Lev. 22:19), which is the house of the sanctuary.
7.	A.	Another explanation of ["Your neck is like the tower of David:" this is the house of the Sanctuary. And] why is it compared to the neck?
	B.	Just as the neck is located in his highest part, so the house of the sanctuary was in the highest place in the world.
	C.	Just as most of the ornaments are hung around the neck, so the priesthood is attached to the house of sanctuary.
	D.	And just as if the neck is removed, a person cannot live, so once the house of the sanctuary was destroyed, [those who hate] Israel have no life.
8.	A.	"built for an arsenal:"
	B.	[Simon:] Four square.
9.	A.	[Since the word for "arsenal' and the words for beauty and ruin use the same consonants,] Hiyya b. R. Bun said, "It was beautiful but is now a ruin.
	B.	"Said the Holy One, blessed be He, 'I am the one who made it a ruin in this world, I am the one who is going to make it beautiful in the world to come.'"

10. A.   [Since the word for "arsenal' and the words for ruin and mouth use the same consonants,] there is another explanation of the word translated arsenal:

B.   It is the ruin for which all mouths pray.

C.   In this connection they have said:

D.   **Those who stand up to say the Prayer outside of the Land turn toward the Land of Israel: "And pray toward their land which you gave their fathers, the city which you have chosen, and the house which I have built for your name" (2 Chr. 6:38). Those who are in the Land of Israel turn toward Jerusalem: "And they pray to you toward this city which you have chosen and the house which I have built for your name" (2 Chr. 6:34). Those who are in Jerusalem turn toward the Temple: "When he comes and prays toward this house" (2 Chr. 6:32). Those who are in the Temple turn toward the Chamber of the Holy of Holies and say the prayer: "When they pray toward this place" (1 Kgs. 8:30) It turns out that those standing in the north face south, those in the south face north, those in the east face west, those in the west face east. Thus all Israel turns out to be praying toward one place" (T. Berakhot 3:16A-F, cf. M. Ber. 4:5-6].**

E.   And how do we know that all Israel is to turn out to pray toward one place?

F.   R. Joshua b. Levi said, "'That is, the temple before the sanctuary' (1 Kgs. 6:17), meaning, it is the Temple toward which all faces are to turn."

G.   So much for the age in which the Temple was standing. How about the time that it lies in ruins?

H.   Said R. Abin, "'built for an arsenal:' [Since the word for "arsenal' and the word for mouth use the same consonants,] the sense is, the Temple for which all mouths pray.

I.   "In connection with reciting the *Shema*, one says, '...who builds Jerusalem.'

J.   "In connection with the Prayer, one says, '...who builds Jerusalem.'

K.   "In connection with the Grace after Meals, one says, '...who builds Jerusalem.'

L.   "Thus: 'that for which all mouths say prayers before the Holy One, blessed be He.'

M.   "He will rebuild it and bring his Presence to dwell in it."

11. A.   One verse of Scripture says, "And my eyes and heart will be there perpetually" (1 Kgs. 9:3), and another says, "I will go and return to my place" (Hos. 5:15):

B.   How are the two to be harmonized?

C.   His face is above, but his heart is below.

D.   **For so it has been taught: [And if he cannot turn his face,] he should direct his heart toward the Chamber of the Holy of Holies [M. Ber. 4:5C].**

E.   R. Hiyya the Elder and R. Simeon b. Halafta:

F.   R. Hiyya the Elder said, "Toward the Holy of Holies that is above."

G.   R. Simeon b. Halafta said, "Toward the Holy of Holies that is here below."

H. Said R. Phineas, "I shall confirm the opinions of both of you: it must be toward the Holy of Holies that is above, which is directly over the Holy of Holies that is here below,

I. "in line with this verse: 'The place O Lord that you have made for you to dwell in' (Ex. 15:17), that is, directly above your dwelling place, the sanctuary above."

12. A. "Mount Moriah" [the consonants of which can be read as bitter or as awe]:

B. R. Hiyya the Elder and R. Yannai:

C. One said, "For from there flows bitterness to the world."

D. And the other said, "For from there flows awe to the world."

13. A. "Ark" [the consonants of which can be read as light or curse]:

B. R. Hiyya the Elder and R. Yannai:

C. One said, "For from there flows light to the world."

D. The other said, "For from there flows a curse to the nations of the world."

14. A. "Sanctuary" [a word that uses the same consonants as the word for speech and for commandments]:

B. The household of R. Hiyya the Elder and R. Yannai:

C. One said, "For from there went forth speech to the nations of the world."

D. The other said, "For from there went forth commandments to the world."

15. A. "whereon hang a thousand bucklers:"

B. Said R. Berekhiah, "Said the Holy One, blessed be He, 'A thousand generations I have folded together and brought him who serves as shield to you, whom your heart has yearned for.' [Simon, p. 198, n. 2: The Torah should have been given after a thousand generations but was actually given after twenty-six.]"

16. A. [Supply "whereon hang a thousand bucklers:"]

B. Said R. Berekhiah in the name of R. Isaac, "Said Abraham before the Holy One, blessed be He, 'Lord of the world, For me have you been made a shield, while for my children are you not made a shield?'

C. "Said to him the Holy One, blessed be He, 'For you I am only a single shield: "I am your shield" (Gen. 15:1).

D. "'But for your children, I shall be many shields: "whereon hang a thousand bucklers."'"

17. A. "all of them shields of warriors:"

B. This refers to the priesthood and the monarchy.

The miscellany before us shows us the remarkable discipline that characterized the prior readings of the base verse and demonstrates that the formal unity undergirded conceptual cogency.

49

Song of Songs Rabbah to Song of Songs 4:5

4:5　　*Your two breasts are like two fawns, twins of a gazelle, that feed among the lilies.*

XLIX:i
1.　A.　"Your two breasts are like two fawns:"
　　B.　This refers to Moses and Aaron.
　　C.　Just as a woman's breasts are her glory and her ornament,
　　D.　so Moses and Aaron are the glory and the ornament of Israel.
　　E.　Just as a woman's breasts are her charm, so Moses and Aaron are the charm of Israel.
　　F.　Just as a woman's breasts are her honor and her praise, so Moses and Aaron are the honor and praise of Israel.
　　G.　Just as a woman's breasts are full of milk, so Moses and Aaron are full of Torah.
　　H.　Just as whatever a woman eats the infant eats and sucks, so all the Torah that our lord, Moses, learned he taught to Aaron: "And Moses told Aaron all the words of the Lord" (Ex. 4:28).
　　I.　And rabbis say, "He actually revealed the Ineffable Name of God to him."
　　J.　Just as one breast is not larger than the other, so Moses and Aaron were the same: "These are Moses and Aaron" (Ex. 6:27), "These are Aaron and Moses" (Ex. 6:26), so that in knowledge of the Torah Moses was not greater than Aaron, and Aaron was not greater than Moses.
2.　A.　R. Abba said, "The matter may be compared to the case of a king who had two first-rate pearls, which he put in the balance.
　　B.　"This one was not greater than that, and that was not greater than this.
　　C.　"So Moses and Aaron were equal."
3.　A.　Said R. Hanina b. R. Pappa, "Blessed is the Omnipresent, who has chosen these two brothers.
　　B.　"For they were created only for the Torah and the glory of Israel."

4. A. R. Joshua of Sikhnin in the name of R. Levi: "There were two [Simon, p. 199, n.1] species of snakes in Alexandria, one of which induced cold, the other heat.

   B. "[Simon, verbatim:] There was a case in which physicians sent for some of them and made a compound out of them with which they healed [snake bites]."

5. A. R. Abbah in the name of R. Simeon: "A mortal cannot put on the poultice before seeing the wound.

   B. "But the One who spoke and thereby brought the world into being is not that way. But rather he puts on the poultice and only afterward inflicts the wound.

   C. "'Behold I will bring it healing and cure and I will cure them' (Jer. 33:6); 'When I would heal Israel' (Hos. 7:1).

   D. "Said the Holy One, blessed be He, 'I have come to heal the transgressions of Israel, and 'Then is the iniquity of Ephraim uncovered and the wickedness of Samaria' (Hos. 7:1).

   E. "But as to the nations of the world, he smites them and then heals them: 'And the Lord will smite Egypt, smiting and healing' (Isa. 19:22),

   F. "smiting through Aaron, healing through Moses."

6. A. Happy are these two brothers, who were created only for the glory of Israel.

   B. That is what Samuel said, "It is the Lord that made Moses and Aaron and brought your fathers up" (1 Sam. 12:6).

7. A. Thus "Your two breasts are like two fawns:"

   B. This refers to Moses and Aaron.

It is unusual to see so much attention to editorial artifice as is revealed by No. 7. But some of the materials that the compilers have chosen – Nos. 4, 5 in particular – do not fit because they have not been composed for the purposes of the present construction. Not only so, but No. 6 so clearly refers us back to No. 3 that the intervening materials are surely out of kilter. Read as Nos. 1-3 and 6-7, the composition is unitary and stunning; it bears a liturgical quality.

XLIX:ii

1. A. "twins of a gazelle:"

   B. R. Joshua of Sikhnin in the name of R. Levi: "Just as in the case of twins, if one of them leaves the breasts, the breasts dry up, so it is written, 'And I cut off the three shepherds in one month [Moses, Aaron, Miriam]' (Zech. 9:8).

   C. "Now is it not the fact that they died only in the same year?

   D. "But the decree concerning them [that they were to die] was made in the same month for all three: 'The princes of the people are gathered in' (Ps. 47:10)."

2. A. R. Yosé says, "Three good providers arose for Israel, and these are they: Moses, Aaron, and Miriam.

   B. "On account of the merit accruing to them were given to them three good gifts: the well, manna, and clouds of glory."

C.   "The manna on account of the merit of Moses, the well on account of the merit of Miriam, and the clouds of glory on account of the merit of Aaron.

D.   "When Miriam died, the well went dry, and they said, 'This is no place of seed or of figs' (Num. 20:5), but the well again returned on account of the merit of Moses and Aaron.

E.   "When Aaron died, the clouds of glory departed: 'And when all the congregation saw that Aaron was dead' (Num. 20:29) may be read not 'saw' but 'feared.'

F.   "So both [the well and the clouds] were restored on account of the merit of Moses.

G.   "But when Moses died, all three of them departed, and never returned,

H.   "the hornet did not cross the Jordan with them,

I.   "and the Israelites never again from that time on saw tranquillity."

3. A.   "that feed among the lilies:"

B.   Said Samuel b. R. Nahmani, "Miriam and Jochebed were the midwives of Israel, and they would shepherd Israel, whose hearts were as soft as lilies.

C.   "And where was the feeding ground of Israel? In Egypt at the Red Sea."

The reading of the base verse in terms of Moses, Aaron, and now Miriam, goes forward in a coherent way. Nos. 1, 2 go over the ground of the foregoing, treating the holy family as equivalent in merit. No. 2 covers the same ground. No. 3 then focuses upon Miriam and Jochebed, which is to say, it is framed for a different theme from the paramount one.

50

Song of Songs Rabbah to Song of Songs 4:6

4:6   *Until the day breathes and the shadows flee,*
I will hie me to the mountain of myrrh and the hill of
frankincense.

L:i

1.   A.   "Until the day breathes:"
      B.   R. Abbahu and R. Levi:
      C.   One said, "[Genesis Rabbah XLVII:VII.1. "Then Abraham took Ishmael his son and all the slaves born in his house [or bought for his money, every male among the men of Abraham's house, and he circumcised the flesh of their foreskins that very day, as God had said to him]" (Gen. 17:23)]
      D.   "When Abraham circumcised himself, his sons, and those who were born of his house, he made a mountain of foreskins, and the sun shone on them, and they putrefied. The stench rose to heaven before the Holy One, blessed be He, like the scent of incense and like the scent of the handful of frankincense thrown onto the offerings made by fire.
      E.   "Said the Holy One, blessed be He, 'When my children will come into transgressions and bad deeds, I shall remember in their behalf that scent and will be filled with mercy for them and convert the attribute of justice into the attribute of mercy for them.'
      F.   "What verse of Scripture indicates it? 'I will hie me to the mountain of myrrh and the hill of frankincense.'"
      G.   R. Levi said, "When Joshua circumcised the children of Israel, he made a mountain of foreskins, and the sun shone on them, and they putrefied. The stench rose to heaven before the Holy One, blessed be He, like the scent of incense and like the scent of the handful of frankincense thrown onto the offerings made by fire.
      H.   "Said the Holy One, blessed be He, 'When my children will come into transgressions and bad deeds, I shall remember in their behalf that scent and will be filled with mercy for them and

		convert the attribute of justice into the attribute of mercy for them.'
	I.	"What verse of Scripture indicates it? 'I will hie me to the mountain of myrrh and the hill of frankincense.'"
2.	A.	"In that same day Abraham circumcised himself" (Gen. 17:26):
	B.	Said R. Berekhiah, "Had Abraham circumcised himself by night, his generation would have said, 'If we had witnessed it, we would not have let him do it.
	C.	"Thus: 'In that same day Abraham circumcised himself.'
	D.	"If anyone is offended, let him say so."
3.	A.	R. Abbahu b. R. Kahana and R. Levi:
	B.	R. Abbahu said, "He felt the pain and was hurt, so that the Holy One, blessed be He, could increase his reward.
	C.	"'He who is born of your household and he who is bought with your money must be circumcised' (Gen. 17:13).
	D.	"Said the Holy One, blessed be He, 'Will an unclean person come and take up the tasks of a clean one? That is not possible. But...must be circumcised.'
	E.	"'I am clean and Abraham is clean; it is right for the person who is clean to take up the task of one who is clean.'"
4.	A.	R. Abin in the name of R. Simeon said, "The Holy One, blessed be He, joined his right hand with Abraham's and circumcised him:
	B.	"'you made the circumcision with him' (Neh. 9:8)."
5.	A.	Another reading of the verse, "I will hie me to the mountain of myrrh:"
	B.	This speaks of Abraham, who is the head of all the righteous men.
	C.	"and the hill of frankincense:"
	D.	This speaks of Isaac, who was offered like a "handful of frankincense on the altar."

The decision to read the base verse in terms of the patriarchs comes prior to any exposition of the pertinent details. The base verse is not fundamental, as is shown by the version of Genesis Rabbah, which works without it. But the reason the passage has been chosen is equally valid, as we see: the base verse's image works perfectly. Once the theme is introduced, then Nos. 2, 3, 4 are carried along. No. 5 reverts to the main point of interest, and is continued in Chapter Fifty-One with Jacob.

51

Song of Songs Rabbah to
Song of Songs 4:7

4:7   *You are all fair, my love; there is no flaw in you.*

LI:i
1.   A.   "You are all fair, my love:"
      B.   This refers to our father, Jacob.
      C.   [Supply: "there is no flaw in you:"]
      D.   For his bed was whole before him, and there was no unfit [descendant] produced upon it.

2.   A.   What is the meaning of the verse, "You are all fair, my love; [there is no flaw in you]"?
      B.   R. Simeon b. Yohai taught on Tannaite authority, "When the Israelites stood before Mount Sinai and said, 'All that the Lord has spoken we will do and obey' (Ex. 24:7),
      C.   "at that moment there were not found among them persons afflicted with flux, persons afflicted with *saraat*, lame, blind, dumb, deaf, lunatics, imbeciles, fools or hangers-on.
      D.   "And with regard to that moment, Scripture says, 'there is no flaw in you.'
      E.   "But once they had sinned, in only a little while there were found among them persons afflicted with flux, persons afflicted with *saraat*, lame, blind, dumb, deaf, lunatics, imbeciles, fools and hangers-on.
      F.   "At that time it was said, 'Let them put out of the camp every leper and all who has suffered a flux' (Num. 5:2)."

3.   A.   Said R. Helbo, "'And he who presented his offering the first day was Nahshon son of Amminadab...on the second day Nethanel son of Zuar made the offering' (Num. 7:12, 18).
      B.   "Why has Judah been treated as subordinate?
      C.   "It was so that Judah should not take pride and say, 'Since I made my offering first of all, I am the greatest among you all.'
      D.   "Rather, the Holy One, blessed be He, credited it to them as though all of them had made their offerings on the first day and on the final day."

53

4. A.   Said R. Eleazar, "'This was the dedication-offering of the altar, in the day when it was anointed' (Num. 7:84).

    B.   "Now had not each one of them made his offering of one basin, one spoon, and the like [on the successive days]? Why does Scripture tote it all up: 'Twelve silver dishes, twelve silver basins, twelve golden pans' (Num. 7:84)?

    C.   "It was so that Judah should not take pride and say, 'Since I made my offering first of all, I am the greatest among you all.'

    D.   "Rather, the Holy One, blessed be He, credited it to them as though all of them had made their offerings on the first day and on the final day."

5. A.   Said R. Berekhiah, "'All these are the twelve tribes of Israel...every one according to his blessing he blessed them' (Gen. 49:28):

    B.   "Since it is stated, 'And he blessed them" (Gen. 49:28), why was it necessary to repeat, '...blessing each with the blessing suitable to them'?

    C.   "This teaches that Jacob our father went and compared them to wild beasts. Since he had bestowed a blessing on Judah as a lion, 'Judah is a lion's whelp' (Gen. 49:9); Dan as a serpent, 'Dan shall be a serpent in the way' (Gen. 49:17); Naphtali as a hind, 'Naphtali is a hind let loose' (Gen. 49:21); and Benjamin as a wolf, 'Benjamin is a wolf that ravens' (Gen. 49:27).

    D.   "Then he drew them together into a single blessing, so stating that all of them are wolves, serpents, fiery serpents, scorpions.

    E.   "That is in line with this verse: 'Dan shall be a snake' (Gen. 49:17), while Moses called him a lion: 'Dan is a lion's whelp' (Deut. 33:22). [Genesis Rabbah XCIX:IV adds:] "In line with this verse [the message is clear]: 'You all are fair, my love, and there is no blemish in you' (Song 4:7)."

6. A.   Said R. Idi, "We find in connection with the offerings made by the princes that what this one offered that one offered.

    B.   "This one brought a burnt-offering and that one brought a burnt-offering, this one brought a meal-offering and that one brought a meal-offering, this one brought a sin-offering and that one brought a sin-offering, this one brought peace-offerings and that one brought peace-offerings.

    C.   "Why was this so?

    D.   "For all of them were flawless and all of them equal with one another."

7. A.   Why did Scripture give the genealogies, in the book of Exodus, for Reuben, Simeon, and Levi [at Ex. 6:14-19, leaving out the others]?

    B.   R. Hanina and R. Levi:

    C.   One said, "It was because their father had spoken critically of them."

    D.   The other said, "It was because Scripture imputed to them genealogies connected with Moses and Aaron."

    E.   Now we do not know who held the one opinion, and who held the other.

    F.   But on the basis of that which R. Yudan in the name of R. Judah b. R. Simeon in the name of R. Huna said, "'The ear that listens to the reproof of life abides among the wise' (Prov. 15:31)," it must

		follow that it is R. Huna who said, "It was because their father had spoken critically of them.
	G.	"It was because they accepted the rebuke of their father that they had the merit of being assigned a genealogy connected to Moses and Aaron.
	H.	"That is why it is said, 'there is no flaw in you.'"
8.	A.	[Supply: Why did Scripture give the genealogies, in the book of Exodus, for Reuben, Simeon, and Levi at Ex. 6:14-19, leaving out the others?]
	B.	R. Judah, R. Nehemiah, and rabbis:
	C.	R. Judah said, "It is because all the other tribes did not guard their genealogies in Egypt, but Reuben, Simeon, and Levi did guard their genealogies in Egypt."
	D.	R. Nehemiah said, "It was because all the other tribes worshipped idols in Egypt, but Reuben, Simeon, and Levi did not worship idols in Egypt."
	E.	Rabbis said, "It is because all the other tribes did not exercise authority over the Israelites in Egypt, while these tribes did exercise authority over the Israelites in Egypt.
	F.	"How was this so? When Reuben died, authority was transferred to Simeon, when Simeon died, authority was transferred to Levi, when Levi died, he proposed to transfer authority to Judah.
	G.	"But an echo came forth and proclaimed, 'Leave it alone until its time shall come.'
	H.	"When did its time come [for authority to be transferred to Judah]?
	I.	"After the death of Joshua: 'And it happened after the death of Joshua...that the Lord said, Judah shall go up' (Judges 1:1)."
9.	A.	[Supply: "His younger kinsman, Othniel the Kenizzite, captured it" (Judges 1:13):]
	B.	He had three names: Judah, Othniel, and Jabez [cf. 1 Chr. 4:9].
	C.	[As to the Judah to whom authority was transmitted,] R. Berekhiah and R. Levi in the name of R. Hama b. R. Hanina: "This is Boaz."
	D.	R. Simon in the name of R. Joshua b. Levi: "It is Othniel."
10.	A.	[Supply: "You are all fair, my love; there is no flaw in you:"]
	B.	"Son of man, the house of Israel has become dross to me, all of them are brass and tin" (Ezek. 22:18).
	C.	By contrast, said Zechariah, "I have seen it as entirely gold: 'I have seen, and behold a candlestick all of gold, with a bowl on top of it...and two olive trees by it' (Zech. 4:2)."
	D.	Two Amoras:
	E.	One said, "The word translated bowl are to be read to spell the word, exile."
	F.	The other said, "The letters of the word translated bowl should be read redemption."
	G.	The one who reads the letters to spell "exile" holds that they went into exile to Babylonia and the Presence of God went with them.
	H.	The one who reads the letters to spell "redemption" holds that the sense is, the one who redeems her is the one who saves her, as in this sense: "Our redeemer, the Lord of hosts is his name" (Isa. 47:4).

I.   Said the Holy One, blessed be He, "Since that is the case, then: 'You are all fair, my love; there is no flaw in you.'"

No. 1 completes the exposition of Chapter Fifty in terms of the patriarchs. No. 2 turns to read the verse in terms of Israel at Sinai. That was the point at which there was no flaw. Why is No. 3, bearing in its wake Nos. 4, 5, 6, 7, 8, 9 parachuted down? The only reason I can suggest is found at 5.E (echoed at 6.D). The whole had already formed a coherent unit, with its own theme and problem, and then the compilers of our document (or some later collaborator-copyist) dropped the entire composite into our compilation. No. 10's position is only marginally less dubious. Here is another case in which available materials, with a more comfortable location somewhere else, have been made to serve the program of our compilers.

52

Song of Songs Rabbah to Song of Songs 4:8

<table>
<tr><td>4:8</td><td>*Come with me from Lebanon, my bride; come with me from Lebanon. Depart from the peak of Amana, from the peak of Senir and Hermon, from the dens of lions, from the mountains of leopards.*</td></tr>
</table>

LII:i

1. A. "Come with me from Lebanon, my bride, come with me from Lebanon:"

   B. Said the Holy One, blessed be He, "'Come with me from Lebanon.'

   C. "There we have learned in the Mishnah: 'They give a virgin twelve months to provide for herself from the time that the husband has demanded her [hand in marriage, that is to accomplish the consummation of the marriage]. [And just as they give a time of preparation to the woman, so they give a time of preparation to a man to provide for himself]' [M. Ketubot 5:2A-B].

   D. [God continues,] "But that is not how I did it. Rather, while you were still occupied with the mortar and brick [of Egyptian bondage] [the words for brick and Lebanon use the same consonants], I lept and redeemed you" [Simon, p. 205, n. 3: "...straight from the bricks and mortar I took you for my bride by giving you the Torah, though you had had no time yet for spiritual preparation"].

2. A. The oleaginous intellect of Ahasuerus allowed "six months of oil of myrrh" (Est. 2:12).

3. A. [Supply: "six months of oil of myrrh" (Est. 2:12)]

   B. R. Judah b. R. Ezekiel said, "This refers to oil of boxwood."

   C. R. Yannai said, "This refers to oil of unripe oils, which removes hair and smoothens the skin."

4. A. [Reverting to 2.A:] [God continues,] "But that is not how I did it."

5. A. R. Berekhiah and R. Jeremiah in the name of R. Hiyya b. R. Abba said, "In Nehardea R. Levi b. Sisi gave the following exposition:

57

B.   """They saw the God of Israel and there was under his feet the like of a brick work of sapphire stone" (Ex. 24:10). This was before they were redeemed.

C.   "'But after they were redeemed, where the brick work was normally kept, there it was put away."

D.   Said R. Berekhiah, "'A brick work of sapphire' is not what is written here, but rather, 'like a brick work of sapphire.' [The meaning is that] both it [the Torah] and all the implements that belong to it were given, it, the basket, and the trowel were given."

6. A.   Bar Qappara said,, "Before the Israelites were redeemed from Egypt, as it were, [the Torah] was written in the firmament. After they were redeemed, it no longer appeared in the firmament.

B.   "What is the Scripture proof for this view? 'It is like the very heaven in its purity' (Ex. 24:10), when it is clear of clouds."

7. A.   Said the Holy One, blessed be He, to them, "When you went into exile in Babylonia, I was with you: 'For your sake I have been sent to Babylon' (Isa. 43:14).

B.   "And when you return to the chosen house in the near future, I shall be with you: 'with me from Lebanon, my bride.'"

8. A.   [Supply: "with me from Lebanon, my bride:"]

B.   Said R. Levi, "It was necessary for Scripture to say only, 'with me *to* Lebanon, my bride.' How come, 'with me *from* Lebanon, my bride'?

C.   "To begin with, he leaps forth out of [and abandons to destruction] the house of the sanctuary, and only then does he exact punishment from the nations of the world [for destroying the place]."

9. A.   Said R. Berekhiah, "In three hours the Holy One, blessed be He, will exact punishment from the wicked Esau and his troops:

B.   "'Now will I arise, says the Lord' (Isa. 33:10). [The word now appears three times in the cited verse, each standing for an hour, so Simon, p. 207, n. 1]."

10. A.   [Supply: "Now will I arise, says the Lord" (Isa. 33:10):]

B.   R. Simeon b. R. Yannai: "'Now will I arise:' so long as she [Israel] is wallowing in the dirt, as it were, so is he.

C.   "And that is in line with what Isaiah says, 'Shake yourself from the dust, arise, and sit down O Jerusalem' (Isa. 52:2).

D.   "At that moment: 'Be silent, all flesh, before the Lord' (Zech. 2:17).

E.   "Why so? 'Because 'he is aroused out of his holy habitation' (Zech. 2:17)."

F.   Said R. Aha, "Like a chicken that shakes its wings free of ashes."

The message is clear, though the formulation bears the burden of interpolations that impede clarity. 1.D makes the point: God redeemed Israel without preparation. No. 2 continues No. 1, and No. 3 is carried in its wake. No. 4 then completes No. 1. Why Nos. 5 and 6? So far as I can see the basic notion is that when the Israelites were redeemed, they got everything they needed; then the theme is the same as No. 1 – getting ready for the marriage. But the point would seem to me the opposite; now it is not without preparation. No. 7, then

8 then reverts to our base verse, but No. 7 makes its own point, which is that God is with Israel in exile and in redemption, and No. 8 has its position as well, which is that God punishes first Israel, then the nations. No. 9 makes the same point, and No. 10 is tacked on because it amplifies the prooftext of No. 9. The whole then is somewhat run-on, even though the opening proposition is compelling.

LII:ii

1.   A.   "Depart from the peak of Amana, [from the peak of Senir and Hermon, from the dens of lions, from the mountains of leopards]:"

      B.   Said R. Huna in the name of R. Justus, "When the exiles [returning to Zion when the Messiah brings them back] reach Taurus Munus, they are going to say a Song.

      C.   "And the nations of the world are going to bring them [Simon, verbatim:] like princes to the Messiah."

      D.   "What verse of Scripture indicates it? 'Depart from the peak of Amana.'

      E.   "The sense of the word for 'depart' is only 'offering,' as in the following verse: 'There is not a present to bring to the man of God' (1 Sam. 9:7)."

2.   A.   [Supply: "There is not a present to bring to the man of God" (1 Sam. 9:7):]

      B.   "It is suitable, but I am not suitable." [Following Simon, p. 207, n. 5: Saul speaks and says that "what he had might have sufficed as a gift for an ordinary person, but not for Samuel."]

3.   A.   [Reverting to 1.E:] "[God speaks,] 'Have I not done as much in the time of Hazael: "So Hazael went to meet him and took a present with him, even of every good thing of Damascus, forty camels' burden" (2 Kgs. 8:9).'

4.   A.   [Supply: "So Hazael went to meet him and took a present with him, even of every good thing of Damascus, forty camels' burden" (2 Kgs. 8:9):]

      B.   Said R. Judah, "And was the entirety of the good things of Damascus merely forty camels' burden?

      C.   "But this serves to tell you that he had in hand precious stones and jewels that were worth in value all the good things of Damascus, thus, 'took a present with him, even of every good thing of Damascus.'"

5.   A.   [Reverting to 3.A:] "But the [nations of the world] are going to bring [following Simon:] them as gifts to the royal messiah: 'And they shall bring all your brethren out of all the nations for an offering to the Lord, upon horses and in chariots and in litters and on mules and upon swift beasts' (Isa. 66:2).

6.   A.   [Supply: "And they shall bring all your brethren out of all the nations for an offering to the Lord, upon horses and in chariots and in litters and on mules and upon swift beasts" (Isa. 66:2):]

      B.   What is the meaning of the word translated "swift beasts"?

      C.   R. Berekhiah in the name of R. Judah said, "They are like old men who cannot ride any sort of vehicle but have to be carried on a litter [by hand]."

7.   A.   [Continuing 5.A:] "That [view, that the nations will present Israel as
           a gift to the Messiah,] is in line with this verse of Scripture: 'Give to
           the Lord families, you peoples' (Ps. 96:7)."
     B.   Said R. Aha, "What is written is not, 'Peoples, give to the Lord the
           families,' but 'give...families, you peoples, give to the Lord glory
           and strength.'
     C.   "[The meaning is,] 'When you bring them, do not bring them in a
           casual way, but with 'glory and strength.'"
8.   A.   How did the Israelites merit [being made a gift to the Messiah
           brought by the nations]?
     B.   It is by reason of the merit that they gained when they said the
           Song at the Sea.
     C.   R. Nahman said, "It was by reason of the merit that was gained by
           the faith with which Abraham believed: 'And he believed in the
           Lord' (Gen. 15:6)."
     D.   [Contrary to the view of E,] R. Helbo in the name of R. Yohanan
           said, "'And Israel saw the great work [which the Lord had wielded
           against the Egyptians, the people feared the Lord; they had faith
           in the Lord and his servant Moses]' (Ex. 14:31).
     E.   "Now he was still leading them, and should they not have
           believed?! Is there someone who can see and yet not believe?
     F.   "Rather, it must be because of the merit gained by the Israelites
           when, while still in Egypt, they yet believed: 'And the people
           believed' (Ex. 4:31)."

No. 1 introduces the basic proposition in what is a very confusing
passage. It is that the nations are going to present a gift to the Messiah
when the Israelites are en route back to Zion, and, following Simon,
Israel is that gift. That is the clear account of No. 1. The word Amana
then is the occasion, since it stands for gift. No. 2 is interpolated,
because it deals with the prooftext of No. 1. No. 3, bearing its burden of
No. 4, then continues 1.E. No. 5, carrying No. 6, brings us back to No. 3.
No. 7 reverts to No. 5. I see No. 8 as a fresh expansion of the
introductory proposition, as my interpolation shows. But one could as
well see No. 8 and what follows as simply a fresh reading of our base
verse, now with an interest in the merit gained by faith; for the word
faith and Amana share the same consonants. Since nothing beyond 8.A
requires the context of Nos. 1-7, that seems to me a likely alternative.
The theme of the merit gained through faith continues in a fresh
reading of our base verse.

LII:iii

1.   A.   Another reading of "Depart from the peak of Amana, [from the
           peak of Senir and Hermon, from the dens of lions, from the
           mountains of leopards]:"
     B.   This refers to Abraham: "And he believed in the Lord" (Gen. 15:6).
2.   A.   "from the peak of Senir:"
     B.   This refers to Isaac.

C.   Just as the letters of the word "Senir" yield the sense "hates the furrow," so Isaac was tried only one time alone.

3. A.   "and Hermon:"
   B.   This refers to Jacob:
   C.   Just as all the good of Hermon is located on the lower slopes,
   D.   so the priesthood derives from Jacob, the Levites derive from Jacob, the monarchy derives from Jacob.

4. A.   "from the dens of lions:"
   B.   This refers to Sihon and Og.
   C.   Just as a lion is proud, so Sihon and Og were proud and strong.
   D.   For the distance from the one to the other was merely a day, and yet this one did not come to help that one, nor did that one come to help this one.

5. A.   "from the mountains of leopards:"
   B.   This refers to the Canaanites.
   C.   Just as the leopard is bold, so these are bold [for they all went out to fight against the Israelites, as is shown in this verse]: "And there was not a man left in Ai" (Josh 8:17).

6. A.   R. Berekhiah in the name of R. Eliezer said, "The Israelites really ought to have recited a song at the fall of Sihon and Og.
   B.   "Hezekiah really ought to have recited a song at the fall of Sennacherib: 'But Hezekiah rendered not according to the benefit done for him' (2 Chr. 32:25).
   C.   "How come? 'For his heart was lifted up' (2 Chr. 32:25)."

7. A.   [Supply: "For his heart was lifted up" (2 Chr. 32:25):"]
   B.   Now you know full well that Hezekiah was king and righteous, and yet you say, "his heart was lifted up"?
   C.   Rather, his heart was too proud to say a song.
   D.   Isaiah came to Hezekiah and his court and said to them, "Sing to the Lord [for he has done gloriously. Let this be made known in all the world" (Isa. 12:5-6)].
   E.   They said to him, "Why should we?"
   F.   "For he has done gloriously."
   G.   They said, "This already has been 'made known in all the world.'"
   H.   Said R. Abba b. Kahana, "Said Hezekiah, 'The Torah with which I am occupied makes atonement for the song [that I have not sung].'"
   I.   Said R. Levi, "Said Hezekiah, 'Why are we supposed to recite the miracles and mighty acts of the Holy One, blessed be He? This is already known from one end of the world to the other!
   J.   "'After all, didn't the orb of the sun stand still in the middle of the firmament, so that the miracles and mighty acts of the Holy One, blessed be He, were already made known from one end of the world to the other!'"

8. A.   R. Ishmael b. R. Yosé in the name of R. Abba says, "Pharaoh, king of Egypt, and Tirhaka, king of Ethiopia, were subject to that same miracle, when they came to the aid of Hezekiah.
   B.   "Sennacherib took note of them, and what did the wicked Sennacherib do to them?
   C.   "In the evening he chained them.

D.   "At midnight the angel went forth and smote the armies of Sennacherib: 'And the angel of the Lord went forth and smote the camp of the Assyrians' (Isa. 37:36).

E.   "Now at dawn Hezekiah got up and found them chained. He said, 'It appears that these have come only to assist me, and he freed them.

F.   "So they went and reported the miracles and mighty acts of the Holy One, blessed be He: 'Thus says the Lord, Egypt's wealth and Nubia's gains [and Sabaites, long of limb, shall pass over to you and be yours, pass over and follow you in fetters, bow low to you and reverently address you: "Only among you is God, there is no other god at all! You are indeed a God who concealed himself, O God of Israel, who brings victory!"]' (Isa. 45:14-15)."

9. A.   [Supply: "Thus says the Lord, Egypt's wealth and Nubia's gains and Sabaites, long of limb, shall pass over to you and be yours, pass over and follow you in fetters, bow low to you and reverently address you: 'Only among you is God, there is no other god at all! You are indeed a God who concealed himself, O God of Israel, who bring victory!'" (Isa. 45:14-15):]

B.   "Egypt's wealth:"

C.   This refers to Pharaoh.

D.   "and Nubia's gains:"

E.   This refers to Tirhaka, king of Ethiopia.

F.   "and Sabaites, long of limb:"

G.   This refers to their troops.

H.   "shall pass over to you:"

I.   This refers to Hezekiah and his company.

J.   "and be yours:"

K.   They are already handed over to you.

L.   "pass over and follow you in fetters:"

M.   In chains.

N.   "bow low to you:"

O.   That is, to Jerusalem.

P.   "and reverently address you:"

Q.   That is, the house of the sanctuary.

R.   And what will they say?

S.   "Only among you is God, there is no other god at all."

T.   Said Isaiah before the Holy One, blessed be He, "Lord of the world, 'You are indeed a God who concealed himself.'"

U.   What is the sense of "indeed"?

T.   [Since the words for indeed and where use the same consonants, the sense is:] "Where are you hiding, O God?"

U.   [Or, alternatively:] "Indeed, you have power, but you are hiding."

V.   He said to him, "'The God of Israel is the one who will bring victory:' I shall come back and take vengeance."

10. A.   [Supply: "Now I know that the Lord will give victory to his anointed, will answer him from his heavenly sanctuary with the mighty victories of his right arm. They call on chariots, they call on horses, but we call on the name of the Lord our God. They collapse and lie fallen, but we rally and gather strength. O Lord grant victory! May the King answer us when we call" (Ps. 20:7-10):]

B.   R. Joshua b. Levi said, "If Hezekiah had said a song at the fall of Sennacherib, he would have been designated as the royal Messiah, and Sennacherib would have been marked as Gog and Magog. But that is not what he did.

C.   "Rather: 'Now I know that the Lord will give victory to his anointed, will answer him from his heavenly sanctuary with the mighty victories of his right arm. They call on chariots, they call on horses, but we call on the name of the Lord our God. They collapse and lie fallen, but we rally and gather strength. O Lord grant victory! May the King answer us when we call.'" [Simon, p. 211, n. 2: Because he did not become the Messiah through his neglect to hymn God, he found it necessary to pray for the future...otherwise this prayer would have been unnecessary.]

Nos. 1, 2, 3 do a fine job of reading the patriarchs into our base verse, that is, the predictable alternative to Israel at the Sea and Sinai. These are the two moments of love. Since the base verse goes on to refer to "lions," and "leopards," we proceed to further and secondary points of clarification. Now the power of the metaphor shifts; it is no longer general, an encompassing celebration of Israel. It is now particular, and we have to point to what traits, in the metaphor, pertain to the specific and identified figure: how do we know that the traits of the lion pertain, and what traits apply. These are the questions that are dealt with at Nos. 4, 5. No. 6 then tacks on a consideration in no way invited by our base verse, and that accounts for the vast composition that enriches the discussion but also considerably diverts attention from the main points. In this sense our compilers, if they were the ones who threw in this mass of material, have had a dual theory of their document: the Song and its specific meanings for Israel's love for God and God's love for Israel, and then a secondary expansion of all manner of themes and images in general. No. 6 forms the bridge, tacked on because of the allusion to Sihon and Og. Then No. 7 is added because of the expansion upon the prooftext of No. 6. That leads us to the expansion of the expansion, No. 8. The prooftext important to No. 8 is then vastly expanded at No. 9, and No. 10 completes the matter. If the whole goes back to the initial compilers, then we have, as I said, two distinct theories of the formation of the document.

53

Song of Songs Rabbah to Song of Songs 4:9

4:9   *You have ravished my heart, my sister, my bride, you have ravished my heart with a glance of your eyes, with one jewel of your necklace.*

LIII:i

1. A.   "You have ravished my heart, my sister, my bride, you have ravished my heart:"

    B.   Said the Holy One, blessed be He, "You had one heart in Egypt, but you gave me two hearts."

    C.   "you have ravished my heart with a glance of your eyes:"

    D.   It was through the blood of the Passover-offering and the blood of circumcision.

    E.   "with one jewel of your necklace:"

    F.   This is Moses, who was unique, the hero of all your tribes.

2. A.   Another interpretation of the verse, "You have ravished my heart, my sister, my bride, you have ravished my heart:"

    B.   Said the Holy One, blessed be He, "You had one heart at the Sea, but you gave me two hearts."

    C.   "you have ravished my heart with a glance of your eyes:"

    D.   "For you stood before me at Mount Sinai and said, 'All that the Lord has spoken we shall do and we shall obey' (Ex. 24:7)."

    E.   "with one jewel of your necklace:"

    F.   this is Moses, who was unique, the hero of all your tribes.

3. A.   Another interpretation of the verse, "You have ravished my heart, my sister, my bride, you have ravished my heart:"

    B.   Said the Holy One, blessed be He, "You had one heart in the wilderness, but you gave me two hearts."

    C.   "you have ravished my heart with a glance of your eyes:"

    D.   This is setting up the tabernacle: "And on the day that the tabernacle was set up" (Num. 9:15).

    E.   "with one jewel of your necklace:"

    F.   This is Moses, who was unique, the hero of all your tribes.

G.   There are those to say, "This refers to the women of the generation of the wilderness, who were virtuous. When that foul deed came around, they went and took counsel among themselves, and did not give a thing of their jewelry to the making of the calf.

H.   "Further, when they heard that, in their menstrual periods, they were prohibited to them, they forthwith went and locked their doors."

4. A.   Another interpretation of the verse, "You have ravished my heart, my sister, my bride, you have ravished my heart:"

  B.   Said the Holy One, blessed be He, "You had one heart in the matter of the spies, but you gave me two hearts."

  C.   [Supply: "you have ravished my heart with a glance of your eyes:"]

  D.   This refers to Joshua and Caleb: "Except for Caleb son of Jephunneh the Kenizzite and Joshua the son of Nun" (Num. 32:12).

  E.   "with one jewel of your necklace:"

  F.   This is Moses, who was unique, the hero of all your tribes.

5. A.   Another interpretation of the verse, "You have ravished my heart, my sister, my bride, you have ravished my heart:"

  B.   Said the Holy One, blessed be He, "You had one heart at Shittim, but you gave me two hearts."

  C.   "you have ravished my heart with a glance of your eyes:"

  D.   This refers to Phineas: "Then arose Phineas and carried out judgment...and that was counted to him for righteousness" (Ps. 106:30-31).

  E.   "with one jewel of your necklace:"

  F.   This is Moses.

The form is nearly perfectly executed; I have repaired the slight flaw at No. 4, and No. 5 breaks the form and so marks the conclusion. Here is a classic example of how "another interpretation" in fact serves to bind a sequence of closely allied, sequential statements of a single proposition. It is that the Israelites did not serve God with a whole heart at times of crisis, but somehow, through heroic individuals (named males, "the women" in general) they muddled through. Simon, p. 211, n. 3, interprets No. 1 in these words: "You had but one heart in Egypt, to sin, but then your better inclination triumphed and you dedicated both hearts." Then the dual heart is the inclination to do good and the inclination to do evil. That seems to me plausible.

54

Song of Songs Rabbah to Song of Songs 4:10

4:10   *How sweet is your love, my sister, my bride! How much better is your love than wine, and the fragrance of your oils than any spice!*

LIV:i

1.   A.   "How sweet is your love, my sister, my bride! How much better is your love than wine:"

     B.   R. Berekhiah and R. Helbo in the name of R. Samuel b. R. Nahman said, "There are ten passages in which Israel is called bride, six here [in the Song of Songs] and four in the prophets.

     C.   "Six here: 'Come with me from Lebanon, my bride; come with me from Lebanon. Depart from the peak of Amana, from the peak of Senir and Hermon, from the dens of lions, from the mountains of leopards' (Song 4:8); 'You have ravished my heart, my sister, my bride, you have ravished my heart with a glance of your eyes, with one jewel of your necklace' (Song 4:9); 'How sweet is your love, my sister, my bride! How much better is your love than wine, and the fragrance of your oils than any spice!' (Song 4:10); 'Your lips distill nectar, my bride; honey and milk are under your tongue; the scent of your garments is like the scent of Lebanon' (Song 4:11); 'A garden locked is my sister, my bride, a garden locked, a fountain sealed' (Song 4:12); 'I come to my garden, my sister, my bride, I gather my myrrh with my spice, I eat my honeycomb with my honey, I drink my wine with my milk. Eat, O friends, and drink; drink deeply, O lovers!' (Song 5:1).

     D.   "And four in the prophets: 'The voice of mirth and the voice of gladness, the voice of the bridegroom and the voice of the bride' (Jer. 7:34); 'And as a bride adorns herself with jewels' (Isa. 61:10); 'And gird yourself with them like a bride' (Isa. 59:18); 'And as the bridegroom rejoices over the bride' (Isa. 62:5).

     E.   "And, correspondingly, the Holy One, blessed be He, puts on ten [nuptial] robes: 'The Lord reigns, he is clothed in majesty' (Ps. 93:1); 'The Lord is clothed' (Ps. 93:1); 'He has girded himself' (Ps.

66

93:1); 'And he put on righteousness as a coat of mail' (Isa. 59:17); 'And he put on garments of vengeance' (Isa. 59:17); ' 'For clothing' (Isa. 59:17); 'This one who is glorious in his apparel' (Isa. 63:1); 'Wherefore is your apparel red' (Isa. 63:2); 'You are clothed with glory and majesty' (Ps. 104:1).

F. "This is so as to exact punishment from the nations of the world, who kept from the Ten Commandments the Israelites, who are [Simon] bound closely around them like the ornaments of a bride."

2. A. "and the fragrance of your oils than any spice:"

B. Said R. Samuel b. R. Nahman, "Just as oil is odorless, but if you scent it, it takes on the fragrance of any number of odors,

C. "so a given verse you interpret and find in it any number of good flavors [Simon: excellent thoughts]."

Both compositions move us away from the particular reading of the Song that has predominated. In No. 1 our base verse provides a prooftext in a florilegium; at No. 2 the interpretation moves us to Torah study, without an intervening assertion that Torah is represented here by some image or other.

55

Song of Songs Rabbah to Song of Songs 4:11

4:11　　*Your lips distill nectar, my bride; honey and milk are under your tongue; the scent of your garments is like the scent of Lebanon.*

LV:i

1.　A.　　"Your lips distill nectar, my bride:"

　　B.　　R. Derosa and R. Jeremiah in the name of R. Samuel b. R. Isaac: "Sixty myriads of prophets arose for Israel in the time of Elijah."

　　C.　　R. Jacob in the name of R. Yohanan said, "One hundred two myriads."

　　D.　　For said R. Yohanan, "From Gibeath to Antipatris were sixty myriads of towns. And you have no more corrupt towns among them all than Beth El and Jericho, the latter because of Joshua's curse, the former because of the fact that Jeroboam's two calves of gold were located there.

　　E.　　"Now one verse of Scripture states, 'And the sons of the prophets who were at Beth El came to Elisha' (2 Kgs. 2:3), and the smallest number of a plural is two."

2.　A.　　[Supply: "And the sons of the prophets who were at Beth El came to Elisha'"(2 Kgs. 2:3):]

　　B.　　[If there were so many prophets,] why were their prophesies not published?

　　C.　　It was because the coming generations had no need of them.

　　D.　　One must then conclude that any prophecy which applies for the here and now and which also was needed for coming generations was published,

　　E.　　and every prophecy that applies for the here and now but for which coming generations had no need was not published.

　　F.　　But in the age to come the Holy One, blessed be He, will collect them and publish all of their prophecies: "And the Lord my God shall come and all the holy ones with you" (Zech. 14:5).

3. A   [Reverting to 1.B:] R. Berekhiah in the name of R. Helbo said, "Just as the Israelites had sixty myriads of male prophets, so they had sixty myriads of female prophets.

    B.   "Solomon came and publicized them: 'Your lips distill nectar, my bride.'"

4. A   [Supply: "Your lips distill nectar, my bride:"] R. Huna and R. Halafta of Caesarea in the name of R. Simeon b. Laqish said, "Just as a bride is adorned with twenty-four adornments, and should she lack one of them, she is null,

    B.   "so a disciple of a sage has to be conversant with the twenty-four books [of the written Torah], and should he lack one of them, he is null."

    C.   R. Huna in the name of R. Simeon b. Laqish: "Just as a bride is modest, so a disciple of a sage has to be modest."

    D.   R. Halafta in the name of R. Simeon b. Laqish: "Just as a bride sits on her throne and says, 'See that I am pure, and this, my bridal accoutrements, gives testimony about me,'

    E.   "so a disciple of a sage likewise must be above all reproach."

5. A   [As to the word translated nectar,] R. Eleazar b R. Simeon and R. Yosé b. R. Hanina and rabbis:

    B.   R. Eleazar b. R. Simeon says, "Whoever teaches words of the Torah in public, and they are not so pleasing to those who hear them as fine flour that one has sifted in a sieve [a word that uses the consonants for the word translated nectar] would have been better off not to have said them."

    C.   R. Yosé [b. R. Hanina] says, "Whoever teaches words of the Torah in public, and they are not so pleasing to those who hear them as honey from the comb, would have been better off not to have said them."

    D.   Rabbis say, ""Whoever teaches words of the Torah in public, and they are not so pleasing to those who hear them as honey and milk mixed together would have been better off not to have said them."

6. A   [As to the word translated nectar,] R.Yohanan and R. Simeon b. Laqish:

    B.   R. Yohanan said, "Whoever teaches words of the Torah in public, and they are not so pleasing to those who hear them as a bride, who gives pleasure to those who see her when she is sitting in her bridal bower, would have been better off not to have said them."

    C.   R. Simeon b. Laqish said, "Whoever teaches words of the Torah in public, and they are not so pleasing to those who hear them as a bride, who gives pleasure to her groom, would have been better off not to have said them."

At Nos. 1-3, our base verse serves as a prooftext. But the reading is not merely casual, for it links the bride of our base verse with prophecy, and, for sages, the disciples of sages now are the counterpart to the prophets then. Thus the disciples of sages are God's brides, and that accounts for the progress through the base verse that we follow at Nos. 4, 5, 6. The metaphor of the bride for the disciple of the sage is now explicit. So, in point of fact, the whole has been composed with a single metaphorization in mind, and the message is delivered with clarity and force; there is nothing random.

LV:ii

1. A. "honey and milk are under your tongue:"

    B. R. Berekhiah said, "There is no drink that is more rotten than the drink that is under the tongue, and yet you say, 'honey and milk are under your tongue'!

    C. "But if there are laws that are obscure under your tongue like honey and milk, laws that are firmly in hand how much the more so!?

    D. Said R. Levi, "Also concerning one who recites Scripture in accord with its [Simon:] proper modulation and intonation, it is said, 'honey and milk are under your tongue.'"

2. A. "the scent of your garments is like the scent of Lebanon:"

    B. "And he came near and kissed him, and he smelled the smell of his clothes" (Gen. 27:27).

    C. Said R. Yohanan, "You have nothing so foul-smelling and gross as washed goatskins, and yet you say, 'And he came near and kissed him, and he smelled the smell of his clothes'!

    D. "But when our father, Jacob, came in, with him came the Garden of Eden: 'See, the smell of my son is like the smell of a field that the Lord has blessed' (Gen. 27:27).

    E. "But when the wicked Esau came in to his father, with him came the [stench of] Gehenna: 'When pride comes, then comes shame' (Prov. 11:2).

    F. "That is why he said to him, 'Who then' (Gen. 27:33), as if to say, '[Since the words for 'then' and 'baked use the same consonants], 'who is baked in this oven?'

    G. "The Holy Spirit replied, 'He who has taken venison' (Gen. 27:33).

3. A. R. Eleazar b. R. Simeon asked R. Simeon b. R. Yosé b. Laqonia, his father-in-law, "Did weaving looms go forth with the Israelites to the Wilderness?"

    B. He said to him, "No."

    C. He said to him, "Then where did they get clothes all those forty years that the Israelites spent in the wilderness?"

    D. He said to him, "It was from the clothing that the ministering angels provided for them to wear: 'I clothed you also with richly woven work' (Ezek. 16:10)."

4. A. [Supply: "I clothed you also with richly woven work" (Ezek. 16:10):]

    B. R. Simai said, "It was purple."

    C. Aqilas translated, "It was embroidered."

5. A. [Reverting to 3.D:] He said to him, "But didn't the clothes wear out?"

    B. He said to him, "Have you never studied Scripture in your entire life? 'Your clothing did not get old on you' (Dt. 8:4)."

    C. He said to him, "But didn't the children grow up?"

    D. He said to him, "Go learn the lesson of the snail, for as it grows, its shell grows with it."

    E. He said to him, "But didn't the clothes need laundering?"

F.   He said to him, "The cloud would rub against them and clean them."

G.   He said to him, "But didn't they burn up [in the fire that went along with the cloud]?"

H.   He said to him, "Go learn the lesson of the asbestos thread, which is cleaned only in fire."

I.   He said to him, "But didn't they breed lice?"

J.   He said to him, "If after they died they did not produce lice, did they produce them when alive?"

K.   "But didn't they have B.O. from the sweat of their bodies?"

L.   He said to him, "They would roll around in the grass by the well: 'He makes me lie down in green pastures' (Ps. 23:2).

M.   "So their good smell wafted from one end of the world to the other.

N.   "And Solomon came and made the matter explicit: 'the scent of your garments is like the scent of Lebanon.'"

No. 1 takes for granted that the lover, God, speaks of the beloved, the disciple of sages. The reading of the first part of the base verse has prepared us for such an interpretation. Nos. 2, 3 work on the reference to garments, but the composition serves Gen. 27:27; it has then been inserted solely for general thematic reasons. No. 4 has its own problem, and our base verse is a mere prooftext; it has not generated the problem that the author has proposed to solve, which is the clothing of the Israelites in the wilderness. The upshot is that our base verse is not here interpreted within the framework of Song Rabbah at all; it is simply used, and once used, it supplies a pretext to insert the entire composition in which it has been used.

56

Song of Songs Rabbah to
Song of Songs 4:12

4:12   *A garden locked is my sister, my bride, a garden locked, a fountain sealed.*

[4:13   *Your shoots are an orchard of pomegranates with all choicest fruits,*
        henna with nard.]

LVI:i

1. A.   "A garden locked is my sister, my bride, [a garden locked, a fountain sealed]:"

    B.   R. Judah b. R. Simon in the name of R. Joshua b. Levi: "[The matter may be compared to the case of] a king who had two daughters, an older and a younger, and who did not take time out to marry them off but left them for many years and went overseas.

    C.   "The daughters went and [Simon, verbatim:] took the law into their own hands, and married themselves off to husbands. And each one of them took her husband's signature and his seal.

    D.   "After a long time the king came back from overseas and heard people maligning his daughters, saying, 'The king's daughters have already played the whore.'

    E.   "What did he do? He issued a proclamation and said, 'Everybody come out to the piazza,' and he came and went into session in the antechamber [holding court there].

    F.   "He said to them, 'My daughters, is this what you have done and have ruined yourselves?'

    G.   "Each one of them immediately produced her husband's signature and his seal.

    H.   "He called his son-in-law and asked, To which of them are you the husband?'

    I.   "He said to him, 'I am the first of your sons-in-law, married to your elder daughter.'

    J.   "He said to him, 'And what is this?'

    K.   "He said to him, 'This is my signature and my seal.'

    L.   "And so with the second.

M.		"Then the king said, 'My daughters have been guarded from fornication, and you malign and shame them! By your lives, I shall carry out judgment against you.'
N.		"So too with the nations of the world: since they taunt Israel and say, '"And the Egyptians made the people of Israel work with rigor" (Ex. 1:13), if that is what they could make them do in labor, how much the more so with their bodies and with their wives'!'
O.		"Then said the Holy One, blessed be He, 'A garden locked is my sister, my bride.'"
2.	A.	[Supply: "A garden locked:"]
	B.	What is the meaning of "A garden locked"?
	C.	Said the Holy One, blessed be He, "My garden is locked up, and yet she is maligned!"
3.	A.	[Continuing the account of 1.O:] said R. Phineas, "Then the Holy One, blessed be He, summoned the angel in charge of pregnancy and said, 'Go and form them with all the distinctive features of their fathers.'
	B.	"And whom did their fathers resemble? The founders of their families, thus of Reuben, 'The families of the Reubenites' (Num. 26:7)."
	C.	Said R. Hoshaiah, "Reuben [produced] the Reubenites, Simeon the Simeonites."
	D.	Said R. Merinus b. R. Hoshaia, "But this is as people say, 'Baronites, Sabronites, Sibuyites.' [Simon, p. 218, n. 2: The name does not prove legitimacy.]"
	E.	R. Huna in the name of R. Idi: "The word 'the' at the beginning of the name and the addition of 'ites' at the end indicates of them that they really are the sons of their designated fathers."
4.	A.	[Supply: "A garden locked is my sister, my bride, a garden locked, a fountain sealed:"]
	B.	Said R. Phineas, "'A garden locked:' this refers to the virgins.
	C.	"'a garden locked:' this refers to the married women.
	D.	"'a fountain sealed:' this refers to the males."
5.	A.	[Leviticus Rabbah XXXII:V.1: "A garden locked is my sister, my bride, a garden locked, a fountain sealed:"]
	B.	It was taught in the name of R. Nathan, "'a garden locked, a fountain sealed:'
	C.	"one refers to vaginal, the other to anal intercourse [neither of which has taken place]."
6.	A.	[Leviticus Rabbah XXXII:V.4:] R. Huna in the name of Bar Qappara: "It was on four counts that the Israelites were redeemed from Egypt:
	B.	"Because they did not change their names [from Jewish to Egyptian ones], because they did not change their language, because they did not gossip, and because they did not go beyond the bounds of sexual decency.
	C.	"Because they did not change their names: Reuben and Simeon – whoever went down Reuben and Simeon came up bearing the same names.
	D.	"They did not call Reuben Rufus, Judah Julian, Joseph Justus, or Benjamin Alexander.

E.   "They did not change their language: elsewhere it is written, 'And a refugee came and told Abram the Hebrew' (Gen. 14:13), and here it is written, 'The God of the Hebrews has met with us' (Ex. 3:18); and 'For my mouth it is that speaks with you' (Gen. 45:12) – all in the holy language.

F.   "Because they did not gossip: 'Speak into the ears of the people and let them ask jewels or silver from their neighbors' (Ex. 11:2). Now you find that this matter of taking away the wealth of Egypt had been set in trust with them for twelve months prior to the exodus, but not a single one of them turned out to have revealed the secret, and not a single one of them ratted on his buddy.

G.   "Because they did not go beyond the bounds of sexual decency: you find that that was the case, for there was only a single Israelite woman who actually did so, and Scripture explicitly identified her: 'And the name of his mother was Shulamit, daughter of Dibri, of the tribe of Dan' (Lev. 24:11). [She was the only Israelite woman who bore a child to an Egyptian man.]"

7. A.   [Leviticus Rabbah XXXII:V.3: R. Huna in the name of R. Hiyya b. Abba] R. Abba b. Kahana said, "Sarah went down to Egypt and fenced herself off from sexual licentiousness, and all the other Israelite women were kept fenced off on account of the merit that she had attained.

B.   "Joseph went down to Egypt and fenced himself off from sexual licentiousness, and all the other Israelite men kept fenced off on account of the merit that he had attained."

C.   Said R. Phineas in the name of R. Hiyya, "It was truly worthy that through the fence that kept people from licentious behavior, Israel should be redeemed."

D.   [Song of Songs Rabbah now adds:] "How do we know it? Because Scripture says, 'A garden locked is my sister, my bride, a garden locked, a fountain sealed,' and then, 'Your shoots are an orchard of pomegranates with all choicest fruits, henna with nard.'"

8. A.   [Supply from Leviticus Rabbah XXXII:V.2: Another interpretation of "A garden locked" (Song 4:12):] R. Phineas in the name of R. Hiyya bar Abba, "Because the Israelites locked themselves up and avoided licentious sexual behavior with the Egyptians, they were redeemed from Egypt. On that account was 'your being sent forth' [that is, 'your shoots'] 'are an orchard of pomegranates with all choicest fruits.' That interpretation is in line with the following: 'And it came to pass, when Pharaoh sent forth...' (Ex. 13:17). [The shoots of Song 4:13) calls to mind the "sending forth' of Pharaoh, and the Israelites were sent forth by virtue of the fact that they had protected the integrity of their 'shoots,' that is, their offspring.]

B.   R. Simeon b. Yohai taught on Tannaite authority, "[The Egyptians were] in the position of someone who inherited a piece of ground that was a dumping ground. The heir was lazy, so he went and sold it for some trifling sum. The buyer went and worked hard and dug up in the dump heap and found a treasure, and with it he built himself a big palace. The buyer would walk about the marketplace, with servants following in a retinue, all on the strength of that treasure that he had bought with the dump heap.

C.   "The seller, when he saw this, he began to choke, saying, 'Woe, what I have lost!'

D.   "So too, when the Israelites were in Egypt, they were enslaved in mortar and bricks, and they were held in contempt by the Egyptians. But when they saw them with their standards, encamped at the sea, in royal array, the Egyptians began to choke, saying, 'Woe, what have we sent forth from our land!'

E.   "That is in line with this verse, 'And it came to pass [a word that contains consonants that can be read, 'woe,'] when Pharaoh had let the people go' (Ex. 13:17)."

9. A.   Said R. Jonathan, "They were in the position of someone who had a field the size of a kor who went and sold it for a piddling sum.

    B.   "The buyer went and dug wells in it and made in it gardens and orchards.

    C.   "When the seller saw this, he began to choke, saying, 'Woe, what I have lost!'

    D.   "So too, when the Israelites were in Egypt, they were enslaved in mortar and bricks, and they were held in contempt by the Egyptians. But when they saw them with their standards, encamped at the sea, in royal array, the Egyptians began to choke, saying, 'Woe, what have we sent forth from our land!'

    E.   "That is in line with this verse, 'And it came to pass [a word that contains consonants that can be read, 'woe,'] when Pharaoh had let the people go' (Ex. 13:17)."

10. A.   R. Yosé says, "They were in the position of someone who had a grove of cedars, who went and sold it for a piddling sum.

    B.   "The buyer went and made of the wood boxes, chests, towers and carriages.

    C.   "When the seller saw this, he began to choke, saying, 'Woe, what I have lost!'

    D.   "So too, when the Israelites were in Egypt, they were enslaved in mortar and bricks, and they were held in contempt by the Egyptians. But when they saw them with their standards, encamped at the sea, in royal array, the Egyptians began to choke, saying, 'Woe, what have we sent forth from our land!'

    E.   "That is in line with this verse, 'And it came to pass [a word that contains consonants that can be read, 'woe,'] when Pharaoh had let the people go' (Ex. 13:17)."

Israel's virginal condition forms the basic motif, and God's address concerning Israel is then identified with both the present condition of Israel, permanently espoused to God, and also Israel in the Exodus from Egypt. But it is the selection of the theme and thesis, not the exposition, that alone is to be credited to our compilers. For the bulk of the materials focus upon the theme and neglect the base verse. No. 1 deals with the base verse only thematically, and of the lot, it is closest to that verse. At least the verse plays an important role, and it is assigned to God; the reference to the Egyptians is critical, since it accounts for all the rest. No. 2 moves from the metaphor of the verse to its language, remaining philologically within the limits of the metaphor. No. 3 then concentrates on the theme, to the exclusion of the base verse.

From No. 4 through No. 7, we deal with the way in which the authorship of Leviticus Rabbah has expounded our base verse, now as an intersecting verse for a base verse of its own. The insertion of No. 8 and following is comprehensible only if we know that Leviticus Rabbah XXXII:V.2 cites both our base verse and the one that follows; then it is "your shoots," yielding, "your being sent forth," that accounts for the entire story. But the sense of the story has nothing to do with the established theme of the sexual purity of Israel; it is, rather, concerning with "a fountain sealed – your shoots/going forth...," with the consequent "an orchard of pomegranates, with all choicest fruits" bearing the sense that the Egyptians had sent forth something of enormous value and realized it only too late. So Nos. 8-10 really serve the following verse, and the framer of Leviticus Rabbah, if he had access to them, correctly omitted them from his composite; our compilers, by contrast, put in everything pertinent and much impertinent, so why not this? Chapter Fifty-Seven treats Nos. 8-10 as focused upon Song 4:13, since it commences, "another matter," as though Nos. 8-10 had dealt with Song 4:13, not 4:12, and the person who added "another matter" was quite right, since the lot really deals with the theme that is coming, not the one that dominates here.

57

Song of Songs Rabbah to Song of Songs 4:13

4:13 *Your shoots are an orchard of pomegranates with all choicest fruits,*
henna with nard.

LVII:i

1. A. Another explanation of the verse, "Your shoots are an orchard of pomegranates:"
   B. [Reading "your shoots" as "the gifts that you have sent" (Simon),] they are like "an orchard of pomegranates,"
   C. as in the speech of ordinary people, for instance, "What did so-and-so send to his betrothed?" "Pomegranates."
2. A. [On the subject of exchanges of gifts between God and Israel,] R. Hanina and R. Simon:
   B. One said, "She [the community of Israel] brought him thirteen things, and he brought her thirteen things.
   C. "She [the community of Israel] brought him thirteen things, as made explicit in the book of Exodus: 'And this is the offering...gold and silver and brass, and blue and purple and scarlet and fine linen and goats' hair, and rams' skins dyed red and sealskins and acacia wood...onyx stones and stones to be set' (Ex. 25:3-7).
   D. "and he brought her thirteen things as spelled out in Ezekiel: 'I clothed you also with embroidered garments [and gave you sandals of tahash leather to wear and wound fine linen about your head and dressed you in silks. I decked you out in finery and put bracelets on your arms and a chain around your neck. I put a ring in your nose and earrings in your ears and a splendid crown on your head]' (Ezek. 16:10-12)."
3. A. [Supply: "I clothed you also with embroidered garments:"]
   B. R. Simoi said, "This is purple."
   C. Aqilas translated, "embroidered work."
4. A. "and gave you sandals of tahash leather to wear:"
   B. the counterpart of the sealskins of the tabernacle.
5. A. "and wound fine linen about your head:"

	B.	the counterpart of the fine linen and goatskins.
6.	A.	"and dressed you in silks:"
	B.	R. Aibu said, "He made them something substantial in the world [the words for substantial and silk share the same consonants]."
	C.	R. Judah b. R. Simon said, "He wrapped them in clouds of glory: 'The pillar of cloud...did not depart' (Ex. 13:22) [the words for silk and depart share the same consonants]."
7.	A.	"I decked you out in finery:"
	B.	This refers to weapons of war.
8.	A.	It has been taught on Tannaite authority:
	B.	R. Simeon b. Yohai says, "The weapon that he gave to them at Horeb has the Ineffable Name of God incised in it.
	C.	"But when they sinned, it was taken away from them."
	D.	How was it taken away from them?
	E.	R. Aibu said, "It peeled away on its own."
	F.	Rabbis say, "An angel came down and peeled it off."
9.	A.	"and put bracelets on your arms:"
	B.	This refers to the tablets of the covenant on which the Ten Commandments are incised:
	C.	"And the tables were the work of God" (Ex. 32:16).
10.	A.	"and a chain around your neck:"
	B.	This refers to teachings of the Torah:
	C.	"bind them perpetually upon your heart, tie them around your neck" (Prov. 6:21).
11.	A.	"I put a ring in your nose:"
	B.	This refers to the holy crown.
12.	A.	"and earrings in your ears:"
	B.	This refers to the plate:
	C.	for we have learned on Tannaite authority:
	D.	The plate was like a thin plate of gold, two fingerbreadths in width, and it went around the forehead from ear to ear.
13.	A.	"and a splendid crown on your head:"
	B.	This refers to the Presence of God:
	C.	"you shall also be a crown of beauty in the hand of God" (Isa. 62:3); "And their king is passed on before them, and the Lord at the head of them" (Mic. 2:13).
14.	A.	[Reverting to 2.B:] what about the other three?
	B.	"You adorned yourself with gold and silver and your apparel was of fine linen, silk and embroidery. Your food was choice flour, honey and oil. You grew more and more beautiful and became fit for royalty. Your beauty won you fame among the nations, [for it was perfected through the splendor which I set upon you]" (Ez. 16:13-14).
15.	A.	"with all choicest fruits, henna with nard:"
	B.	R. Huna said, "She brought him thirteen things, and he brought her twenty-six things, as is the way of the groom to double the wedding gift [Hebrew: marriage settlement] of the bride:
	C.	R. Aha said, "She brought him utensils and spices, and he brought her utensils and spices, utensils through Moses, spices through Solomon:

D.　"'And she gave the king a hundred and twenty talents of gold and of spices a very great quantity, and precious stones; there came no more such abundance of spices as those that the Queen of Sheba gave to King Solomon' (1 Kgs. 10:10)."

E.　R. Simon said, "She brought him utensils and spices that were counted out, but he brought her utensils and spices that were beyond all counting.

F.　"Solomon came along and made it explicit: 'with all choicest fruits, henna with nard.'"

The basic message is an exchange of gifts, resting on the reading of "shoots" in the sense of "what has been sent," that is, gifts. No. 2 is of course defective, since we have no saying for "the other," but rather a sustained reading of the cited passage of Ezekiel. There is no point in revising 15.B, since the exposition now focuses on the second part of our base verse, which is cited, and since, more to the point, Huna is matched with Aha and Simon.

LVII:ii

1. A　Another reading of the verse, "Your shoots are an orchard of pomegranates :"

B.　[Reading "your shoots" as though it spoke of irrigated ground, since the words for "shoots" and "irrigated ground" share the same consonants (Simon, p. 222, n. 6):]

C.　the Holy One, blessed be He, is going to make you like an orchard of pomegranates in the age to come.

D.　And what is the sense here?

E.　It is akin to the well of Miriam.

2. A　Where did the Israelites get libation wine for all those forty years that they spent in the desert?

B.　R. Yohanan said, "From the well, and from it came most of the things that gave them pleasure."

C.　For said R. Yohanan, "The well would bring up for them all kinds of herbs, vegetables, and trees.

D.　"You may know that that was so, for when Miriam died, the well stopped, and they said, 'It is no place of seed, figs, or vines' (Num. 20:5)."

E.　R. Levi said, "They got it from the grapecluster, in line with this verse: 'They cut down from there a branch with one cluster of grapes' (Num. 13:23)."

F.　Is such a thing possible?

G.　Said R. Abba b. Kahana, "The fruit was unusually fat at that time."

H.　Rabbis said, "They got the wine from what the gentile traders were selling to the Israelites."

I.　It was taught on Tannaite authority by R. Ishmael, "The gentiles' wine at that time was not forbidden to Israelites."

No. 1 moves the discussion on from an exchange of gifts to another sense altogether; it is that in the age to come – we now move beyond the nuptials in the wilderness – God will make the Israelites into a flourishing orchard, so the base verse is made to indicate. The rest is an agglutinative essay on the theme of the well and related questions.

LVII:iii

1. A.   Another reading of the verse, "Your shoots are an orchard of pomegranates :"
    B.   [Reading "your shoots" as though it spoke of irrigated ground, since the words for "shoots" and "irrigated ground" share the same consonants:]
    C.   the Holy One, blessed be He, is going to make you like an orchard of pomegranates in the age to come.
    D.   And what is the sense here?
    E.   It is akin to the stream: "All kinds of trees for food will grow up on both banks of the stream. Their leaves will not wither nor their fruit fail; they will yield new fruit every month, because the water for them flows from the Temple. Their fruit will serve for food and their leaves for healing" (Ezek. 47:12).

2. A.   [Supply: "Their fruit will serve for food and their leaves for healing" (Ezek. 47:12):]
    B.   What is the meaning of the word for "healing"?
    C.   Said R. Yohanan, "It means [Simon:] a laxative.
    D.   "[Simon, p. 223, n. 7:] Its food helps digestion."

3. A.   [Supply: "Their fruit will serve for food and their leaves for healing" (Ezek. 47:12): What is the meaning of the word for "healing"?]
    B.   Rab and Samuel:
    C.   One said, "It was to loosen the upper mouth [relieving a speech impediment (cf. Simon)]."
    D.   The other said, "It was to loosen the lower mouth [relieving barrenness]."
    E.   R. Hanina and R. Joshua b. Levi:
    F.   One said, "It was to loosen the upper mouth [relieving a speech impediment (cf. Simon)]."
    G.   The other said, "It was to loosen the lower mouth [relieving barrenness]."

We move from the well in the wilderness to the stream in the messianic age, with everything else in place: the prooftext and the secondary amplification of the prooftext. What must come next will be the Messianic era, and the repertoire is complete.

LVII:iv

1. A.   Another reading of the verse, "Your shoots are an orchard of pomegranates :"
    B.   [Reading "your shoots" as though it spoke of irrigated ground, since the words for "shoots" and "irrigated ground" share the same consonants:]
    C.   the Holy One, blessed be He, is going to make you like an orchard of pomegranates in the age to come.
    D.   And what is the sense here?
    E.   It is akin to Elijah, of blessed memory.

F.   For we have learned in the Mishnah:

G.   The family of the house of Seriphah was in Transjordan, and Ben Zion put it out by force. And there was another family there, which Ben Zion drew near by force. It is families of this sort that Elijah will come to declare unclean and to declare clean, to put out and to draw near.

H.   R. Judah says, "To draw near but not to put out."

I.   R. Simeon says, "To smooth out disputes."

J.   And sages say, "Not to put out or to draw near, but to make peace in the world,

K.   "as it is said, 'Behold I will send you Elijah the prophet...and he will return the heart of the fathers to the children and the heart of the children to the fathers' (Mal. 4:23-24)." [M. Ed. 8:7D-J].

The exposition is complete, and all the "other interpretations" add up to a single proposition, which is the full and complete message of God to Israel at their betrothal.

58

Song of Songs Rabbah to Song of Songs 4:14

4:14   *nard and saffron, calamus and cinnamon,*
with all trees of frankincense, myrrh and aloes, with all chief
spices —

LVIII:i

1. A. "nard and saffron, calamus and cinnamon, with all trees of frankincense, myrrh and aloes, with all chief spices:"
    B. "nard:"
    C. Nard-oil.
    D. "and saffron:"
    E. As stated.
    F. "calamus:"
    G. This is sweet calamus: "And of sweet calamus" (Ex. 30:23).
    H. "and cinnamon:"
    I. R. Huna in the name of R. Yosé says, "Cinnamon used to grow in the Land of Israel, and goats and deer would munch on it."
    J. "[with all trees of frankincense], myrrh:"
    K. Oil of myrrh.
    L. "and aloes:"
    M. R. Yassa said, "This is [Simon:] foliatum [an ointment or oil prepared from leaves of spikenard (Simon, p. 225, n. 1)]."
    N. Why is it called "aloes" [which is spelled with letters that may be read, "tents"]?
    O. R. Abba b. R. Yudan in the name of R. Judah said, "Because it comes by way of tents [through Bedouin]."
    P. And rabbis say, "Because it spreads when in a tent['s contained space]."

2. A. And where did the Israelite women get their ornaments to please their men through the forty years that they spent in the wilderness?
    B. R. Yohanan said, "From the well: 'a garden fountain, a well of living water and flowing streams from Lebanon' (Song 4:15)."

C.   R. Abbahu said, "From the manna: '[translated by Simon as:] Myrrh and aloes and cassia are all your garments, from what is eaten with the tooth' (Ps. 45:9).

D.   "'From what is eaten with the tooth' did the modest and righteous Israelite women adorn themselves and please their men all the forty years that they spent in the wilderness."

3. A.   "For behold the Lord commands and the great house will be made into ruins and the small one into clefts" (Amos 6:11):

B.   "Ruins" are not the same as "clefts,"

C.   for a ruin yields fragments, and a cleft does not.

No. 1 accomplishes the phrase-by-phrase clarification of our base verse. No. 2 is dropped down because of the appearance of myrrh and aloes in the prooftext, C. I do not know why No. 3 is included, and I also do not understand what it means; Simon's footnote, p. 225, n. 6, seems to me as good as we can hope to get.

59

Song of Songs Rabbah to Song of Songs 4:15

4:15   *a garden fountain, a well of living water and flowing streams from Lebanon.*

LIX:i

1. A.   "a garden fountain, a well of living water:"
   B.   Said R. Yohanan, "Forty-eight times the word 'well' is written in the Torah, corresponding to the forty-eight ways through which the Torah is given, thus: 'a garden fountain, a well of living water.'"
2. A.   "and flowing streams from Lebanon:"
   B.   Said R. Azariah, "This one flows a bit in one matter, and that one flows a bit in one matter, until the law stands forth like [a cedar of] Lebanon."
   C.   Said R. Tanhuma, "This one [Simon:] fastens a little and that one fastens a little, until the law stands forth like well-joined beams."

No. 1 invokes the metaphor for purposes of representing the Torah. Simon, p. 226, n. 3, prefers to assign No. 2 to Song 5:13, where we have a reference to "cheeks," a word that shares the consonants of the word for "beam." The mixture of "flow" of B with "Lebanon," surely a great tree and not a stream, certainly is somewhat confusing.

60

Song of Songs Rabbah to Song of Songs 4:16

4:16   *Awake, O north wind, and come, O south wind! Blow upon my garden,*
let its fragrance be wafted abroad. Let my beloved come to his garden,
and eat its choicest fruits.

LX:i

1. A.   "Awake, O north wind, and come, O south wind:" [I give the version of Genesis Rabbah XXII:V.2, which begins: "And Abel brought of the firstlings of his flock and of their fat portions" (Gen. 4:4).]

    B.   R. Eleazar and R. Yosé bar Hanina:

    C.   R. Eleazar [Song: Eliezer] says, "The children of Noah [when they made offerings] offered their sacrifices in the status of peace-offerings. [They kept portions of the sacrificial beast, e.g., the hide, and burned up on the fire only the fats, that is, minimal sacrificial parts.]"

    D.   R. Yosé bar Hanina said, "They prepared them in the status of whole-offerings [burning up the entire animal and not keeping any portions for the sacrificer and sacrificer]."

    E.   R. Eleazar objected to the view of R. Yosé bar Hanina, "And is it not written, 'And of their fat portions' (Gen. 4:4)? It was an offering in the status of one the fat portions of which are burned up on the altar [and not eaten by the sacrificer]."

    F.   How does R. Yosé bar Hanina treat this passage? He interprets it to refer to the fat animals [and not to the portions of those that were offered up, but only referring to "the best of the flock"].

    G.   R. Eleazar objected to the view of R. Yosé bar Hanina, "And lo, it is written: 'And he sent the young men of the children of Israel, who offered burnt-offerings and sacrificed peace-offerings of oxen unto the Lord' (Ex. 24:5)? [This was before revelation, and hence would indicate that the children of Noah, belonging to the category of the Israelites at that time, prior to the Torah, in fact

85

offered not only whole-offerings but also peace-offerings, just as Eleazar maintains.]"

H. How does R. Yosé bar Hanina treat this verse? He interprets the reference to "peace-offerings" to mean that they offered up the beasts with their hides, without flaying them and cutting them into pieces. [So even though the verse refers to peace-offerings, in fact the animals were offered up as whole-offerings, hide and all.]

I. R. Eleazar objected to R. Yosé bar Hanina, "And is it not written, 'And Jethro, Moses' father-in-law, took a burnt-offering and sacrifices' (Ex. 18:12)? [The reference to a burnt-offering would suffice, so the inclusion of the further reference to "sacrifices" indicates that there was an offering made in a different classification, hence, peace-offerings.]"

J. How does R. Yosé bar Hanina deal with this verse? He accords with the view of him who said that Jethro came to Moses *after* the giving of the Torah, [at which point Jethro was in the status of an Israelite. Hence the type of offering Jethro gave would indicate only what Israelites did when they made their sacrifices and would not testify to how children of Noah, prior to the giving of the Torah, in general offered up their animals.]

K. [We shall now deal with the point at which Jethro rejoined Moses.] Said R. Huna, "R. Yannai and R. Hiyya the Elder differed on this matter."

L. R. Yannai said, "It was prior to the giving of the Torah that Jethro came."

M. R. Hiyya the Elder said, "It was after the giving of the Torah that Jethro came."

N. Said R. Hanina, "They did not in fact differ. The one who said that it was prior to the giving of the Torah that Jethro came holds that the children of Noah offered peace-offerings [in addition to offerings in accord with the rules governing the classification of whole-offerings]. The one who maintains that it was after the giving of the Torah that Jethro came takes the position that the children of Noah offered up animals only in the status of whole-offerings."

O. The following verse supports the view of R. Yosé bar Hanina, "Awake, O north wind" (Song 4:16) refers to the whole-offering, which was slaughtered at the north side of the altar. What is the sense of "awake"? It speaks of something that was asleep and now wakes up.

P. "And come, you south" (Song 4:16) speaks of peace-offerings, which were slaughtered [even] at the south side of the altar. And what is the sense of "come"? It speaks of a new and unprecedented practice. [Hence the rules governing peace-offerings constituted an innovation. Freedman, trans. *Genesis Rabbah*, p. 184, n. 1: Thus it was only now, after the giving of the Torah, that the practice of sacrificing peace-offerings was introduced.]

Q. R. Joshua of Sikhnin in the name of R. Levi: "Also the following verse supports the view of R. Yosé bar Hanina: 'This is the Torah governing the preparation of the whole-offering, that is the whole-

	offering [of which people already are informed]' (Lev. 6:2) meaning, that whole-offering that the children of Noah used to offer up.
R.	"When by contrast the passage speaks of peace-offerings, it states, 'And this is the law of the sacrifice of peace-offerings' (Lev. 7:11), but it is not written, '*which they offered up*,' but rather, 'which they *will* offer up' (Lev. 7:11), meaning, only in the future. [Hence peace-offerings' rules, allowing the sacrificer and sacrificer a share in the animal that is offered up, represented an innovation, not formerly applicable, in support of the view of R. Yosé bar Hanina that such offerings' rules constituted an innovation.]"
S.	[Reverting to the text of Song:] How does R. Eliezer interpret this same verse, "Awake, O north wind, and come, O south wind"?
T.	When the exiles living in the North will wake up and come and encamp in the south, as in this verse, "Behold I will bring them from the north country and gather them from the uttermost parts of the earth" (Jer. 31:8).
U.	When Gog and Magog, who are situated in the north, come and fall upon the south: "And I will turn you around and lead you on and I will cause you to come up" (Ezek. 39:2).
V.	When the Messiah, located in the north, will awake and come and rebuild the Temple, which is located in the south: "I have awakened one from the north and he has come" (Isa. 41:25).

2.	A.	"Blow upon my garden, let its fragrance be wafted abroad:"
	B.	Said R. Huna in the name of R. Joshua b. R. Benjamin b. R. Levi, "It is because in this age, when the south wind blows, the north wind does not, and when the north wind blows, the south wind does not.
	C.	"But in the age to come, the Holy One will bring [Simon:] a strong clearing wind into the world, and he will lead both winds to blow together, and both of them will serve: 'I will say to the north, give up, and to the south, do not hold back' (Isa. 43:6)."
3.	A.	"Let my beloved come to his garden:"
	B.	Said R. Yohanan, "The Torah here teaches you proper conduct,
	C.	"specifically, that the groom should not enter 'the marriage canopy' until the bride gives him permission to do so:
	D.	"'Let my beloved come to his garden.'"

No. 1 is parachuted down only because one of its prooftexts is our base-text; Nos. 2, 3, by contrast, do wish to read our base-text in line with the broader program of the compilers.

Part Five

PARASHAH FIVE

Song of Songs - Chapter Five

5:1   *I come to my garden, my sister, my bride,*
      I gather my myrrh with my spice,
      I eat my honeycomb with my honey,
      I drink my wine with my milk.
      Eat, O friends, and drink;
      drink deeply, O lovers!

5:2   *I slept, but my heart was awake.*
      Hark! my beloved is knocking.
      "Open to me, my sister, my love,
      my dove, my perfect one;
      for my head is wet with dew,
      my locks with the drops of the night."

5:3   *I had put off my garment,*
      how could I put it on?
      I had bathed my feet,
      how could I soil them?

5:4   *My beloved put his hand to the latch,*
      and my heart was thrilled within me.

5:5   *I arose to open to my beloved,*
      and my hands dripped with myrrh,
      my fingers with liquid myrrh,
      upon the handles of the bolt.

5:6   *I opened to my beloved,*
      but my beloved had turned and gone.
      My soul failed me when he spoke.
      I sought him, but found him not;
      I called him, but he gave no answer.

5:7   *The watchmen found me,*
      as they went about in the city;
      they beat me, they wounded me,
      they took away my mantle,
      those watchmen of the walls.

5:8   *I adjure you, O daughters of Jerusalem,*
if you find my beloved,
that you tell him
I am sick with love.

5:9   *What is your beloved more than another beloved,*
O fairest among women!
What is your beloved more than another beloved,
that you thus adjure us?

5:10   *My beloved is all radiant and ruddy,*
distinguished among ten thousand.

5:11   *His head is the finest gold;*
his locks are wavy,
black as a raven.

5:12   *His eyes are like doves,*
beside springs of water,
bathed in milk,
fitly set.

5:13   *His cheeks are like beds of spices,*
yielding fragrance.
His lips are lilies,
distilling liquid myrrh.

5:14   *His arms are rounded gold,*
set with jewels.
His body is ivory work,
encrusted with sapphires.

5:15   *His legs are alabaster columns,*
set upon bases of gold.
His appearance is like Lebanon,
choice as the cedars.

5:16   *His speech is most sweet,*
and he is altogether desirable.
This is my beloved, and this is my friend,
O daughters of Jerusalem.

61

Song of Songs Rabbah to Song of Songs 5:1

5:1   *I come to my garden, my sister, my bride, I gather my myrrh with my spice, I eat my honeycomb with my honey, I drink my wine with my milk. Eat, O friends, and drink; drink deeply, O lovers!*

LXI:i

1.   A.   "I come to my garden:"

     B.   Said R. Menahem, son-in-law of R. Eleazar b. R. Abonah, in the name of R. Simeon b. R. Yosenah, "'I come to the garden' is not what is written, but rather, 'I come to *my* garden.'

     C.   "The sense is, 'to my bridal chamber,' the place that had been my principal home to begin with.

     D.   "For was not the principal dwelling of the Presence of God to begin with in the lower realm: 'And they heard the voice of the Lord God walking in the garden' (Gen. 3:8)?"

2.   A.   [Genesis Rabbah XIX:VII.2 commences, "And they heard the voice of the Lord God walking in the garden" (Gen. 3:8):] Said R. Abba bar Kahana, "The word is not written, 'move,' but rather, 'walk,' bearing the sense that [the Presence of God] lept about and jumped upward.

     B.   "[The point is that God's presence leapt upward from the earth on account of the events in the garden, as will now be explained. The principal location of the Presence of God was meant to be among the creatures down here.] When the first man sinned, the Presence of God moved up to the first firmament. When Cain sinned, it went up to the second firmament. When the generation of Enosh sinned, it went up to the third firmament. When the generation of the Flood sinned, it went up to the fourth firmament. When the generation of the dispersion [at the tower of Babel] sinned, it went up to the fifth. On account of the Sodomites it went up to the sixth, and on account of the Egyptians in the time of Abraham it went up to the seventh.

C.   "But, as a counterpart, there were seven righteous men who rose up: Abraham, Isaac, Jacob, Levi, Kahath, Amram, and Moses. They brought the Presence of God [by stages] down to earth.

D.   "Abraham had merit and so brought it from the seventh to the sixth, Isaac brought it from the sixth to the fifth, Jacob brought it from the fifth to the fourth, Levi brought it down from the fourth to the third, Kahath brought it down from the third to the second, Amram brought it down from the second to the first. Moses brought it down to earth."

E.   Said R. Isaac, "It is written, 'The righteous will inherit the land and dwell therein forever' (Ps. 37:29). Now what will the wicked do? Are they going to fly in the air? But that the wicked did not make it possible for the Presence of God to take up residence on earth [is what the verse wishes to say].

F.   "Rather, the righteous made it possible for the Presence of God to take up residence on the earth.

G.   "What verse of Scripture so indicates? 'The righteous will inherit the land and dwell therein forever' (Ps. 37:29). They will made it possible for the Presence of God to dwell upon it: 'He who inhabits eternity, whose name is Holy' (Isa. 57:15)."

3. A. And when did the Presence of God come to rest upon the earth? It was on the day on which the tabernacle was set up: "And it came to pass on the day that Moses had made an end of setting up the tabernacle" (Num. 7:1).

B.   [Pesiqta deRab Kahana I:I.1 commences, "I have come back to my garden, my sister, my bride (Song 5:1):] R. Azariah in the name of R. Simon said, "[The matter may be compared to the case of] a king who became angry at a noblewoman and drove her out and expelled her from his palace. After some time he wanted to bring her back. She said, 'Let him renew in my behalf the earlier state of affairs, and then he may bring me back.'

C.   "So in former times the Holy One, blessed be He, would receive offerings from on high, as it is said, 'And the Lord smelled the sweet odor' (Gen. 8:21). But now he will accept them down below."

D.   [Song now adds:] "I come to my garden, my sister, my bride,

4. A. "I gather my myrrh with my spice:"
B.   This refers to the incense of spices and the handful of frankincense.
C.   "I eat my honeycomb with my honey:"
D.   This refers to the limbs of the burnt-offering and the innards of the Most Holy Things.
E.   "I drink my wine with my milk:"
F.   This refers to the libations and the innards of Lesser Holy Things.
G.   "Eat, O friends:"
H.   This refers to Moses and Aaron.
I.   "and drink; drink deeply, O lovers:"
J.   This refers to Nadab and Abihu, who got drunk to their sorrow.

5. A. Said R. Idi, "David wanted to make his offering in line with the offering of the princes: 'I will offer you burnt-offerings of fatlings with the sweet smoke of rams; I will offer bullocks with goats' (Ps. 66:15).

B.   "Now what offering involved bullocks and rams and goats?

C.   "You must say that it was the offering of the princes: 'And for the sacrifice of the peace-offerings, two oxen' (Num. 7:17)."

6.   A.   [Supply from the text, which gives these words after D, below]: "Eat, O friends:" this refers to the princes.

B.   "drink deeply, O lovers:" this refers to the nobles.

C.   Why does [the Song] refer to the princes as friends?

D.   Said R. Simeon b. Yosina, "[The reason is that the princes and nobles are given special standing in the conditions of their dedicatory-offerings, which no other individuals are ever accorded, as I shall now explain:] In every other circumstance an individual does not present as an offering a sin-offering made as a free-will-offering [but only as an obligatory one], while here a sin-offering is brought voluntarily.

E.   "In every other circumstance the offering brought by an individual does not override the restrictions involving uncleanness and the Sabbath, while here the offering brought by an individual does override the restrictions involving uncleanness and the Sabbath.

F.   "In all other circumstances, an individual does not present a sin-offering except in the case of a[n unwitting] sin, while here an individual does present a sin-offering not in the case of a[n unwitting] sin."

7.   A.   [In connection with the anomalous rules governing the offering of the princes,] another explanation of the phrase, "Eat, O friends:"

B.   Said R. Berekhiah, "The matter may be compared to the case of a king who made a banquet and invited guests, and a dead creeping thing fell into the soup. If the king had declined to eat it, all of them would have declined to eat it. The king put out his hand [to serve himself] so everybody else did too. [That accounts for the acceptance of the offerings under the special rules, setting aside restrictions ordinarily in force.]"

8.   A.   [In connection with the anomalous rules governing the offering of the princes,] said R. Yannai, "The matter may be compared to the case of a king who made a banquet and invited guests to come to him, and he [Simon:] went around among them, saying to them, 'I hope you like it, I hope you enjoy it.'"

9.   A.   [In connection with the anomalous rules governing the offering of the princes,] said R. Abbahu, "The matter may be compared to the case of a king who made a banquet and invited guests to come, and when they had eaten and drunk, he said, 'Take this good helping and give it to the host.'

B.   "Thus here: 'I come to my garden, my sister, my bride, I gather my myrrh with my spice, I eat my honeycomb with my honey,' so you eat too.

C.   "'I drink my wine with my milk.' You too: 'Eat, O friends, and drink; drink deeply, O lovers.'"

Nos. 1-2 interpret the base verse to speak of God's espousal of Israel in the form of the Presence of God at rest in Israel. Since this involves the tabernacle, Nos. 3ff. deal with that closely aligned metaphor. No.

3 makes explicit the notion that the Presence of God is in the tabernacle. No. 4 then explains how the verse at hand refers to the tabernacle and the offerings there. I assume that No. 5 is parachuted down because it refers to the offering of the princes, and that becomes important not only because the tabernacle was dedicated through the princes' offering, but also because at No. 6 we invoke the special rules governing their making that offering; so No. 5 is not an accidental accretion, even though, from our perspective, it impedes the exposition. No. 6 is read as I do by moving the language that appears in the printed text at the end to the beginning, that is, A-C, as marked. Nos. 7, 8, 9 then work on the same matter, now supplying parables to explain the facts given earlier. This is a beautiful piece of composition, since, as we see, a variety of available materials are sewn together to make a kind of tapestry with a coherence all its own.

62

Song of Songs Rabbah to Song of Songs 5:2

5:2   *I slept, but my heart was awake. Hark! my beloved is knocking. "Open to me, my sister, my love, my dove, my perfect one; for my head is wet with dew, my locks with the drops of the night."*

LXII:I

1.   A.   "I slept, but my heart was awake:"
     B.   Said the Community of Israel before the Holy One, blessed be He, "Lord of the world, 'I slept:' as to the religious duties,
     C.   "'but my heart was awake:' as to acts of loving kindness.
     D.   "'I slept:' as to acts of righteousness.
     E.   "'but my heart was awake:' in doing them.
     F.   "'I slept:' as to the offerings.
     G.   "'but my heart was awake:' as to reciting the *Shema* and saying the Prayer.
     H.   "'I slept:' as to the house of the sanctuary.
     I.   "'but my heart was awake:' as to synagogues and study-houses.
     J.   "'I slept:' as to the end of days.
     K.   "'but my heart was awake:' as to redemption.
     L.   "'I slept:' as to redemption.
     M.   "'but the heart' of the Holy One, blessed be He, 'was awake' to redeem me."

2.   A.   Said R. Hiyya b. R. Abba, "Where do we find that the Holy One, blessed be He, is called the heart of Israel?
     B.   "It is in the present verse: 'God is the rock, my heart, and my portion forever' (Ps. 73:26)."

3.   A.   "Hark! my beloved is knocking:"
     B.   This is through Moses, in his saying, "Thus saith the Lord, 'About midnight I will go out into the midst of Egypt'" (Ex. 11:4).

4.   A.   "Open to me:"
     B.   R. Yasa said, "Said the Holy One, blessed be He, to Israel, 'My children, "open to me" an opening of repentance no larger than the eye of a needle, and I shall widen it into a gateway through which wagons and carriages can pass.'"

5. A. R. Tanhuma and R. Hunia and R. Abbahu in the name of R. Simeon b. Laqish: "It is written, 'Let be and know that I am God' (Ps. 46:11).

    B. "Said the Holy One, blessed be He, to Israel, '"Let" your evil deeds "be, and know that I am God."'"

6. A. R. Levi said, "If the Israelites were to repent even a single day, they would forthwith be redeemed and the son of David would immediately come.

    B. "What verse of Scripture indicates it? 'For he is our God and we are the people of his pasture and the flock of his hand. Today, if you would only listen to his voice' (Ps. 95:7)."

7. A. R. Judah and R. Levi said, "Said the Holy One, blessed be He, to Israel, '"Let" your evil deeds "be," and repent even for as much as the blinking of an eye, "and know that I am God."'"

8. A. "my sister:"

    B. [God speaks:] "For they became my blood relatives in Egypt by carrying out two religious duties, the blood of the Passover and the blood of circumcision,

    C. "'And when I passed by you and saw you wallowing in your blood, I said to you, In your blood live' (Ezek. 16:6) – that is, in the blood of the Passover.

    D. "'Yes, in your blood live' (Ezek. 16:6) – the blood of circumcision."

9   A. "my love:"

    B. [God speaks:] "For they became my lovers at the Sea,

    C. "saying, 'This is my God and I will glorify him' (Ex. 15:2); 'The Lord shall reign for ever and ever' (Ex. 15:18).

10. A. "my dove:"

    B. [Supply: God speaks: "For they became my dove] at Marah,

    C. "where they were subjected to commandments and distinguished by all the religious duties, acts of righteousness, and good deeds, just as a dove is distinguished: 'There he made for them a statute and an ordinance' (Ex. 15:25)."

11. A. "my perfect one:"

    B. [Supply: God speaks:] "My wholly devoted one,

    C. "who became wholly at one with me at Sinai, saying, 'All that the Lord has said we will do and obey' (Ex. 24:7)."

12. A. [Supply: "my perfect one:"]

    B. R. Yannai said, "My twin [since the words for perfect and twin use the same consonants].

    C. "[God speaks:] 'It is as though I were not greater than she, nor she greater than I.'"

13. A. [Supply: "my perfect one:"]

    B. [Since the words for perfect and twin use the same consonants], R. Joshua of Sikhnayya in the name of R. Levi: "'My twin:' just as in the case of twins, if one of them gets a headache, the other one hurts, so it is as though the Holy One, blessed be He, said, 'I will be with him in trouble' (Ps. 91:15)."

14. A. "For my head is wet with dew:"

    B. "The earth trembled, the heavens also dripped" (Ps. 68:9).

    C. "my locks with the drops of the night:"

    D. "Yes, the clouds dripped water" (Judges 5:4).

The parsing of the base verse governs throughout, though the accretions enrich the passage in an unusual measure. The point of No. 1 is not clear in all the details, but it comes through overall. Even though Israel's present condition is not ideal, still, she keeps the faith, the contrast at H-I telling the story. No. 2 is necessary to fill out the details of No. 1. Nos. 3, 4, 5 proceed to the successive clauses; the reading of the base verse is coherent, even though the details stand each on its own. Because of 4.B, Nos. 5, 6, 7 are dropped in. No. 8 then reverts to the clause-by-clause exposition, and the remainder systematically makes the same point about God's intense love affair with Israel, always appealing to the redemption at the Sea and Israel at Sinai as the initial moments of the eternal affair. The success of this passage derives from the economy of its form – so simple as "a few words" + "this is...," so that the weight of the statement is carried by the images and metaphors, not by propositions or syllogisms. The poetry of the Song is allowed to speak without meddling exposition in prose by the "commentators," rather, our compilers, and those whose writings they compile, join in the Song: image for image.

63

Song of Songs Rabbah to Song of Songs 5:3

5:3   *I had put off my garment, how could I put it on?*
I had bathed my feet, how could I soil them?

LXIII:i
1. A.   "I had put off my garment, how could I put it on:"
   B.   Said R. Yohanan, "Even the simplest of simpletons knows how to take off and put on a coat, and yet you say, 'I had put off my garment, how could I put it on'?"
   C.   R. Hanina and R. Yohanan say, "On the day that Nebuchadnezzar made war against Israel, he removed from them two garments that mark greatness, the garment of the priesthood and the garment of the throne."
2. A.   "I had bathed my feet:"
   B.   Of the filth of idolatry.
   C.   "I knew that the dust of that place [Babylonia] would lead me to idolatry. Even so: My beloved put his hand to the latch, and my heart was thrilled within me.'"

The reading of the present verse is brief, and the whole continues in Chapter Sixty-Four. No. 1 is somewhat awry, and we have a better version of Yohanan's statement in the next chapter. But the basic theme is clearly established, namely, Israel among the nations by God's hand.

64

Song of Songs Rabbah to Song of Songs 5:4

[5:3   *I had put off my garment, how could I put it on? I had bathed my
        feet, how could I soil them?]*
5:4   *My beloved put his hand to the latch, and my heart was thrilled
        within me.*

LXIV:i
1. A.   [Supply: "My beloved put his hand to the latch, and my heart was
          thrilled within me:"]
    B.   Said R. Abba b. Kahana, "How come the 'latch' is mentioned, and
          it is a place that grows vermin!
    C.   "But this is what the Community of Israel said before the Holy
          One, blessed be He, 'Lord of the world, all the miracles that you
          have done for me through Cyrus – would it not have been better
          to have done them through Daniel and through a righteous man?
    D.   "Nonetheless: 'my heart was thrilled within me.'"
2. A.   [Supply: "and my heart was thrilled within me:"]
    B.   Said R. Azariah, "Said the Holy One, blessed be He, 'I make a
          good decree. You say, "my heart was thrilled within me," but I also
          have said, "My bowels, my bowels, I writhe in pain" (Jer. 4:19).'"
3. A.   Another explanation of the verse, "I had put off my garment, how
          could I put it on:"
    B.   Said R. Yohanan in the name of R. Simeon b. Laqish, "Even the
          simplest of simpletons knows how to take off and put on a coat,
          and yet you say, 'I had put off my garment, how could I put it on'?"
    C.   "But what is the point? It is because sleep at Pentecost is
          pleasant, and the night is brief [Simon, p. 2345, n. 6: yet Israel
          awoke to receive the Torah]."
    D.   Said R. Yudan, "And they were not even bitten by fleas."
4. A.   "I had bathed my feet:"
    B.   Of the filth of idolatry.
    C.   "I knew that the dust of that place [Babylonia] would lead me to
          idolatry. Even so: My beloved put his hand to the latch, and my
          heart was thrilled within me.'"

D.   Said R. Ammi, "Like a poor man seeking alms."
E.   Nonetheless: "my heart was thrilled within me:"
F.   And so he says to me, "Therefore my heart yearns for him. I will surely have compassion on him, says the Lord" (Jer. 31:20).

This go-around makes more sense than the prior one. The message of No. 1 is that Israel is pleased with what God does, no matter through whom he does it. I am not entirely sure how No. 2 fits or what its message is. No. 3 goes over the ground of the foregoing, but now it is easy to follow, linking Israel at Pentecost to the present metaphor. No. 4 is equally an improvement on the earlier version, in enriching the presentation of the main point.

65

Song of Songs Rabbah to Song of Songs 5:5

5:5   *I arose to open to my beloved, and my hands dripped with myrrh, my fingers with liquid myrrh, upon the handles of the bolt.*

LXV:i

1. A.   "I arose to open to my beloved:"
   B.   "I arose," and not the nations of the world.
2. A.   R. Jacob b. R. Abinah was translating in the presence of R. Isaac: "It is written, 'Then arose the heads of fathers' houses of Judah and Benjamin and the priests and the Levites' (Ezra 1:5).
   B.   "Judah, because he was king,
   C.   "Benjamin, because the house of the sanctuary was in his alloted property,
   D.   "the priests, because of the liturgical labor,
   E.   "the Levites, because of the musical labor. [These were the ones who accepted Cyrus's permission to return to Zion. They all had work to do there.]"
3. A.   "I arose to open to my beloved:"
   B.   For repentance.
4. A.   "and my hands dripped with myrrh:"
   B.   [Since the words for myrrh and bitterness use the same consonants, the sense is,] with bitterness.
   C.   For Cyrus made the decree, saying, "Whoever has crossed the Euphrates has crossed [and must stay over there], and whoever has not crossed may never cross."
5. A.   Said R. Yohanan, "It is written, 'The sun was darkened in his going forth' (Isa. 13:10).
   B.   "Would that that day had been dark and [the sun] not risen.
   C.   "Cyrus went about touring the city, and saw the city abandoned. He said, 'How come this city is abandoned? Where are the gold-workers, where are the silver-workers?'
   D.   "They said to him, 'But are you not the one who made the decree, saying, 'All the Jews are to go forth and rebuild the house of the sanctuary!'

E.   "'And among their numbers were the gold-workers, and among
     their numbers were the silver-workers. Now they have gone up to
     build the sanctuary.'

F.   "At that moment he made the decree, saying, 'Whoever has
     crossed the Euphrates has crossed [and must stay over there], and
     whoever has not crossed may never cross.'"

6. A.   Daniel and his companions and friends went up at that time.
         They said, "It is better that we should eat a meal of the food of the
         Land of Israel and say the Blessing over Food in the Land of Israel
         [since the blessing refers to the produce of the Land in
         particular]."

    B.   But Ezra and his companions and friends did not go up at that
         time.

    C.   Why did Ezra not go up at that time?

    D.   Because he had to clarify his learning [Simon: complete his
         studies] before Baruch b. Neriah.

    E.   Then why did Baruch b. Neriah not go up too?

    F.   But they said that Baruch b. Neriah was a very large man and
         feeble and unable to be carried even in a litter."

7. A.   Said R. Simeon b. Laqish, "It was on account of the sanctity [of the
         sanctuary] that Ezra did not go up at that time. For had Ezra gone
         up at that time, Satan would have had an occasion to cavil, and
         say, 'It is better that Ezra should serve as the high priest than that
         Joshua b. Jehozadak should serve in the high priesthood.'

    B.   "But Joshua b. Jehozadak was a high priest who was a son of a high
         priest, but Ezra, even though he was a righteous man, still was not
         suited to serve in the high priest as much as he was."

8. A.   Said R. Simon, "It is difficult before the Holy One, blessed be He,
         to uproot a genealogy from its proper place."

9. A.   "upon the handles of the bolt:"

    B.   [Since the word for bold and bar use the same consonants,] for
         from that point the Euphrates was blocked off before them.

10. A.   Another explanation of the verse, ""I arose [to open to my
         beloved, my fingers with liquid myrrh, upon the handles of the
         bolt]:"

    B.   "I arose," and not the nations of the world.

    C.   "to open to my beloved:"

    D.   in repentance.

    C.   "my fingers with liquid myrrh:"

    D.   in bitterness.

    E.   For I said to the calf, "These are your gods, Israel" (Ex. 32:4).

    F.   "my fingers with liquid myrrh:"

    G.   Nonetheless, the Master bypassed it, forgiving my [Simon:]
         provocation: "And the Lord repented of the evil" (Ex. 32:14).

    H.   "upon the handles of the bolt:"

    I.   For from that moment the way was closed before them, so that
         they might not enter the Land of Israel.

Both explanations invoke as their generative image the two prior
points at which Israel entered the land. It appears, therefore, that
"arose to open to my beloved" then stands for "arose" to enter the Land,

with God and Israel joining in the venture. The first explanation runs through the return to Zion in the time of Ezra, the second, brief one, which is in precisely the same model, the Exodus from Egypt in the time of Moses. The basic conception in both cases concerns not entering the land, that is, those who stayed behind and then were prevented from doing so by Cyrus, or those who sinned and were denied entry by God. Nos. 1-10 bear a burden of interpolation, but the message is clear, and the remainder, of course, is pellucid. Both components of the reading of the base verse are equally required to make the point that the compilers wished to set forth.

66

Song of Songs Rabbah to Song of Songs 5:6

5:6   *I opened to my beloved, but my beloved had turned and gone. My soul failed me when he spoke. I sought him, but found him not; I called him, but he gave no answer.*

LXVI:i

1.   A.   "I opened to my beloved, but my beloved had turned and gone:"
   B.   He [Simon] became peevish and was filled with anger against me.
   C.   "My soul failed me when he spoke:"
   D.   When Cyrus spoke and decreed that those who had not yet crossed the Euphrates might not do so.
   E.   "I sought him, but found him not; I called him, but he gave no answer."

2.   A.   Another explanation for the verse, "I opened to my beloved, but my beloved had turned and gone:"
   B.   He [Simon] became peevish and was filled with anger against me, like a pregnant woman.
   C.   "My soul failed me when he spoke:"
   D.   From the sound of his first act of speech, when he said, "I am the Lord your God" (Ex. 20:1).
   E.   "I sought him, but found him not; I called him, but he gave no answer."

The reading of Chapter Sixty-Five continues. Simon, p. 237, n. 2, explains 2.D as follows: The very love which He showed in saying this to me made my heart fail me when I realized that I had repaid it by making the Golden Calf.

67

Song of Songs Rabbah to Song of Songs 5:7

5:7   *The watchmen found me, as they went about in the city; they beat me, they wounded me, they took away my mantle, those watchmen of the walls.*

LXVII:i

1. A.   "The watchmen found me, as they went about in the city:"
   B.   This refers to Tattenai, the Governor on the other side of the river, and his allies.
   C.   "they beat me, they wounded me:"
   D.   They issued an indictment against the inhabitants of Judah and Jerusalem.

2. A.   "they took away my mantle, those watchmen of the walls:"
   B.   ["of the walls:"] of Jerusalem.
   C.   Said R. Abba b. R. Kahana, "In the past, the wall was built of stone of ten cubits and of eight, but here, 'it is built of great stones' (Ezra 5:8), meaning, stones that can be rolled around."

3. A.   Another explanation of the verse,"The watchmen found me:"
   B.   This refers to the tribe of Levi: "They have watched your word" (Dt. 33:9).
   C.   "as they went about in the city:"
   D.   That is in line with the following: "Go to and fro from gate to gate" (Ex. 32:27).
   E.   "they beat me, they wounded me:"
   F.   "And slay every man his brother" (Ex. 32:27).

4. A.   "they took away my mantle:"
   B.   This refers to weapons of war.

5. A.   It has been taught on Tannaite authority:
   B.   R. Simeon b. Yohai says, "The weapon that he gave to them at Horeb has the Ineffable Name of God incised in it.
   C.   "But when they sinned, it was taken away from them."
   D.   How was it taken away from them?
   E.   R. Aibu said, "It peeled away on its own."
   F.   Rabbis say, "An angel came down and peeled it off."

6. A.   "those watchmen of the walls:"
    B.   The walls of the Torah.

The reading of the passage in the context of the return to Zion continues at Nos. 1, 2. No. 3 reverts to the incident of the Golden Calf, now to the Levites' role in the repression. No. 5 is attached to 4.B, as is predictable. No. 6 then shifts the ground of metaphor, since no one has introduced the matter of the Torah as a generative motif here.

68

Song of Songs Rabbah to Song of Songs 5:8

5:8   *I adjure you, O daughters of Jerusalem, if you find my beloved,*
      that you tell him I am sick with love.

LXVIII:i
1.   A.   "I adjure you, O daughters of Jerusalem, if you find my beloved,
          that you tell him I am sick with love:"
     B.   Just as a sick person yearns for healing, so the generation in Egypt
          yearned for redemption.

The motif of the original redemption recurs.

69

Song of Songs Rabbah to Song of Songs 5:9

5:9   *What is your beloved more than another beloved, O fairest among women! What is your beloved more than another beloved, that you thus adjure us?*

LXIX:i

1. A.   "What is your beloved more than another beloved, O fairest among women:"

    B.   The nations of the world say to Israel, "'What is your beloved more than another beloved?'

    C.   "What is God more than other divinities? That patron more than other patrons?"

The dialogue of Song 5:9 leads right into Song 5:10, as we shall now see.

70

Song of Songs Rabbah to Song of Songs 5:10

[5:9 *What is your beloved more than another beloved, O fairest among women! What is your beloved more than another beloved, that you thus adjure us?*]

5:10 *My beloved is all radiant and ruddy, distinguished among ten thousand.*

LXX:i

1. A. The Israelites answer them, "'My beloved is all radiant and ruddy."
   B. "radiant:" to me in the land of Egypt,
   C. "and ruddy:" to the Egyptians.
   D. "radiant:" in the land of Egypt, "For I will go through the land of Egypt" (Ex. 12:13).
   E. "and ruddy:" "And the Lord overthrew the Egyptians" (Ex. 14:27).
   F. "radiant:" at the Sea: "The children of Israel walked upon dry land in the midst of the sea" (Ex. 14:29).
   G. "and ruddy:" to the Egyptians at the Sea: "And the Lord overthrew the Egyptians in the midst of the sea" (Ex. 14:27).
   H. "radiant:" in the world to come.
   I. "and ruddy:" in this world.

2. A. R. Levi b. R. Hayyata made three statements concerning the matter:
   B. "'radiant:' on the Sabbath.
   C. "'and ruddy:' on the other days of the week.
   D. "'radiant:' on the New Year.
   E. "'and ruddy:' on the other days of the year.
   F. "'radiant:' in this world.
   G. "'and ruddy:' in the world to come.

3. A. "distinguished among ten thousand:"
   B. Said R. Abba b. R. Kahana, "A mortal king is known by his ceremonial garments, but here, he is fire and his ministers are fire: 'And he came from the myriads holy' (Dt. 33:2).
   C. "He is marked in the midst of 'the myriads holy.'"

The contrasts that are drawn underline, at No. 1, the redemption; now Israel is one thing, its enemies the other; then, No. 2, the metaphor is made to refer to the holy way of life, and No. 3 concludes by having the lover refer to God.

71

Song of Songs Rabbah to
Song of Songs 5:11

5:11   *His head is the finest gold; his locks are wavy, black as a raven.*

LXXI:i
1.   A.   "His head is the finest gold; his locks are wavy, black as a raven:"
      B.   "His head:"
      C.   This refers to the Torah: "The Lord made me as the beginning of his way" (Prov. 8:22) [and the words for beginning and head are the same].

2.   A.   R. Hunia in the name of R. Simeon b. Laqish: "By two thousand years did the Torah precede the creation of the world.
      B.   "What verse of Scripture indicates it? 'Then I was by him as a nursling, and day by day I was his delight' (Prov. 8:30).
      C.   "and the day of the Holy One, blessed be He, is a thousand years: 'For a thousand years in your sight are but as yesterday when it is past' (Ps. 90:4)."

3.   A.   "...is the finest gold:"
      B.   This refers to teachings of the Torah:
      C.   "More to be desired are they than gold, yes, than much fine gold" (Ps. 19:11).

4.   A.   "his locks are wavy:"
      B.   this refers to [Simon:] "the ruled lines in the scroll."

5.   A.   "black as a raven:"
      B.   this refers to the letters.

6.   A.   Another explanation of the phrase, "his locks are wavy:"
      B.   [since the word for wavy can be divided into the words, heaps], it means, heaps upon heaps.

7.   A.   Another explanation of the phrase, "his locks are wavy:"
      B.   [since the word for his locks yields letters that can be read as strokes, that is, mere ornamentations, and can also be read as thorns] R. Azariah says, "Even things that you regard as mere strokes in the Torah are [Simon:] thorns upon thorns [Simon, p. 239, n. 7: raise all manner of knotty problems]."
      C.   R. Eliezer and R. Joshua say, "Heaps upon heaps."

8. A.   Another explanation of the phrase, "his locks are wavy:"
    B.   [since the word for his locks yields letters that can be read as
           strokes, that is, mere ornamentations, and can also be read as
           thorns] R. Azariah says, "Even things that you regard as mere
           strokes in the Torah are heaps upon heaps.

9. A.   With whom do they endure?
    B.   "black as a raven:"
    C.   "With him who gets up early and works late into the night [a word
           that uses the same consonants as raven] in laboring over them."

10. A.   R. Yohanan and R. Simeon b. Laqish:
    B.   R. Yohanan said, "The harvest ['threshing floor'] of the Torah takes
           place only by night.
    C.   "What verse of Scripture so indicates? 'She rises also while it is
           yet night' (Prov. 31:15); 'Arise, cry out in the night' (Lam. 2:19)."
    D.   R. Simeon b. Laqish said, "It is by day and by night,
    E.   "in line with the following: 'You shall meditate on it day and night'
           (Josh. 1:8)."
    F.   Said R. Simeon b. Laqish, "Well did R. Yohanan teach me, that
           the harvest ['threshing floor'] of the Torah takes place only by
           night."
    G.   Said R. Simeon b. Laqish, "When I was working on the Torah by
           day, it was by night that it illuminated me: 'You shall meditate on
           it day and night' (Josh. 1:8)."

11. A.   [Supply: "his locks are wavy:"]
    B.   [Following the version of Leviticus Rabbah XIX:II.1ff.] [With
           reference to the word for wavy, the letters of which yield the word
           heaps,] R. Yohanan of Sepphoris interpreted the verse to speak of
           heaps of dirt:
    C.   "What does a fool say? 'Who can ever hope to remove this pile of
           dirt?'
    D.   "What does a smart person say? 'Lo, today, I'll take away two
           basket loads, and tomorrow I'll take away two, and in the end I'll
           take away the entire pile.'
    E.   "So a stupid person says, 'Who in the world can study the whole
           Torah? The tractate of Damages [referring to Baba Qamma,
           Babqa Mesia, and Baba Batra] has thirty chapters and the
           tractate of Utensils has thirty chapters [of Mishnah teachings].'
    F.   "What does a smart person say? 'Lo, I'll learn two laws today, and
           two laws tomorrow, until I have finished reciting the entire Torah.'"

12. A.   R. Yannai said, "'Wisdom is unattainable to the fool' (Prov. 24:7).
    B.   "The matter may be compared to the case of a loaf of bread
           suspended in the air in a house.
    C.   "What does a fool say? 'Who can bring it down?'
    D.   "What does a smart person say? 'Didn't somebody else go and
           hang it up? So I'll go and bring two sticks and tie them together
           and I'll pull it down.'
    E.   "So what does a fool say? 'Who can ever learn the Torah which is
           in the heart of a sage?'
    F.   "What does a wise man say? 'Didn't he learn it from somebody
           else? So I'll study two laws by day and two laws by night until I
           have learned the entire Torah just like him.'"

13. **A.** Said R. Levi, "The matter may be compared to a basket with a hole. The owner hired workers to fill it up.

    B. "What does a fool say? 'What good can I do? The basket takes in here what it lets out there.'

    C. "What does a smart person say? 'Do I not collect a wage for each barrel?'

    D. "So what does a fool say? 'What good do I do if I learn Torah and then forget it?'

    E. "But what does a wise man say? 'Does the Holy One, blessed be He, not pay a reward for the effort?'"

14. **A.** R. Levi said, "[As to the statement, 'His locks are in curls,' read as, heaps upon heaps, mounds upon mounds, as the letters yield both meanings,] even things that you regard in the Torah as useless thorns in fact are mounds.

    B. "They have the power to destroy the entire world and to turn it into a mound.

    C. "That is in line with this statement: 'And it shall be a mound forever, it shall never be rebuilt' (Dt. 13:17)."

15. **A.** "Hear O Israel, the Lord our God, the Lord is one" (Dt. 6:4):

    B. If you turn the D of "one" into an R, you get "another," so you will destroy the world.

    C. "You shall not bow down to any other god" (Ex. 34:14):

    D. If you turn the R of other into a D [yielding, one], you will destroy the world.

    E. You will not profane my holy name" (Lev. 22:32);

    F. If you turn the H of the word profane into an H, you will destroy the entire world [by reading, You will not praise my holy name"].

    G. "Every soul will praise the Lord" (Ps. 103:6).

    H. If you turn the H into a different H, you will destroy the entire world [by reading, "Every soul will profane the Lord"].

    I. "They have acted deceptively against the Lord" (Jer. 5:12).

    J. If you turn the B into a K, you will destroy the entire world [by reading, "They have acted deceptively like the Lord"].

    K. "Against the Lord they have acted treacherously" (Hos. 5:7).

    L. If you turn the B into a K, you will destroy the entire world [by reading, "They have acted treacherously like the Lord"].

    M. "There is none holy like the Lord" (1 Sam. 2:2).

    N. If you turn the B into a K, you will destroy the entire world [by reading, "There is nothing holy in the Lord"].

    O. "For there is none beside you" (1 Sam. 2:2):

    P. For R. Abba b. R. Kahana said, "Everything wears out, but you do not wear out.

    Q. "'For there is none beside you' – for there is none that wears you out' [no one can outlive you or supersede you]."

16. **A.** "black as a raven:"

    B. R. Alexander b. Hadrin and R. Alexander Qaroba [Leviticus Rabbah XIX:II.5.A: R. Alexandri b. R. Agri and R. Alexandri bar Habrin, following Magulies reading, p. 419, n. 5] say, "If everybody in the world got together to bleach one wing of a raven, they could not do it. So if all the nations of the world got together to uproot a single teaching from the Torah, they could not do it.

	C.	"From whom do you derive that lesson?
	D.	"From King Solomon. It was because he tried to uproot a single teaching from the Torah that he came under indictment."
	E.	Who indicted him?
	F.	R. Judah b. Levi said, "It was the letter Y in the word *Yarbeh* [increase, he shall increase] that indicated him [as will now be explained]."
17.	A.	R. Simeon b. Yohai taught on Tannaite authority, "The book of Deuteronomy went up and spread itself out before the Holy One, blessed be He, saying to him, 'Lord of the world! Solomon has uprooted me and made me into a forgery. For any legal document in which two or three minor matters are found to be null is entirely null.
	B.	"'Now lo, King Solomon wants to pull out one of my Y's.
	C.	"'It is written, "He will not multiply [*yrbh*] wives for himself" (Dt. 17:17), but he has multiplied [*hrbh*] wives for himself.
	D.	"'"He will not multiply horses for himself" (Dt. 17:16), but he has multiplied horses for himself.
	E.	"'"He will not multiply silver and gold" (Dt. 17:17) but he has multiplied silver and gold.'
	F.	"Said to him the Holy One, blessed be He, 'Go your way. Lo, Solomon and a hundred like him will be null, but a single Y of yours will never be null.'"
18.	A.	[Genesis Rabbah XLVII:I.2:A "You shall not call her name Sarai, but Sarah shall be her name" (Gen. 17:15):]
	B.	Said R. Joshua b. Qorha, "The Y [that the Holy One, blessed be He, took away from the name of Sarai] went fluttering above, before the Holy One, blessed be He, saying, 'Lord of all ages, because I am the smallest of all the letters you took me out of the name of that righteous woman, the wife of that righteous man, Abraham, and you have called her Sarah!'
	C.	"Said the Holy One, blessed be He, to it, 'In the past you were in the name of a woman and at the end of the letters of the name. Now I shall put you in the name of a male, and as the first of the letters of his name: "And Moses called Hoshea ben Nun Yehoshua'" (Num. 13:16)."
	D.	[Genesis Rabbah adds: Said R. Mana, "In the past she was princess for her own people, now she shall be princess for all humankind." (Freedman, p. 400, n. 1: He holds that both Sarai and Sarah denote princess, but that the latter is more comprehensive.)]
19.	A.	R. Eleazar b. R. Abinah in the name of R. Aha: "For twenty-six generations the A [alef] complained before the Holy One, blessed be He, 'Lord of the world, you have set me at the head of the alphabet, but you created the world not with me but with the B [which is the second letter of the alphabet].
	B.	"'For it is said, "In [B] the beginning, God created the heaven and the earth" (Gen. 1:1).'
	C.	"Said to him the Holy One, blessed be He, 'My world and all that is in it were created only on account for the merit accruing to the

Torah: "The Lord for the sake of wisdom founded the earth" (Prov. 23:19).

D.   '"Tomorrow I shall be revealed and shall give the Torah to Israel, and I shall put you at the head of the Ten Commandments, and with you I shall open first of all: "I [spelled with the A, anokhi] am the Lord your God" (Ex. 20:2).'"

20. A.   Bar Huta said, "Why is the letter called '*alef*'?

B.   "For it [Simon:] holds good for a thousand [*elef*] generations: 'The word which he commanded to a thousand generations' (Ps. 105:8)."

21. A.   [Supply: Another explanation of the phrase, "his locks are wavy, black as a raven:"]

B.   R. Judah interpreted the verse to speak of disciples of sages:

C.   "'his locks are...black as a raven:' this refers to disciples of sages.

D.   "For even though they appear ugly and sallow in this world, in the world to come, 'The appearance of them will be like torches, they will run to and fro like lightning' (Nah. 2:5)."

22. A.   [Supply: Another explanation of the phrase, "his locks are wavy, black as a raven:"]

B.   R. Samuel b. R. Isaac interpreted the verse to speak of the sections of the Torah:

C.   "'his locks are...black as a raven:' this refers to sections of the Torah that appear too ugly and dark to be recited in public,

D.   "[but] said the Holy One, blessed be He, 'To me they are sweet.'

E.   "[That reading of the letters of the word that yields either raven or sweet is in line with this verse:] 'Then shall the offering of Judah and Jerusalem be pleasant to the Lord' (Mal. 3:4).

F.   "For lo, the passage of the Scripture that deals with the male who has a flux and the passage of the Scripture that deals with a female who has a flux not during her menstrual cycle [Lev. 15:2, Lev. 15:19, respectively] are not stated together, but this is given by itself and that is given by itself: 'If any man has an issue out of his flesh' (Lev. 15:2), 'And if a woman has an issue' (Lev. 15:19)."

23. A.   Said R. Simeon b. Levi, "The Torah that the Holy One, blessed be He, gave –

B.   "the leather was white fire, the writing was black fire, it was fire, hewn of fire, formed of fire, given in fire:

C.   "'At his right hand was a fiery Torah to them' (Dt. 33:2).

The base verse is now to be compared to the Torah, which God admires as the speaker. Everything else flows from that one point, which, as a matter of fact, is made explicit at the outset. With that in hand, the compilers can hardly have been faulted for combining the massive materials before us, most of which pertain to the theme, but few of which do more than restate images that contain and realize the same theme. That seems to me to capture the nature of discourse in Song of Songs Rabbah, and it further seems to me the right way to respond to the Song. Over and over again, what we have as expansion, elaboration, and explanation is simply repetition of the base verse's image as interpreted: if this stands for Torah, then the language at hand ("his head," "finest gold," "locks," "wavy," "black," "raven") will be asked to link up to the image of the Torah, disciples of the Torah, the Torah as an object, and the like.   That forms the hermeneutic of our document and permits us to predict, at any given point, what is likely to happen.   That is to say, we can make sense of the materials that are selected, or we can understand the materials that are made up, because we grasp the processes of thought – here, thought through imagination and emotion – of the authorship of the Song of Songs and of Song of Songs Rabbah, both.   Once at No. 1 the Torah is introduced, then No. 2 is as good as anything to follow; it belongs, since it expands on the prooftext of No. 1.   Nos. 3, 4, 5, 6, 7 make the same point over and over again.   Nos. 8, 9 continue along these same lines.   No. 10 belongs because of the reference to "black as a raven," hence by extension, by night, so it seems to me.   Nos. 11-13 go over the same ground over and over again, made relevant by the intersection in the same consonants of the words for locks and heaps.   That same confluence of meanings within the same letters accounts for Nos. 14-15. No. 16 then reverts to the sense, "black as a raven," now to deal with "uproot a single teaching from the Torah."   Here the metaphor used in our base verse triggers reference to the metaphor that occurs in the quite autonomous item at hand, "bleach the wing of a raven/uproot a single teaching from the Torah."   And since prior to insertion here, Nos. 17, 18, 19, 20 had been conglomerated into a sizable essay on the theme of the permanence of the letters of the alphabet in each of their usages in the Torah, the whole was parachuted down.   No. 22 then reverts to our base verse and makes its own point, parallel to the one about the disciples of sages being ugly now but beautiful in the world to come; the same applies to passages of the Torah.   No. 23 concludes with a kind of hymn.   The whole is a perfect case of how the principles of agglutination and accretion yield a document of the remarkable cogency and aesthetic perfection such as this one.

72

Song of Songs Rabbah to Song of Songs 5:12

5:12   *His eyes are like doves, beside springs of water, bathed in milk,*
        fitly set.

LXXII:i

1. A.   "His eyes are like doves:"
    B.   "his eyes" – this refers to the Sanhedrin, which is the eyes of the
          congregation:
    C.   "Then it shall be, if it be done before the eyes of the congregation"
          (Num. 15:24).
    D.   A human body has two hundred forty-eight limbs, and all of them
          follow the lead of the eyes.
    E.   So too the Israelites can do nothing except by the word of their
          Sanhedrin.

2. A.   "beside springs of water:"
    B.   For [the Israelites] are strengthened [a word that uses the same
          consonants as springs] by the water of the Torah.
    D.   For said R. Hama b. Uqba, "Words of Torah strengthen all those
          who are occupied in them for as much as is required."

3. A.   "bathed in milk:"
    B.   This refers to the laws, which people clean with their teeth until
          they make them as spotless as milk.

4. A.   "fitly set:"
    B.   On the fulness [the words for fitly and fulness use the same
          consonants] of the Torah.

5. A.   Another interpretation of "fitly set:"
    B.   On the fulness of Jerusalem: "full of justice" (Isa. 1:21).

6. A.   R. Phineas in the name of R. Hoshaia the Elder: "There were four
          hundred eighty synagogues in Jerusalem,
    B.   "corresponding to the numerical value of the letters of the word
          'full' (in the verse, 'full of justice,' Isa. 1:21)."

7. A.   [Supply: another interpretation of "fitly set:"]
    B.   Said R. Tanhuma, "'fitly set' – this provides something [the word
          for 'provide' and 'fitly' using the same consonants] and that one

117

provides something until the law comes forth like the Lebanon."
[cf. LXIX:i.2. A. "and flowing streams from Lebanon (Song 4:15)."
Said R. Azariah, "This one flows a bit in one matter, and that one
flows a bit in one matter, until the law stands forth like [a cedar of]
Lebanon."]

C.   Said R. Tanhuma, "This one [Simon:] fastens a little and that one
fastens a little, until the law stands forth like well-joined beams."

Israel is now described by God, the lover, with special reference to
the institutions and processes of the law, thus No. 1, the Sanhedrin,
No. 2, legal study, No. 3, 4, the legal process. Nos. 5, 6 are tacked on for
thematic purposes; they do not make the same point as Nos. 1-4. No. 7
is then borrowed from elsewhere, as noted; it fits much better in
Chapter Fifty-Nine, since, after all, whence "Lebanon"?

73

Song of Songs Rabbah to Song of Songs 5:13

5:13   *His cheeks are like beds of spices, yielding fragrance. His lips are lilies, distilling liquid myrrh.*

LXXIII:i

1. A.   "His cheeks are like beds of spices:"
   B.   Said R. Yannai, "In my time there were two companies, and we would go out onto the street to work on the Torah,
   C.   "and the reasoning that one party would set forth was not the same as that which the other one set forth."

2. A.   "yielding fragrance:"
   B.   Said R. Tanhuma, "Just as the chest of the spice dealer holds all kinds of spices,
   C.   "so a disciple of a sage has to be full of Scripture, Mishnah, Talmud, laws, and lore."

3. A.   [Supply: another interpretation of "yielding fragrance:"]
   B.   The priesthood and the Levites, deriving from Jacob.

4. A.   "His lips are lilies:"
   B.   This refers to a disciple of sages who is fluent in his study of the Mishnah, for his lips "distill liquid myrrh."
   C.   "distilling liquid myrrh:"
   D.   This refers to a disciple of sages who is not fluent in his study of the Mishnah, for, while his lips "distill liquid myrrh," nonetheless [his learning] is transient, so he has to go over and clarify what he has learned.

The established motif of God's describing the virtues of the disciple of sages is worked out through the sustaining metaphor.

74

Song of Songs Rabbah to Song of Songs 5:14

5:14   *His arms are rounded gold, set with jewels.*
         His body is ivory work, encrusted with sapphires.

LXXIV:i

1. A.   "His arms are rounded gold:"
   B.   This refers to the tablets of the covenant: "And the tablets were the work of God" (Ex. 32:16).
2. A.   "rounded gold:"
   B.   This refers to words of Torah: "More to be desired are they than gold, yes, than much fine gold" (Ps. 19:11).
3. A.   [Supply: "rounded gold:"]
   B.   Said R. Joshua b. R. Nehemiah, "There was a miracle involved [in the tablets],
   C.   "for they were made of hard stone and yet they rolled up [the words for rounded and rolled using the same consonants]."
4. A.   R. Menahema in the name of R. Abun said, "They were hewn from the orb of the sun.
   B.   "How were they written? Five on one tablet, five on the other, in line with the verse: 'his arms are rounded gold.'"
   C.   That [B, five on one side, five on the other] accords with the position of R. Hananiah b. Gamaliel: "'And he wrote them upon two tablets of stone' (Dt. 4:13)."
   D.   Rabbis said, "There were ten on one tablet: 'And he declared to you his covenant, which he commanded you to perform, even the ten words, and he wrote all of them upon each of two tablets of stone' (Dt. 4:13)."
   E.   R. Simeon b. Yohai said, "There were twenty on one tablet and twenty on the other: 'And he wrote them on two tablets of stone (Dt. 4:13), twenty on this tablet, twenty on that."
   F.   R. Simai says, "There were forty on this tablet and forty on that: 'Tablets that were written on both their sides, on the one side and on the other' (Ex. 32:15) – in a square."
5. A.   [Supply: "set with jewels:"]

B.   Hananiah, son of the brother of R. Joshua, said, "Between each of the Ten Commandments were written all of the passages and details of the Torah."

C.   When R. Yohanan would set forth Scripture and would come to this verse, "set with jewels," he would say, "Well did Hananiah, son of the brother of R. Joshua, teach me. For just as in the case of great waves, where there are small ripples between each one, so between each of the Ten Commandments were written all of the passages and details of the Torah."

6. A.   "set with jewels:"

    B.   This refers to the Talmud,

    C.   which resembles the Great Sea: "Unto Tarshish" (Jonah 1:3) [the words for jewels and Tarshish sharing the same consonants], "All the rivers run into the sea" (Qoh. 1:7) [Simon, p. 246, n. 3: so is the Talmud, which embraces all].

7. A.   "His body is ivory work:"

    B.   This refers to the book of Leviticus.

    C.   Just as the belly has the heart on one side and the intestines on the other and it is in the middle,

    D.   so the book of Leviticus has two books fore, and two books aft, and it is in the middle.

8. A.   "ivory work:"

    B.   Just as out of a block of ivory you may make any number of nails or javelins,

    C.   so the book of Leviticus contains any number of religious duties, any number of details, any number of arguments *a fortiori*, any number of cases involving the rendering of an offering refuse, any number of cases involving the rendering of an offering left over.

9. A.   "encrusted with sapphires:"

    B.   [Study of the Torah] drains the strength of people, for it is as hard as sapphire. [The words for encrusted and drain the strength use the same consonants.]

    C.   R. Yudan and R. Phineas:

    D.   R. Yudan said, "If you want to maintain that sapphire is soft, take note of the case of a man who brought a sapphire to Rome to sell. The purchaser said, '...on condition that I may test it, so let us test it by breaking a little piece off it.' They put it on the anvil and begin to hit it with the hammer. The anvil cracked, the hammer broke in two, but the sapphire stood firm and lost nothing.

    E.   "That is in line with this verse: 'encrusted with sapphires.'"

10. A.   Said R. Abba b. R. Mammel, "If a person tires himself in studying the Torah and law, in the end he will be made a sapphire through them."

    B.   Rabbis said, "Whoever is made a charm through words of the Torah in the end will be made a king by them: 'A divine sentence is in the lips of the king' (Prov. 16:10)."

11. A.   R. Eliezer b. R. Simeon:

    B.   Ass-drivers came to his father to buy grain from the town.

    C.   They saw him sitting at the oven. His mother would take [a hot roll from the oven] and he would eat it, his mother would take [a hot roll from the oven] and he would eat it – until he ate up all the rolls.

D. They said, "Woe! there is an evil snake in that man's belly. It appears that this one is going to bring a famine to the world."

E. He heard what they were saying.

F. When they went out to buy their burden of grain, he took their asses and brought them up to the roof.

G. They came looking for their asses and did not find them.

H. They raised their eyes and saw them situated on the roof.

I. They went to his father and repeated the story to him.

J. He said to them, "Is it possible that you made him hear some offensive statement?"

K. They said to him, "No, my lord, but this is what happened."

L. He said to them, "Then why did you call the evil eye down upon him [by grudging him his meal]? Was he eating something that belonged to you? Or is it your job to provide him with his meals? Is not the One who created him the one who also created his food? Still, go speak to him in my name, and he will bring them down for you."

M. The latter miracle was more difficult than the former.

N. When he brought them up, he brought them up one by one, but when he brought them down, he brought them down two by two.

O. But when he was engaged in the study of the Torah, even his cloak he was unable to bear.

P. That is in line with this verse: "encrusted with sapphires." [For study of the Torah drains the strength of people].

12. A. A member of the household in the establishment of Rabban Gamaliel had the habit of taking a basket carrying forty *seahs* of grain and bringing it to the baker.

B. He said to him, "All this wonderful strength is in you, and you are not engaged in the Torah?"

C. When he got involved in the Torah, he would begin to take thirty, then twenty, then twelve, then eight *seahs*, and when he had completed a book, even a basket of only a single *seah* he could not carry.

D. And some say that he could not even carry his own hat, but others had to take it off him, for he could not do it.

E. That is in line with this verse: "encrusted with sapphires." [For study of the Torah drains the strength of people].

The established motif for interpreting the metaphor is worked out now with reference to two components, first, the Ten Commandments, second, the study of the Torah. Nos. 1, 2, 3, 4, 5, 6 develop that theme, with nothing of intense interest to add; Nos. 7-8 then make an autonomous point; and Nos. 9ff. work on the other motif. Here the play on the word for sapphire yields the proposition that Torah study is enervating. I do not grasp the point of No. 10; Simon, p. 247, has "if a man grows faint over the study of Torah...he will ultimately become able to conjure with them...whoever is able to conjure with the words of Torah will finally become a king over them...'divination is in the lips of the king.'" That seems a plausible reading, since the point of the story of Eliezer b. R. Simeon is that he could conjure; that that is a miracle is made explicit. But then 11.O-P contradicts the point of the story, since it is now a physical action that he did, and that is coherent with No. 12. I am therefore inclined to read the story of Eliezer not as cogent with No. 10 but as an illustration of the power that someone loses when he studies the Torah; the correlation between the enormous meal and the enormous strength hardly requires us to introduce the conception of a miracle, other than the obvious one, N, of brute force. That leaves No. 10 as something of an anomaly, and, as I said, I cannot claim to understand it.

75

Song of Songs Rabbah to Song of Songs 5:15

5:15　　His legs are alabaster columns, set upon bases of gold.
　　　　His appearance is like Lebanon, choice as the cedars.

LXXV:i

1.　A.　["His legs are alabaster columns, set upon bases of gold. His appearance is like Lebanon, choice as the cedars:"]

　　B.　"His legs:" refer to the world.

　　C.　"alabaster columns:" for the world rests on the six days of creation: "For in six days did God create the world" (Ex. 20:11).

　　D.　"set upon bases of fine gold:" this refers to the sections of the Torah, which are interpreted both in light of what precedes them and also in light of what follows them. [Leviticus Rabbah XXV:VIII:i.D: This refers to words of the Torah, "which are more to be desired than fine gold" (Ps. 19:11), then: ...sections of the Torah.]

2.　A.　To what may they be compared?

　　B.　To a column that has a base on the bottom and a capitol on the top.

　　C.　So there are sections of the Torah to be interpreted both in light of what precedes them and also in light of what follows them. [This will now be illustrated.]

3.　A.　How do we know that that is the rule concerning what precedes them?

　　B.　"If a man lies carnally with a woman who is a slave" (Lev. 19:20-22).

　　C.　And immediately following: "When you come into the land and plant all kinds of trees for food" (Lev. 19:23).

　　D.　Now what has one matter got to do with the other?

　　E.　But it is to teach that one who weeds and farms with his fellow gradually becomes part of the household. Since he comes and goes in his house, he becomes suspect of having sexual relations with the other's slave girl.

　　F.　He says, "Is it not a sin-offering that I now owe? Is it not a guilt-offering that I know owe? I'll bring a sin-offering, I'll bring a guilt-offering."

4. A. For R. Yudan in the name of R. Levi said, "Those who in this world treat slave girls as though they were sexually permitted are destined to hang by the scalp of their head in the world to come.

B. "This is in line with the following verse of Scripture: 'But God will shatter the heads of his enemies, the hair crown of him who walks in his guilty ways' (Ps. 68:21)."

C. What is meant by "walking in his guilty ways"?

D. Everybody says, "Let that man go in his guilt, let that man go in his guilt."

5. A. Passages of the Torah also may be interpreted in light of what follows them – how so?

B. "For three years it shall be as though uncircumcised for you" (Lev. 19:23).

C. And further, "You shall not eat any flesh with the blood in it" (Lev. 19:26).

D. [What has one thing go to do with the other?] Said the Holy One, blessed be He, to Israel, "You are prepared to wait for the uncircumcised fruit tree for three years, and for your wife do you not wait, while she observes the period of her menstruation?

E. "For your uncircumcised tree you are prepared to wait for three years, and for the meat of your beast are you not prepared to wait until the blood is fully drained from it?"

6. A. Who observed the religious duty governing the blood?

B. It was Saul, for it is said, "Then they told Saul, Behold the people are sinning against the Lord by eating with the blood. And he said, You have dealt treacherously; roll a great stone to me here. And Saul said, Disperse yourselves among the people and say to them, Let every man bring his ox or his sheep and slay them here; and eat, but do not sin against the Lord by eating with the blood" (1 Sam. 14:33-34).

C. What is meant by "here"?

D. Rabbis say, "A knife fourteen fingers long did he show them, and the numerical value of the letters of the word for 'here' adds up to that number, so he said to them, 'In this manner will you slaughter and eat meat, [with a knife of proper length]."

E. How did the Holy One, blessed be He, reward him?

F. It was in the day of battle with the Philistines: "So on the day of the battle there was neither sword nor spear found in the hand of any of the people with Saul and Jonathan, but with "Saul and Jonathan his son weaponry was found. And the garrison of the Philistines went out to the pass of Michmash" (1 Sam. 13:22).

G. First it says, "was not found," and then it says, "But...was found"! Who provided it for him?

H. R. Haggai in the name of R. Isaac said, "An angel provided him with the needed weapons."

I. And rabbis say, "The Holy One, blessed be He, provided him with the needed weapons." First it says, "was not found," and then it says, "But...was found"! Who provided it for him?

J. R. Haggai in the name of R. Isaac said, "An angel provided him with the needed weapons."

K.   And rabbis say, "The Holy One, blessed be He, provided him with the needed weapons."

7. A.   It is written, "And Saul built an altar to the Lord; it was the first altar built to the Lord" (1 Sam. 14:35).

    B.   How many altars had the earlier generations already built – Noah, Abraham, Isaac, Jacob, Moses, Joshua – and yet you say, "it was the first altar built to the Lord"!

    C.   What it means is this: "he was the first of the kings to build one."

    D.   Said R. Yudan, "Because he was ready to give his life for this matter, Scripture treated it in his behalf as if he were the first one who built an altar to the Lord."

8. A.   Said R. Simeon b. Yosé b. Lagoniah, "Now in this world, one person builds a building, and someone else uses it.

    B.   "One person may plant a tree, but someone else eats its fruit.

    C.   "But of the world to come: 'They shall not build and another inhabit, they shall not plant and another eat...they shall not work in vain' (Isa. 65:22-23); 'And their seed shall be known among the nations, and their offspring among the peoples; all who see them shall acknowledge them, that they are the seed which the Lord has blessed' (Isa. 61:9)."

The entire passage serves equally well at Leviticus Rabbah XXV:VIII, as indicated. The sole point of contact is the opening lines, which invite the amplification about reading one passage in light of others fore and aft, a fundamental hermeneutical principle. Only the opening parsing is relevant here, and the main point, then, is that the description of the lover pertains to the world and the Torah, which God loves. So God is still the speaker here.

76

Song of Songs Rabbah to Song of Songs 5:16

5:16 *His speech is most sweet, and he is altogether desirable. This is my beloved, and this is my friend, O daughters of Jerusalem.*

LXXVI:i

1. A. "His speech is most sweet:"
   B. "For thus says the Lord to the house of Israel, seek me and live" (Amos 5:4).
   C. Do you have a candy sweeter to the palate than this?
   D. "As I live, says the Lord God, I have no pleasure in the death of the wicked" (Ezek. 33:11).
   E. Do you have a candy sweeter to the palate than this?
   F. "For I have no pleasure in the death of him who dies, says the Lord God, repent and live" (Ezek. 18:32).
   G. Do you have a candy sweeter to the palate than this?
   H. "When the wicked man turns away from his wickedness...and does what is lawful and right, he shall save his soul alive" (Ezek. 18:27).
   I. Do you have a candy sweeter to the palate than this?
   J. Said R. Simeon b. Laqish, "But that is on condition that he regret what he had done."
   K. How so?
   L. R. Simeon b. Yohai taught on Tannaite authority, "Lo, if someone was righteous his entire life, but at the end he turned wicked, in his regard Scripture says, 'As for the wickedness of the wicked, he shall not stumble thereby in the day that he turns from his wickedness' (Ezek. 33:12)."
   M. Said R. Yohanan, "Not only so, but all the transgressions that he has committed does the Holy One, blessed be He, count as acts of merit: 'Myrrh and aloes and cassia are all your garments' (Ps. 45:9).
   N. "[That is to say,] 'All the acts of treachery [a word that uses the same consonants as the word for garments] that you have

127

committed against me, lo, they are like myrrh and aloes before me.'"

2. A. It has been taught on Tannaite authority: How old was Abraham when he recognized his creator?

B. R. Hananiah and R. Yohanan both said, "He was forty-eight years old when Abraham recognized his creator."

C. [Genesis Rabbah XCV:III: R. Levi in the name of] R. Simeon b. Laqish: "He was three years old."

D. "How do we know? It is stated, 'because Abraham obeyed my voice and kept my charge,' that is, he listened to the voice of his creator and kept his charge [for the years numbered by the numerical value of the consonants in the word] 'because' and since he lived 175 years, and the letters of the word for 'because' bear the numerical value of 172, he was three years of age when he converted."

E. Said R. Levi, "When he could lift up his heel from the ground [that is, at the age of one year]."

3. A. [Leviticus Rabbah XXVII:VI.2ff.:] Said R. Samuel b. R. Nahman, "On three occasions the Holy One, blessed be He, came to engage in argument with Israel, and the nations of the world rejoiced, saying, 'Can these ever [dare] engage in an argument with their creator? Now he will wipe them out of the world.'

B. "One was when he said to them, 'Come, and let us reason together, says the Lord' [Isa. 1:18]. When the Holy One, blessed be He, saw that the nations of the world were rejoicing, he turned the matter to [Israel's] advantage: 'If your sins are as scarlet, they shall be white as snow' [Isa. 1:18].

C. "Then the nations of the world were astonished, and said, 'This is repentance, and this is rebuke? He has planned only to amuse himself with his children.'

D. "[A second time was] when he said to them, 'Hear, you mountains, the controversy of the Lord' [Mic. 6:2], the nations of the world rejoiced, saying, 'How can these ever [dare] engage in an argument with their creator? Now he will wipe them out of the world.'

E. "When the Holy One, blessed be He, saw that the nations of the world were rejoicing, he turned the matter to [Israel's] advantage: 'O my people, what have I done to you? In what have I wearied you? Testify against me' [Mic. 6:3]. 'Remember what Balak king of Moab devised' [Mic. 6:5].

F. "Then the nations of the world were astonished, saying, 'This is repentance, and this is rebuke, one following the other? He has planned only to amuse himself with his children.'

G. "[A third time was] when he said to them, 'The Lord has an indictment against Judah, and will punish Jacob according to his ways' [Hos. 12:2], the nations of the world rejoiced, saying, 'How can these ever [dare] engage in an argument with their creator? Now he will wipe them out of the world.'

H. "When the Holy One, blessed be He, saw that the nations of the world were rejoicing, he turned the matter to [Israel's] advantage. That is in line with the following verse of Scripture: 'In the womb he [Jacob = Israel] took his brother [Esau = other nations] by the heel [and in his manhood he strove with God. He strove with the angel and prevailed, he wept and sought his favor]'" (Hos. 12:3-4).

4. A.   Said R. Yudan [b. R. Simeon], "The matter may be compared to a widow who was complaining to a judge about her son. When she saw that the judge was in session and handing out sentences of punishment by fire, pitch, and lashes, she said, 'If I report the bad conduct of my son to that judge, he will kill him now.' She waited until he was finished. When he had finished, he said to her, 'Madam, this son of yours, how has he behaved badly toward you?'

    B.   "She said to him, 'My lord, when he was in my womb, he kicked me.'

    C.   "He said to her, 'Now has he done anything wrong to you?'
    D.   "She said to him, 'No.'
    E.   "He said to her, 'Go your way, there is nothing wrong in the matter [that you report].'

    F.   "[Lev. R. adds:] So, when the Holy One, blessed be He, saw that the nations of the world were rejoicing, he turned the matter to [Israel's] advantage:

    G.   "'In the womb he took his brother by the heel' (Mic. 12:3). [Then the nations of the world were astonished, saying, 'This is repentance and this is rebuke, one following the other? He has planned only to amuse himself with his children.']"

    H.   R. Eleazar b. R. Simon said, "The God of Jacob, our father, has paid honor to him."

5. A.   "His speech is most sweet:"
    B.   R. Azariah and R. Aha in the name of R. Yohanan said, "When the Israelites heard at Sinai, 'I,' their souls fled: 'If we hear the voice...any more, then we shall die' (Dt. 5:22); 'My soul failed me when he spoke' (Song 5:16).

    C.   "The word went back before the Holy One, blessed be He, and said, 'Lord of the world, you live and endure, and your Torah lives and endures, and you have sent me to corpses – all of them have died!'

    D.   "At that moment the Holy One, blessed be He, went and sweetened the word for them: 'The voice of the Lord is powerful, the voice of the Lord is full of majesty' (Ps. 29:4)."

6. A.   [Supply: "The voice of the Lord is powerful, the voice of the Lord is full of majesty" (Ps. 29:4):]
    B.   Said R. Hama b. R. Hanina, "'The voice of the Lord is powerful' for youths, 'the voice of the Lord is full of majesty' for the mature."

7. A.   It has been taught on Tannaite authority by R. Simeon b. Yohai, "The Torah that the Holy One, blessed be He, gave to Israel restored their souls to them:
    B.   "'The Torah of the Lord is perfect, restoring the soul' (Ps. 19:8)."

8. A.   Another interpretation of the verse, "His speech is most sweet:"
    B.   The matter may be compared to the case of a king who scolded his son, and the son was afraid and lost heart.

C.   When the king saw that his son had lost heart, he began to hug and kiss him and appease him, saying to him, "What's with you? Are you not my only son? Am I not your father?"

D.   So when the Holy One, blessed be He, spoke: "I am the Lord your God," their spirit forthwith departed.

E.   Since they had died, the angels began to hug and kiss them, saying to them, "What's with you? Don't be afraid! 'You are children of the Lord your God' (Dt. 14:1)."

F.   And the Holy One, blessed be He, sweetened the word in their mouths and said to them, "Are you not my children? 'I am the Lord your God.' You are my people, you are precious to me."

G.   So he began to appease them until their souls were restored, and they began to [Simon:] entreat him.

H.   Thus: "His speech is most sweet."

9.   A.   The Torah began to seek mercy for Israel before the Holy One, blessed be He.

B.   She said before him, "Lord of the world, is there such a thing as a king who marries off his daughter and also kills one of his householders?

C.   "Everyone is happy on my account, but your children are dying."

D.   Forthwith their souls were restored: "The Torah of the Lord is perfect, restoring the soul" (Ps. 19:8).

10. A.   R. Aha and R. Tanhum b. R. Hiyya in the name of R. Yohanan: "'And sanctify my Sabbaths' (Ez. 20:20).

B.   "How do you sanctify it? Sanctify it with food and drink and clean clothing: 'For it is a sign between me and you throughout your generations that you may know that I am the Lord' (Ex. 31:13).

C.   "'I the Lord am faithful to pay a good reward to you.'"

11. A.   Said R. Hiyya b. R. Abba, "Under ordinary circumstances someone works for a householder, and because he gets himself all dirty with mud, the other pays his salary.

B.   "But the Holy One, blessed be He, is not that way.

C.   "Rather, he admonishes the Israelites, saying to them, 'Do not make yourselves dirty with evil, and I will pay you a good reward: 'You shall not make yourselves detestable with any swarming thing' (Lev. 11:43), 'You shall not make any cuttings in your flesh...I am the Lord' (Lev. 19:28).

D.   "'I the Lord am faithful to pay a good reward to you in the world to come.'"

12. A.   R. Yudan in the name of R. Hama b. R. Hanina and R. Berekhiah in the name of R. Abbahu: "It is written, 'And I have set you apart from the peoples' (Lev. 20:26).

B.   "Had Scripture said, 'I shall separate the peoples from you,' there would have been no stance for (the enemies of) Israel, but 'I shall separate you from the nations' bears the analogy to one who filters out the bad from the good.

C.   "Once he had separated out the bad, he does not sift any more.

D.   "But he keeps on sifting the good.

E.   "So had Scripture said, 'I shall separate the peoples from you,' there would have been no stance for (the enemies of) Israel, but 'I shall separate you from the nations' means, 'to be be mine, for my name forever.'"

F.   Said R. Aha, "On this basis [we learn] that the Holy One, blessed he he, told the nations to repent and he would bring them under his wings."

13. A.   Said R. Levi, "Whatever the Israelites do is different from what the nations of the world do, whether as to ploughing, sowing, planting, reaping, sheaf gathering, threshing, garnering, wine vintaging, in roofs, firstborn, meat, shaving, or even counting.

B.   "ploughing:' 'You shall not plough with an ox and an ass together' (Dt. 22:10).

C.   "sowing:' 'You shall not sow your vineyard with two kinds of seed' (Dt. 22:9).

D.   "planting:' 'Then you shall count the fruit thereof as forbidden' (Lev. 19:23).

E.   "reaping:' 'And when you reap the harvest of your land, you shall not wholly reap the corner' (Lev. 19:9).

F.   "sheaf gathering:' 'If you forget a sheaf in the field' (Dt. 24:19).

G.   "threshing:' 'You shall not muzzle an ox in his treading out the grain' (Dt. 25:4).

H.   "garnering, wine vintaging:' 'You shall not delay to offering the fulness of your harvest and the outflow of your presses' (Ex. 22:28); "As to the grain of your threshing floor and the fulness of your winepress' (Num. 18:27);

I.   "in roofs:' 'You shall make a parapet for your roof' (Dt. 22:8).

J.   "shaving:' 'neither shall you mar the corners of your beard' (Lev. 19:27).

K.   "or even counting:' 'when you take the sum of the children of Israel' (Ex. 30:12);

L.   "and the Israelites count the days by the moon, but the nations of the world by the sun."

14. A.   R. Berekhiah made two statements, one in the name of Kahana, one in the name of R. Levi.

B.   The one in the name of Kahana: "She [Israel] praises him, and he [God] praises her.

C.   "She praises him from above and moves downward, he starts from below and moves upward.

D.   "[At Song 5:11-15] she praises him from above and moves downward, for he was among the beings of the upper world and brought his Presence to dwell among the creatures of the lower world.

E.   "And he praises her from below to above, for she is at the lowest level, and he will raise her up: 'The Lord your God will set you on high' (Dt. 28:1)."

F.   In the name of R. Levi he said, "It is like the case of a king who betrothed a noble lady and said, 'I want to see her.'

G.   "When he had seen her, he began to praise her and count her virtues: 'You are stately as a palm tree' (Song 7:7).

H.   "For her part, she said, 'I want to see him,' and when she saw him, she began to praise him: 'His speech is most sweet, and he is altogether desirable.'"

The printed text starts Parashah Six here. No. 1 gives a variety of examples of how sayings of the Torah are most sweet; these sayings concern the power of repentance to achieve full and complete forgiveness. I cannot account for the inclusion of Nos. 2-3. No. 4, bearing in its wake No. 5, 6 reverts to our base verse. No. 7, bearing No. 8 alongside, offers yet another reading, all the time with the point of reference now God and the Torah and the act of revelation. What follows seems to me rather random; there certainly is no clear connection to our base verse. until the very end. The connection among the compositions derives from a general theme, namely, Israel and the nations. The principle that holds the whole together seems to me essentially agglutinative, since I see no well-crafted proposition that is served in a systematic way by what is at hand.

Part Six
PARASHAH SIX

Song of Songs - Chapter Six

6:1   *Whither has your beloved gone,*
O fairest among women?
Whither has your beloved turned, that we may seek him with
    you?

6:2   *My beloved has gone down to his garden,*
to the beds of spices,
to pasture his flock in the gardens,
and to gather lilies.

6:3   *I am my beloved's, and my beloved is mine;*
he pastures his flock among the lilies.

6:4   *You are beautiful as Tirzah, my love,*
comely as Jerusalem,
terrible as an army with banners.

6:5   *Turn away your eyes from me,*
for they disturb me —
Your hair is like a flock of goats,
moving down the slopes of Gilead.

6:6   *Your teeth are like a flock of ewes*
that have come up from the washing,
all of them bear twins,
not one among them is bereaved.

6:7   *Your cheeks are like halves of a pomegranate,*
behind your veil.

6:8   *There are sixty queens and eighty concubines,*
and maidens without number.

6:9   *My dove, my perfect one, is only one,*
the darling of her mother,
flawless to her that bore her.
The maidens saw her and called her happy;
the queens and concubines also,
and they praised her.

6:10   *"Who is this that looks like the dawn,*

fair as the moon, bright as the sun,
terrible as an army with banners?"

6:11   *I went down to the nut orchard*
to look at the blossoms of the valley,
to see whether the vines had budded,
whether the pomegranates were in bloom.

6:12   *Before I was aware, my fancy set me*
in a chariot beside my prince.

6:13   *Return, return, O Shulammite,*
return, return that we may look upon you.
Why should you look upon the Shulammite,
as upon a dance before two armies?

77

The Song of Songs to
Song of Songs 6:1

6:1   *Whither has your beloved gone, O fairest among women?*
       Whither has your beloved turned, that we may seek him with
       you?

LXXVII:I
1. A.   "Whither has your beloved gone, O fairest among women:"
    B.   The nations of the world [here] speak to Israel, "'Whither has your
          beloved gone?' From Egypt to the Sea to Sinai.
    C.   "'Whither has your beloved turned?'"
    D.   And Israel answers the nations of the world, "How come you're
          asking about him, when you have no share in him?
    E.   "Once I had cleaved to him, can I depart from him? Once he had
          cleaved to me, can he depart from me? Wherever he may be, he
          comes to me."

Now the speaker is the nations, the addressee is Israel, and the
issue is Israel's relationship to God. It is one of love and cannot be
sundered.

135

78

Song of Songs Rabbah to Song of Songs 6:2

6:2   *My beloved has gone down to his garden, to the beds of spices, to pasture his flock in the gardens, and to gather lilies.*

LXXVIII:i

1. A.   "My beloved has gone down to his garden, to the beds of spices, [to pasture his flock in the gardens, and to gather lilies]:"

    B.   Said R. Yosé b. R. Hanina, "As to this verse, the beginning of it is not the same as the end, and the end not the same as the beginning.

    C.   "The verse had only to say, 'My beloved has gone down to pasture in his garden,' but you say, 'in the gardens'!

    D.   But 'my beloved' is the Holy One, blessed be He;

    E.   "'to his garden' refers to the world.

    F.   "'to the beds of spices' refers to Israel.

    G.   "'to pasture his flock in the gardens' refers to synagogues and schoolhouses.

    H.   "'and to gather lilies' speaks of picking [taking away in death] the righteous that are in Israel."

2. A.   What is the difference between when old folks die and when young people die?

    B.   R. Judah and R. Abbahu:

    C.   R. Judah says, "When a candle goes out on its own, it is good for it and good for the wick, but when the candle does not go out on its own, it is bad for it and bad for the wick."

    D.   R. Abbahu said, "When a fig is picked in its season, it is good for it and good for the fig tree. When it is not picked in its season, it is bad for it and bad for the fig tree."

3. A.   There was the case involving R. Hiyya b. R. Abba and his disciples, and some say, R. Aqiba and his disciples, and some say, R. Joshua and his disciples.

    B.   They had the custom of going into session and studying under a fig tree. Every day the owner of the fig tree would get up in the morning and pick his fig.

C.   They said, "We should change our place, perhaps he suspects us [of stealing his fruit]."

D.   What did they do? They went and held their sessions in another location.

E.   The owner of the fig tree got up but did not find them. He went and looked for them until he found them, He said to them, "My lords, there was a single religious duty that you were carrying out for me, and you want to hold it back from me!"

F.   They said to him, "God forbid!"

G.   "Then why did you leave your place and go into session in another location?"

H.   They said, "We were concerned that you might suspect us."

I.   He said to them, "God forbid. But I shall tell you on what account I get up early to pick my fig. It is because once the sun shines on the figs, they get rotten."

J.   They immediately returned to their place.

K.   One day they found that he had not gathered. They took some of them and opened them up and found them wormy.

L.   They said, "Well did the master of the fig tree speak. And if he knows the season of his fig and picks it, so does the Holy One, blessed be He, know when it is the season of the righteous to remove them, so he takes them up."

4. A.   Said R. Samuel b. R. Nahman, "[The matter may be compared] to the case of a king who had an orchard and planted in it rows of nut trees, apple trees, and pomegranates, and handed them over to his son.

B.   "When the son did the father's will, the king would go and make the rounds all over the world and see which planting was particularly attractive and would uproot it and bring it and plant it in that orchard. But when his son did not carry out his will, the king would see which planting in the orchard was particularly fine, and he would uproot that one.

C.   "So is the case with Israel: when they carry out the will of the Omnipresent, he picks out a righteous person among the nations of the world, for instance, Jethro or Rahab, and brings him and cleaves him to Israel. But when Israel does not do the will of the Holy One, blessed be He, he identifies a righteous, upright, virtuous, and God-fearing person among them and takes him up from their midst."

5. A.   When R. Hiyya b. R. Avia, the son of the sister of Bar Qappara, died, they said to R. Yohanan, "Go in and take leave of him [with an appropriate eulogy]."

B.   He said to them, "Let R. Simeon b. Laqish go up, for he is his disciple and knows his formidable [virtue]."

C.   R. Simeon went up and took his leave of him [in this language], "'My beloved has gone down to his garden:'

D.   "The Holy One, blessed be He, knows the great deeds of R. Hiyya b. R. Avia and has removed him from the world."

6. A.   When R. Simon b. R. Zabedi died, R. Ila went up to take leave of him: "'But wisdom, where shall it be found? And where is the place of understanding? The deep says, It is not in me, and the

sea says, It is not with me...it is hid from the eyes of all living and kept close from the birds of the air' (Job 28:12, 14, 21).

B. "Four things are of worldly use, but if lost, they can be replaced, and these are they:

C. "'For there is a mine for silver and a place for gold which they refine. Iron is taken out of the dirt and brass is cast out of stone' (Job 28:1-2).

D. "But as to a disciple of a sage, if he dies, who will present us with his substitute?

E. "And we who have lost R. Simon, whence shall we find his like?"

F. Said R. Levi, "The tribes [of Jacob] found something: 'And their hearts failed them, and they turned trembling' (Gen. 42:28).

G. "We, who have lost R. Simon b. R. Zabedi, whence shall we find his substitute?

H. "That is in line with the statement, 'But wisdom, where shall it be found? And where is the place of understanding? The deep says, It is not in me, and the sea says, It is not with me...it is hid from the eyes of all living and kept close from the birds of the air' (Job 28:12, 14, 21)."

7. A   When R. Bun b. R. Hiyya died, R. Zira went up to take leave of him: "'Sweet is the sleep of a working man' (Qoh. 5:11):

B. "Let me tell you what R. Bun resembles:

C. "A king who had a vineyard, which he hired workers to keep. Now there was one worker there, who was paid for his work more than all the others.

D. "When the king saw how remarkably zealous he was at his work, he took him by the hand and began walking with him up and down.

E. "At evening the workers came to collect their wages, and that worker came to collect his wage along with them. And the king gave him his wage the same as theirs.

F. "They workers began to complain and said to him, 'Our Lord, King, we worked hard all day long, and this one worked only two or three hours for the day, but he takes the same wage that we do!'

G. "The king said to them, 'Why are you complaining? This one accomplished in two or three hours what you people did not accomplish in the entire day of work!'

H. "So R. Bun b. R. Hiyya accomplished in the twenty-eight years in which he studied the Torah what an accomplished disciple did not accomplish in a hundred years."

I. Said R. Yohanan, "Whoever is engaged in Torah study in this world, even in the world to come will not be accorded the right to sleep,

J. "but they will bring him to the house of study of Shem and Aber, Abraham, Isaac, Jacob, Moses and Aaron.

K. "And how long? Until: 'I will make you a great name, like the name of the great ones that are in the earth' (2 Sam. 7:9)."

No. 1 completes the treatment of our base verse. 1.H accounts for the inclusion of the rest. But even 1.H hardly prepares us for what interests our compilers, which is announced at No. 2 and is then carried out in a sequence of cogent stories. These account, first for the early death of some, then for the death of disciples, then for the early death of disciples; that is to say, beyond No. 5, the subject gradually shifts from the issue at hand to the distinct question of why sages die young. Nos. 6 & 7 therefore ought to have been joined prior to insertion, and had they been left out, we should have missed nothing important to the context of our base verse.

79

Song of Songs Rabbah to Song of Songs 6:3

6:3 *I am my beloved's, and my beloved is mine; he pastures his flock among the lilies.*

Our compilation contains nothing on this verse.

80

Song of Songs Rabbah to Song of Songs 6:4

6:4   *You are beautiful as Tirzah, my love, comely as Jerusalem, terrible as an army with banners.*

LXXX:i

1. A.   "You are beautiful as Tirzah, my love:"
    B.   R. Judah b. R. Simon interpreted the verse to speak of the offerings:
    C.   "'You are beautiful as Tirzah, my love:' this refers to the offerings, for you win my favor [a word that uses the same consonants as Tirzah] through offerings: 'It shall be accepted for him to make atonement for him' (Lev. 1:4).
    D.   "'comely as Jerusalem:' this refers to the Holy Things which are [kept] in Jerusalem: 'As the flock for sacrifice, as the flock of Jerusalem' (Ezek. 36:38)."

2. A.   Another interpretation: "You are beautiful as Tirzah, my love:"
    B.   This refers to the women of [Simon, verbatim:] the generation of the wilderness.
    C.   For said Rabbi, "The women of the wilderness were virtuous. They went and restrained themselves and did not contribute their jewelry to the work of making the golden calf.
    D.   "They said, 'If the Holy One, blessed be He, could pulverize the sturdy idols, how much the more so the flaccid ones!'"

3. A.   "comely as Jerusalem:"
    B.   For whoever wanted to find models of Peor could go and find them in Jerusalem:
    C.   "Whose graven images did exceed those of Jerusalem and of Samaria" (Isa. 10:10).

The first explanation – the sacrifices – is cogent; the second splits into two parts. But in point of fact Nos. 2-3 read together refer to the opposite of valid sacrifices to God, which is the invalid adoration of the golden calf. So the whole holds together.

LXXX:II

1. A. Another reading of the verse, ""You are beautiful as Tirzah, my love:"
    B. When you want [a word that uses exactly the same consonants as Tirzah].

2. A. When you desire, you do not have to learn anything from anybody else.
    B. Who told them to present wagons and oxen to bear the tabernacle? Was it not on their own that they brought them? Thus: "And they brought their offering before the Lord, six covered wagons" (Num. 7:3).

3. A. [Supply: "And they brought their offering before the Lord, six covered wagons" (Num. 7:3):
    B. The six wagons corresponded to the six firmaments.
    C. But are there not seven firmaments?
    D. Said R. Abun, "What belongs to the king is exempt from taxes."
    E. They corresponded to the six earths, [that is to say, the six Hebrew names for earth, which are] *eres, arqa, adamah, ge, siah, neshiah,* and *tebel.*
    F. And it is written, "He will judge the world with righteousness" (Ps. 98:9).
    G. The six correspond to the six divisions of the Mishnah;
    H. to the six days of creation;
    I. to the six matriarchs, Sarah, Rebecca, Rachel, Leah, Zilpah, and Bilhah.

4. A. [Supply: "And they brought their offering before the Lord, six covered wagons" (Num. 7:3):]
    B. The word for "covered" means that they were like a canopy;
    C. it means they were distinguished;
    D. arranged in order;
    E. the host [a word that uses the same consonants as the word for covered] of the Levites was in charge of them.
    F. It was taught on Tannaite authority in the name of Nehemiah, "They were like arched carriages, so that the utensils of divine service should not split."

5. A. "twelve oxen:"
    B. Corresponding to the twelve princes.

6. A. "A wagon for every two of the princes, and for each one an ox:"
    B. This teaches that they did not purchase them on the market, but this one brought an ox, and that one brought an ox, this one brought a wagon, and that one brought a wagon [out of his own resources].

7. A. "And they offered them before the tabernacle:"
    B. This teaches that they handed them over to the ownership of the community.

8. A. "And the Lord spoke to Moses, saying" (Num. 7:4):
    B. What is the meaning of "saying"?
    C. Said the Holy One, blessed be He, to him, "Go and say to them words of praise and consolation."

9. A. Said R. Hoshaia, "Said the Holy One, blessed be He, 'I credit it to you as though I had needed to bear with it the burden of my world, and you brought it to me.'

   B. "At that moment Moses was afraid and thought to himself, 'Is it possible that the Holy Spirit had departed from me and come to rest on the princes? Or perhaps some other prophet has arisen and made a new law?'

   C. "Said to him the Holy One, blessed be He, 'Moses! If I had spoken to them to bring, I would have told you to tell them. But 'take it of them, that they may be....'"

10. A. [Supply: "take it of them, that they may be:"]

    B. It was from them that the matter had come.

11. A. And who had advised them?

    B. Said R. Simon, "It was the tribe of Issachar.

    C. "They said to them, 'As to this tabernacle that you people are making, is it going to fly in the air? Make wagons for it, so that it may be borne upon them.'

    D. "That is why Scripture praises the tribe of Issachar: 'And of the children of Issachar, men who had understanding of the times' (1 Chr. 12:33)."

12. A. [Supply: "And of the children of Issachar, men who had understanding of the times:"]

    B. What is the meaning of "who had understanding of the times"?

    C. R. Tanhuma said, "The seasons."

    D. R. Yosé of Caesarea said, "The intercalation of the calendar."

13. A. "to know what Israel should do" (1 Chr. 12:33):

    B. For they knew how to heal skin disease.

14. A. "The heads of them were two hundred" (1 Chr. 12:33):

    B. This speaks of the two hundred chiefs of the Sanhedrin who derived from Issachar.

15. A. "and all their brothers were subject to their commandment" (1 Chr. 12:33):

    B. This teaches that all their brothers would make the law conform to their ruling, as though it were law revealed to Moses from Sinai.

16. A. [Reverting to No. 2:] At that time Moses said before the Holy One, blessed be He, "Lord of the world, what happens if one of the oxen dies, or one of the wheels breaks, so the offering of the princes will be invalid, and all of the work in making the tabernacle will be null!"

    B. Forthwith: "The Lord spoke to Moses, saying, Take it from them, that they may be to do the service" (Num. 7:4).

17. A. [Supply: "The Lord spoke to Moses, saying, Take it from them, that they may be to do the service" (Num. 7:4):]

    B. The sense is that they should live and endure for ages to come.

    C. How long did they endure?

    D. R. Yudan and R. Huna in the name of Bar Qappara: "To Gilgal: 'In Gilgal they sacrificed bullocks, yes, their altars were as heaps in the furrows of the field' (Hos. 12:12)."

    E. Where did they offer them?

    F. R. Abun said, "In Nob they offered them."

    G. R. Abba said, "In Gibeon they offered them."

H.   Levi said, "In Shiloh they offered them."

I.   And rabbis said, "In the eternal house they offered them."

J.   R. Hama said, "The verse of Scripture supporting the view of rabbis is as follows: 'And king Solomon offered the sacrifice of oxen' (2 Chr. 7:5).

K.   "What Scripture says is not, 'a sacrifice of oxen,' but, 'the sacrifice of oxen.' And which one is that? One must say, it is 'the two wagons and four oxen' (Num. 7:7), and further, 'the four wagons and eight oxen' (Num. 7:8)."

L.   [Reverting to C, above:] R. Meir says, "They still endure, and they have never been blemished, nor have they grown old, nor have they turned *terefah,* but they are still living and enduring.

M.   "And that yields an argument *a fortiori:*

N.   "if to the oxen, who were assigned by man to the work of the altar, were given long life so that they should live and endure for ages to come, the Israelites, who cleave [on their own initiative] to the Life of the Ages, all the more so!

O.   "'But you who cleaved to the Lord your God are alive, every one of you, this day' (Dt. 4:4)."

No. 2 is tacked on to No. 1, and everything beyond that point is spun out of No. 2's reference; this is a sustained exposition of the verses pertinent to the offering of the princes, Num. 7:2ff., and related matters. Only a few passages seem to me even to draw near to our fundamental proposition, which is that Israel learns on its own. No. 9 seems to me to allude to that conception. But beyond 9.A, nothing restores the initial proposition to the fore. No. 10 seems to me to make the desired point, but it is scarcely elucidated, and No. 11 raises the question of who had thought it up. Then the exposition of the key verse of No. 11 follows. I am not clear on how No. 16 makes the point we started to set forth, since it is God who supplies the necessary knowledge; here they do not think it up. The rest then expounds more of Num. 7:4ff. The whole seems to me not to make a serious contribution to the exposition of the base verse of Song of Songs. It has been worked out to provide a commentary to the base verses of Numbers and of Chronicles, respectively.

81

Song of Songs Rabbah to Song of Songs 6:5

6:5   *Turn away your eyes from me, for they disturb me – Your hair is like a flock of goats, moving down the slopes of Gilead.*

LXXXI:i

1. A.   "Turn away your eyes from me:"
   B.   R. Azariah in the name of R. Judah b. R. Simon: "[The matter may be compared] to the case of a king who was enraged against the queen and pushed her out and drove her away from the palace.
   C.   "What did she do? She went and pressed her face against a pillar outside the palace.
   D.   "When the king went by, the king said, 'Take her away from before me, for I can't bear it.'
   E.   "Thus when the court is in session and decrees fasts and individuals afflict themselves, the Holy One, blessed be He, says, 'I can't bear it.'"
2. A.   "for they disturb me:"
   B.   They made me stretch my hands forth against my world.
   C.   When the court decrees a fast and children afflict themselves, the Holy One, blessed be He, says, "I can't bear it."
3. A.   "for they disturb me:"
   B.   They made me king over them and said, "The Lord will be king forever and ever."
   C.   When the court decrees a fast and the aged afflict themselves, the Holy One, blessed be He, says, "I can't bear it."
4. A.   "for they disturb me:"
   B.   They accepted my dominion over them at Sinai and said, "Whatever the Lord has spoken we shall do and obey" (Ex. 24:7); "I will make mention of Rahab and Babylon as among those who know me" (Ps. 87:4):
5. A.   R. Phineas in the name of R. Hama b. R. Hanina b. R. Pappa: "'Among the rebellious also that the Lord might dwell there' (Ps. 68:19):

145

B.   '"Even though they are rebellious, the Holy One, blessed be He, brings his Presence to dwell among them.

C.   "On account of what merit? On account of the merit of their saying. 'Whatever the Lord has spoken we shall do and obey' (Ex. 24:7)."

6. A. "Your hair is like a flock of goats:"

    B. Just as a goat is despised, so Israel was despised at Shittim:

    C. "And Israel abode in Shittim" (Num. 25:1).

God is the speaker. The point of the first reading is to underline that God responds not only to Israel's actions and condition, but also to Israel's penitence, which disturbs him; the pattern is repeated from Nos. 1-2 through Nos. 3-4. The second prooftext of 4.B is not obviously pertinent. The reason for No. 5's inclusion is self-evident at 4.B. No. 6 is free-standing and joined only because of the base verse. But LXXXII:i.1 continues the pattern and completes it; so there is a proposition that joins the final item here and the next to come.

82

Song of Songs Rabbah to Song of Songs 6:6

6:6 *Your teeth are like a flock of ewes that have come up from the washing, all of them bear twins, not one among them is bereaved.*

LXXXII:i

1. A. "Your teeth are like a flock of ewes:"
   B. Just as a ewe is modest, so the Israelites were modest and virtuous in the war against Midian.
2. A. R. Huna in the name of R. Aha said, "It was because not one of them put on the phylactery of the head prior to the one that goes on the arm.
   B. "For if one of them had put on the phylactery of the head before the one that goes on the arm, Moses would not have praised them, and they would not have emerged from there whole and complete.
   C. "One must therefore conclude that they were truly righteous."
3. A. "All of them bear twins:"
   B. When they would go in two by two to [a Midianite] woman, one of them would blacken her face, the other would remove her jewelry.
   C. The women would say to them, 'Are we not among those whom the Holy One, blessed be He, created that you should behave in such a way toward us?'
   D. The Israelites would say to them, "It is not enough for you that we have gotten ours on your account!"
   E. "And the Lord said to Moses, Take all the chiefs of the people and hang them up" (Num. 25:4).
4. A. "Not one among them is bereaved:"
   B. Not one of them was suspected of committing a transgression.

The theme of Nos. 1, 3 is the war against Midian, contrasting with the Israelite conduct at Shittim; the whole then completes the foregoing. No. 2 was inserted prior to the inclusion of the composition

147

here, since it has no place in the present exposition. The same theme concerning Midian continues in the next chapter.

83

Song of Songs Rabbah to Song of Songs 6:7

6:7   *Your cheeks are like halves of a pomegranate, behind your veil.*

LXXXIII:i
1. A.   "Your cheeks are like halves of a pomegranate:"
   B.   At that moment at which they returned from the war against Midian, Moses began to praise them: "Even the emptiest among you is as loaded with religious duties and good deeds as a pomegranate is loaded with seeds.
   C.   "For whoever has the opportunity to commit a transgression and is saved from it and did not commit it has carried out a great religious duty.
   D.   "behind your veil:"
   E.   [Moses continues,] "And there is no need to add, those who are modest and restrained among you."

We now complete the account of Midian, translated into praise of Israel for its sexual restraint.

84

Song of Songs Rabbah to Song of Songs 6:8

6:8   *There are sixty queens and eighty concubines, and maidens
       without number.*

LXXXIV:i

1. A.   "There are sixty queens and eighty concubines:"
    B.   R. Hiyya of Sepphoris and R. Levi interpret the verse to speak of
         the nations of the world.
    C.   R. Hiyya said, "'Sixty and eighty' add up to one hundred and forty;
         forty of them have a language but not writing, forty have no
         language but have writing.
    D.   "'and maidens without number:' the rest of them have neither
         writing nor a language of their own.
    E.   "Might one suppose that Israel too is in that condition?
    F.   "Scripture states, 'And to the Jews according to their writing and
         according to their language' (Est. 8:9)."
    G.   R. Levi said, "'Sixty and eighty' add up to one hundred and forty;
         seventy of them know who their fathers were but do not know who
         their mothers were, seventy of them know who their mothers were
         but do not know who their fathers were.
    H.   "'and maidens without number:' [the rest of them] do not know
         either their fathers or their mothers.
    I.   "Might one suppose that Israel too is in that condition?
    J.   "Scripture states, 'And they declared their genealogies after their
         families, by their fathers' houses' (Num. 1:18)."

The subject shifts from Israel and God to the nations of the world.
Why so? A glance at what follows explains: "There are sixty queens
and eighty concubines, and maidens without number. My dove, my
perfect one, is only one, the darling of her mother, flawless to her that
bore her. The maidens saw her and called her happy; the queens and
concubines also, and they praised her." The upshot is that these queens
and concubines praise Israel, "my perfect one," flawless to her that bore

her; the nations then praise Israel, and that accounts for the present reading; in context, it is difficult to fault the exegetes' choice of referent. Not only so, but the present program – predictably – continues in the next chapter.

85

Song of Songs Rabbah to
Song of Songs 6:9

6:9   *My dove, my perfect one, is only one, the darling of her mother,*
       flawless to her that bore her. The maidens saw her and called
       her happy; the queens and concubines also, and they praised
       her.

LXXXV:i

1. A.   ["There are sixty queens and eighty concubines, and maidens
          without number.] My dove, my perfect one, is only one, [the
          darling of her mother, flawless to her that bore her. The maidens
          saw her and called her happy; the queens and concubines also,
          and they praised her]:"

    B.   "My dove, my perfect one, is only one:" this is Abraham,
          "Abraham was one" (Ezek. 33:24).

    C.   "the darling of her mother:" this is Isaac, the only son his mother
          bore.

    D.   "flawless to her that bore her:" this is Jacob, our father, who was
          the preferred child of the one who bore him, because he was
          wholly righteous.

    E.   "The maidens saw her and called her happy:" this refers to the
          tribal progenitors [the sons of Jacob], "And the report was heard in
          Pharaoh's house saying, Joseph's brothers have come" (Gen.
          45:16).

    F.   Another reading of "The maidens saw her and called her happy:"
          this refers to Leah, "Happy I am, for the daughters will call me
          happy" (Gen. 30:13).

    G.   "the queens and concubines also, and they praised her:" this
          refers to Joseph, "And Pharaoh said to his servants, Can we find
          such a one as this" (Gen. 41:38).

    H.   "If we go from one end of the world to the other, we are not going
          to find such a one as this: 'For as much as God has shown you all
          this, there is none so discreet and wise as you' (Gen. 45:39)."

152

2. A.   R. Isaac interpreted the verse to speak of components of the Torah: "'There are sixty queens:' this refers to the sixty tractates of laws [in the Mishnah].

    B.   "'And eighty concubines:' this refers to the sections of the book of Leviticus.

    C.   "'and maidens without number:' there is no end to the Supplements [*toseftaot*].

    D.   "'My dove, my perfect one, is only one:' They differ from one another, even though all of them derive support for their conflicting views from a single prooftext, a single law, a single argument by analogy, a single argument *a fortiori*."

3. A.   R. Yudan b. R. Ilai interpreted the verse to speak of the tree of life and the Garden of Eden:

    B.   "'There are sixty queens:' this refers to the sixty fellowships of righteous persons who are in session in the Garden of Eden under the tree of life, engaged in study of the Torah."

4. A.   It has been taught on Tannaite authority:

    B.   [Genesis Rabbah XV:VI.1 begins: "And out of the ground the Lord God made to grow [every tree that is pleasant to the sight and good for food], the tree of life [also in the midst of the garden, and the tree of the knowledge of good and evil]" (Gen. 2:9)]: It was a tree that spread out over all living things.

    C.   [Said R. Judah bar Ilai,] "The tree of life is so large that it takes five hundred years to walk across it, and all the waters of creation branched out from under it."

    D.   R. Yudan in the name of R. Judah bar Ilai: "It is not the end of the matter that the foliage of the tree is so large as to require a journey lasting for five hundred years, but even the trunk of the tree also is a journey of five hundred years in diameter."

5. A.   It has been taught on Tannaite authority:

    B.   The water that drains from a kor of land can irrigate a tarqab of land [one sixtieth of a kor];

    C.   the water that drains from Ethiopia can irrigate Egypt.

    D.   Now Egypt is a journey of forty days, four hundred parasangs square, and is one sixtieth the size of Ethiopia; Ethiopia is a journey of more than seven years, and is one sixtieth the size of the whole world; the length of the whole world is five hundred years' journey, the breadth the same, and it is one four hundredth of Gehenna. So the extent of Gehenna is two hundred thousand years' journey.

    E.   It follows that the world is to Gehenna as is the lid of a pot to the pot; the world is one sixtieth of Eden, and Eden is beyond all measuring.

6. A.   [Continuing 3.B:] "'and eighty concubines:' this refers to the eighty fellowships of mediocre students who are in session and study the Torah beyond the tree of life.

    B.   "'and maidens without number:' there is no limit to the number of disciples.

    C.   "Might one suppose that they dispute with one another? Scripture says, 'My dove, my perfect one, is only one:' all of them derive support for their unanimous opinion from a single prooftext, a single law, a single argument by analogy, a single argument *a fortiori*."

7. A. Rabbis interpret the verse to speak of those who escaped from Egypt:

    B. "'There are sixty queens:' this refers to the sixty myriads aged twenty and above who went forth from Egypt.

    C. "'and eighty concubines:' this refers to the eighty myriads from the age of twenty and lower among the Israelites who went forth from Egypt.

    D. "'and maidens without number:' there was no limit nor number to the proselytes."

8. A. R. Berekhiah in the name of R. Levi said, "The nations of the world are enumerated but actual figures are not given [following Simon, p. 267, n. 1].

    B. "They are enumerated: 'The sons of Japheth: Gomer and Magon' (Gen. 10:2).

    C. "But the Israelites are both enumerated and also toted up:

    D. "'Those that were numbered of them, according to the number of all the males' (Num. 3:22):

    E. "'those that were numbered' speaks of the enumeration.

    F. "'according to the number' speaks of the toting up."

9. A. Along these same lines:

    B. "And Joab gave up the sum of the number of the people to the king" (2 Sam. 24:9):

    C. "sum" refers to the enumerating,

    D. "numbering" is the toting up.

10. A. If you maintain that we are giving testimony concerning ourselves,

    B. has not the wicked Balaam given testimony concerning us?

    C. For it is written, "Who has counted the dust of Jacob" (Num. 23:10) – this speaks of the enumeration;

    D. "and numbered the stock of Israel" (Num. 23:10) – this speaks of the toting up.

11. A. Another explanation: "My dove, my perfect one, is only one:" this speaks of the community of Israel, "And who is like your people, like Israel, a nation that is singular in the earth" (2 Sam. 7:23).

    B. "the darling of her mother:" "Attend to me, O my people, and give ear to me, O my nation" (Isa. 51:4), with the word for "my nation" spelled to be read "my mother."

    C. "flawless to her that bore her:" R. Jacob translated in the presence of R. Isaac, "Beside her, there is no child belonging to the one who bore her."

    D. "The maidens saw her and called her happy:" "and all the nations shall call you happy" (Mal. 3:12).

    E. "the queens and concubines also, and they praised her:" "And kings shall be your foster fathers" (Isa. 59:23).

Now that we have the nations of the world praising Israel, we proceed to identify what traits of Israel are under discussion. Predictably, these can be associated with the patriarchs and with Israel in Egypt, at the Sea, and then before Sinai; these represent the recurrent topics. No. 1 then has the nations praise Israel as a social entity, that is, the family of Abraham, Isaac, Jacob, then the tribes. No. 2 proceeds to have the glory of Israel identified with the Torah; but we are shading off from our original reading, because now it is not the nations of the world who praise Israel, but the queens and concubines who do so are the components of the Torah. No. 3, continued at 6, with Nos. 4-5 interpolated, remain within that same symbolic system, revising it only in the interesting detail that the Torah study is identified with life in the Garden of Eden. That No. 3 has been broken off from No. 6 is self-evident. No. 7 then forms a rather pointless complement to No. 6, for the thematic reason that is self-evident. Then No. 8 carries in its wake Nos. 9, 10 – a totally agglutinative composition that has been added for further agglutinative considerations! No. 11 then moves on from Torah study to the community of Israel. So the three principal points of application of our base verse are, first, Israel vis-à-vis the nations of the world, then the genealogy of the family of Abraham, Isaac, Jacob, then Torah, and finally, Israel. I cannot imagine a more satisfying repertoire of meanings identified with the social component of the system.

86

Song of Songs Rabbah to Song of Songs 6:10

6:10   *"Who is this that looks like the dawn, fair as the moon, bright as the sun, terrible as an army with banners?"*

LXXXVI:i

1.   A.   "Who is this that looks like the dawn:"
   - B.   There is the following story:
   - C.   R. Hiyya and R. Simeon b. R. Halafta at dawn were going in the valley of Arbel, and they saw the morning star coming up.
   - D.   Said R. Hiyya the Elder to R. Simeon b. R. Halafta, "That is how the redemption of Israel will break forth: 'Though I sit in darkness, the Lord is a light for me' (Mic. 7:8) – at first it comes bit by bit, but then it sparkles, and afterward it breaks forth with great power, and finally it overspreads the sky.
   - E.   "So at the outset: 'In those days, while Mordecai sat in the king's gate' (Est. 2:21);
   - F.   "then: 'Mordecai went forth from the presence of the king in royal apparel' (Est. 8:15);
   - G.   "and finally: 'The Jews had light and gladness' (Est. 8:16)."

2.   A.   "like the dawn:"
   - B.   might one suppose, just as the dawn has no shadow, so is the case with Israel?
   - C.   Scripture states to the contrary, "fair as the moon.'
   - D.   Might one suppose, just as the moon does not give a pellucid light, so is the case for Israel?
   - E.   Scripture states to the contrary, "bright as the sun,"
   - F.   in line with this verse: "But they who love him are as the sun when he goes forth in his power" (Judges 5:31).
   - G.   Might one suppose, just as the sun can be oppressive, so is the case with Israel?
   - H.   Scripture states, "fair as the moon,"
   - I.   in line with this verse: "How precious is your loving kindness, O God, and the children of men take refuge in the shadow of your wings" (Ps. 36:8).

156

J.	Might one suppose, just as with the moon, sometimes it is defective, sometimes full, so with Israel?
K.	Scripture says, "bright as the sun."
L.	Might one suppose, just as the sun serves by day but not by night, so is the case with Israel?
M.	Scripture says, "fair as the moon."
N.	Just as the moon serves by day and also by night, "and to rule over the day and the night" (Gen. 1:18), so Israel is one and the same both in this world and the world to come.
O.	Might one say, just as the sun and the moon do not cause fear, so as the case with Israel?
P.	Scripture says, "terrible as an army with banners:"
Q.	Like the armies with banners above, for instance, Michael and his standard, Gabriel and his standard.
R.	And how do we know that they inspire fear?
S.	"As for their rings, they were high and they were dreadful" (Ez. 1:18)."
T.	R. Joshua says, "It is fear that is inspired here below, for instance, like that brought about by the generals, commanders, and field marshalls [of Rome]."
U.	And how do we know that these inspire fear?
V.	"A fourth beast [Rome], dreadful and terrible and very strong" (Dan. 7:7).

3.
A.	[Supply: "terrible as an army with banners:"]
B.	R. Yudan and R. Huna –
C.	R. Yudan in the name of R. Eliezer, son of R. Yosé the Galilean, and R. Huna in the name of R. Eliezer the Modiite:
D.	[The former said,] "What is written here is not 'like standards' but 'an army with banners,'
E.	Meaning, 'like the generation that was on the verge of going into exile,' [since the word for 'army with banners' and the words for 'being carried into captivity' share the same consonants].
F.	"Now which one was that?
G.	"It was the generation of Hezekiah: 'A day of trouble and of rebuke' (Isa. 37:3).
H.	"Now how do we know that they inspired fear? 'So that he was exalted in the sight of all nations' (2 Chr. 32:23)."
I.	R. Huna in the name of R. Eliezer the Modiite: ""What is written here is not 'like standards' but 'an army with banners,'
J.	meaning, 'like the generation that was on the verge of going into exile,' [since the word for 'army with banners' and the words for 'being carried into captivity' share the same consonants] – but which was not taken into exile after all!
K.	"And which one was that?
L.	"It is the generation of the royal messiah: 'For I will gather all nations against Jerusalem to battle' (Zech. 14:2).
M.	""Now how do we know that he inspires fear? 'And he will smite the land with the rod of his mouth' (Isa. 11:4)."

4.
| A. | R. Eleazar in the name of R. Yosé b. R. Jeremiah: "At that time, the Israelites will be forced to go from one stopping place to another." |

5.   A.   R. Joshua of Sikhnin says, "Said the Congregation of Israel, 'The
                 Holy One, blessed be He, has brought me to 'the wine cellar'
                 which is Sinai.'
     B.   "There were Michael and his standard, Gabriel and his standard.
     C.   "She said, 'Would that we might journey with the array of that
                 which is above.'
     D.   "At that moment said the Holy One, blessed be He, 'Since my
                 children yearn to be set forth by [heavenly] standards, let them
                 encamp by standards: 'The children of Israel shall pitch by their
                 fathers' houses; every man with his own standard according to the
                 insights' (Num. 2:1)."

No. 2 serves the book of Esther; I assume it has ended up here
because there is a reference to the dawn, but the item has no
contribution to make to our document. No. 2, by contrast, provides a
sustained and rather winning exercise on all three components of our
base verse, though admittedly the "army with banners" component
trails off. No. 2.T-V do not seem to me apropos. No. 3 works on the
language of the third clause, but the passage takes no interest in the
context at hand, so far as I can see. I cannot account for the inclusion of
No. 4. No. 5 is autonomous, directing its attention to the general theme
of banners or standards; it too is scarcely relevant here. If these
materials form part of the program of the original compilers, then the
agglutinative principle has misled them to amass what is at best a
compilation of thematically somewhat germane materials. The
contrast between No. 2 and the rest is stunning.

87

Song of Songs Rabbah to Song of Songs 6:11

6:11   *I went down to the nut orchard to look at the blossoms of the valley, to see whether the vines had budded, whether the pomegranates were in bloom.*

LXXXVII:i
1. A.   Another explanation of the phrase, "I went down to the nut orchard:"
    B.   Said R. Joshua b. Levi, "The Israelites are compared to a nut tree:
    C.   "just as a nut tree is pruned and improved thereby, for, like hair that is trimmed and grows more abundantly, and like nails that are trimmed and grow more abundantly,
    D.   "so is the case with Israel, for they are pruned of the return on their work, which they gave to those who labor in the Torah in this world, and it is for their good that they are so pruned, for that increases their wealth in this world and the reward that is coming to them in the world to come."
2. A.   R. Joshua of Sikhnin in the name of R. Levi said, "Just as, while in the case of other plantings, if you cover their roots when they are planted, they prosper, and if not, they do not prosper,
    B.   "in the case of a nut tree, if you cover its roots when it is planted it does not do well,
    C.   "so as to Israel: 'He who covers his transgressions will not prosper' (Prov. 28:13)."
3. A.   [Supply: "the nut orchard:"]
    B.   Said R. Elasa, "Scripture ought to have said, 'to a vegetable patch.
    C.   "Why then 'nut orchard'?
    D.   "This serves to teach that he gave them the staying power of trees and the sheen of a vegetable patch."
4. A.   [Supply: "the nut orchard:"]
    B.   R. Azariah made two statements:
    C.   "Just as in the case of a nut, the husk guards the fruit, so the unlettered people in Israel strengthen [those who are engaged in]

study of the Torah: 'It is a tree of life to those who strengthen her' (Prov. 83:18)."

D.   He made another statement: "Just as if a nut falls into the mud, you take it and wipe it and rinse it and wash it and it is perfectly fine for eating, so in the case of Israel, however they are made filthy in transgressions throughout the days of the year, the Day of Atonement comes along and covers over their sins: 'For on this day shall atonement be made for you, to cleanse you' (Lev. 16:30)."

5. A.   [Supply: "the nut orchard:"]

    B.   R. Judah b. R. Simon says, "Just as a nut has two shells, so the Israelites have two religious duties, the act of circumcision and the act of cutting away the flesh of the penis."

6. A.   Another explanation of the phrase, "I went down to the nut orchard:"

    B.   Said R. Simeon b. Laqish, "Just as a nut tree is unwrinkled – "

    C.   **For we have learned in the Mishnah, "Also on the smooth trunk of nut trees" [M. Peah 4:1] –**

    D.   "so whoever climbs to the top of it and does not pay attention to how he is climbing will fall down and die and get his from the nut tree,

    E.   "so whoever exercises authority over the community in Israel and does not pay a mind to how he governs Israel in the end will fall and get his on their account:

    F.   "'Israel is the Lord's holy portion, his first fruits of the increase, all who consume him will be held guilty' (Jer. 2:3)."

7. A.   Another explanation of the phrase, "I went down to the nut orchard:"

    B.   Just as a nut is a toy for children and a treat for kings,

    C.   so are the Israelites in this world on account of transgression: "I am become a joke to all my people" (Lam. 3:14),

    D.   but in the world to come: "kings will be your foster fathers" (Isa. 49:23).

8. A.   Another explanation of the phrase, "I went down to the nut orchard:"

    B.   Just as in the case of a nut tree, there are soft ones, medium ones, and hard ones,

    C.   so in the case of Israel, there are those who carry out acts of righteousness [through charity] on their own volition, there are those whom you ask and will give, and there are those whom you ask and who do nothing.

    D.   Said R. Levi, "There is the saying: 'the door that you don't open for a religious duty you will open for the doctor.'"

9. A.   Another explanation of the phrase, "I went down to the nut orchard:"

    B.   just as in the case of a nut, a stone breaks it,

    C.   so the Torah is called a stone, [and] the impulse to do evil is called a stone.

    D.   The Torah is called a stone: "And I will give you the tablets of stone" (Ex. 24:12).

    E.   The impulse to do evil is called a stone: "And I will take away the stony heart out of your flesh" (Ezek. 36:26).

F. Said R. Levi, "[The matter may be compared to the case of] a lonely spot, which is infested with terrorists. What does the king do? He assigns there brigades to guard the place so that the terrorists will not attack travellers on the way.

G. "So said the Holy One, blessed be He, 'The Torah is called a stone, and the impulse to do evil is called a stone.

H. "'Let stone guard stone.'"

10. A. Another explanation of the phrase, "I went down to the nut orchard:"

B. Just as a stone cannot deceive the customs collector because it is betrayed by its rattle,

C. So with the Israelites, in any place to which one of them goes, he cannot say, "I'm not a Jew."

D. Why not?

E. Because he is a marked man: "All who see them will recognize them, that they are the seed which the Lord has blessed" (Isa. 61:9).

11. A. Another explanation of the phrase, "I went down to the nut orchard:"

B. Just as in the case of a nut, if you have a full bag of nuts in hand, you can still put in any amount of sesame seeds and mustard seeds and there will be room for them,

C. so how many proselytes have come and been attached to Israel: "Who has counted the dust of Jacob" (Num. 23:10).

12. A. Another explanation of the phrase, "I went down to the nut orchard:"

B. Just as in the case of a nut, if you take one out of the pile, all the rest fall down on one another,

C. so in the case of Israel, if one of them is smitten, all of them feel it:

D. "Shall one man sin and you will be angry with all the congregation" (Num. 16:22).

13. A. [Supply: Another explanation of the phrase, "I went down to the nut orchard:"]

B. Said R. Berekhiah, "Just as a nut is divided into four chambers with a hole in the middle,

C. "so the Israelites were ensconced in the wilderness by four standards, into four camps, with the tent of meeting in the middle:

D. "'Then the tent of meeting...shall set forward in the midst of the camps' (Num. 2:17)."

14. A. Another explanation: "I went down to the nut orchard:"

B. This is the world.

C. "to look at the blossoms of the valley:"

D. This is Israel.

E. "to see whether the vines had budded:" this refers to synagogues and houses of study.

F. "whether the pomegranates were in bloom:"

G. This refers to children who are in session, occupied with the Torah, sitting row by row like pomegranate seeds."

I do not think our compilers and authors of the individual compositions can be better represented than by this fully realized exercise, in which the base verse yields a large variety of metaphorizations for Israel – all of which make the same rather limited number of points. What do the compilers say through their readings of the metaphor of the nut tree for Israel? First, Israel prospers when it gives scarce resources for the study of the Torah or for carrying out religious duties (Nos. 1, 4, and, I assume, No. 8 and for different reasons No. 13 fall into this group); second, Israel sins but atones, and Torah is the medium of atonement (Nos. 2, 3, 4, 9); third, Israel is identified through carrying out its religious duties, e.g., circumcision (Nos. 5, 10); fourth, Israel's leaders had best watch their step (No. 6); fifth, Israel may be nothing now but will be in glory in the coming age (No. 7); sixth, Israel has plenty of room for outsiders but cannot afford to lose a single member (Nos. 11, 12). Only No. 13 is anomalous, and not really so: Israel forms Israel by reason of the tent of meeting that is in the middle of the whole. These several propositions rework the basic word symbols: Israel, Torah, religious duty, saying the same thing in a variety of ways.

88

Song of Songs Rabbah to Song of Songs 6:12

6:12   *Before I was aware, my fancy set me in a chariot beside my prince.*

LXXXVIII:i

1. A.   "Before I was aware, my fancy set me in a chariot beside my prince:"

     B.   It was taught on Tannaite authority by R. Hiyya, "The matter may be compared to the case of a princess who went out gathering stray sheaves.

     C.   "The king turned out to be passing and recognized that she was his daughter.

     D.   He sent out his friend to take her and seat her with him in the carriage.

     E.   "Now her girlfriends were surprised at her and said, 'Yesterday you were gathering stray sheaves, and today you are seated in a carriage with the king.'

     F.   "She said to them, 'Just as you are surprised at me, so I am surprised at myself, and I recited in my own regard the following verse of Scripture, 'Before I was aware, my fancy set me in a chariot beside my prince.'

     G.   "Thus too when the Israelites were enslaved in Egypt in mortar and bricks, they were rejected and despised in the view of the Egyptians.

     H.   "But when they were freed and redeemed and made prefects over everyone in the world, the nations of the world expressed surprise, saying, 'Yesterday you were working in mortar and bricks, and today you have been freed and redeemed and made prefects over everyone in the world!'

     I.   "And the Israelites replied to them, 'Just as you are surprised at us, so we are surprised at ourselves,' and they recited in their own regard, 'Before I was aware, my fancy set me in a chariot beside my prince.'"

2   A.   Another explanation of the verse, "'Before I was aware, my fancy
            set me in a chariot beside my prince:'"
    B.   Scripture speaks of the righteous Joseph.
    C.   Yesterday: "His feet they hurt with fetters, his person was laid in
            iron" (Ps. 105:18).
    D.   Today: "And Joseph was the governor over the land" (Gen. 42:6).
    E.   So in his own regard he recited the verse, "Before I was aware, my
            fancy set me in a chariot beside my prince."

3. A.   Another explanation of the verse, "'Before I was aware, my fancy
            set me in a chariot beside my prince:'"
    B.   Scripture speaks of David.
    C.   Yesterday he was escaping from Saul.
    D.   Today: "David was king" (2 Sam. 8:15).
    E.   So in his own regard he recited the verse, "Before I was aware, my
            fancy set me in a chariot beside my prince."

4. A.   Another explanation of the verse, "'Before I was aware, my fancy
            set me in a chariot beside my prince:'"
    B.   Scripture speaks of Mordecai.
    C.   Yesterday: "He put on sackcloth with ashes" (Est. 4:1).
    D.   Today: "And Mordecai went forth from the presence of the king in
            royal apparel of blue and white" (Est. 8:15).
    E.   So in his own regard he recited the verse, "Before I was aware, my
            fancy set me in a chariot beside my prince."

5. A.   Another explanation of the verse, "'Before I was aware, my fancy
            set me in a chariot beside my prince:'"
    B.   Scripture speaks of the Community of Israel.
    C.   The Community of Israel says to the nations of the world, "'Do not
            rejoice against me, O my enemy; though I have fallen, I shall
            arise' (Mic. 7:8).
    D.   "When I dwelled in darkness, the Holy One, blessed be He,
            brought me forth to light: 'Though I sit in darkness, the Lord is a
            light to me' (Mic. 7:8)."
    E.   So in her own regard she recited the verse, "Before I was aware,
            my fancy set me in a chariot beside my prince."

6. A.   Justus, a tailor in Sepphoris, went up to the government and was
            received by the king.
    B.   The king said to him, "Ask me for something, and I shall give it to
            you."
    C.   He said to him, "Make me the duke of our locale."
    D.   The king gave it to him.
    E.   After he had assumed the position, he left it.
    F.   And those who knew him said, "It's the same man," but others who
            knew him said, "It's not the same."
    G.   One of them said to them, "When he goes through the market, if
            he glances at that tailor's seat on which he used to sit and stitch, it
            is the same man, but if not, it is not the same man."
    H.   He passed through the market and began to look at the stool on
            which he had sat and stitched, so they knew that he was the same
            man.
    I.   He said to them, "You are surprised at me, but I am more
            surprised at myself than you are."

J.   And they recited in his regard the verse, "Before I was aware, my fancy set me in a chariot beside my prince,"

K.   meaning, with me the Prince, the Eternal, walked.

The basic attitude is that what will happen to Israel in time to come will surprise not only the nations, but also Israel herself. That is the point of No. 1. We then proceed with Joseph, David, and Mordecai, all of whom went from difficult circumstances to the heights, and then the Community of Israel, for whom they stand, No. 5. No. 6 completes the composition with an essentially independent entry, which turns out to work well with the foregoing; if I had to point to a perfect execution of a complex program – parable, then a systematic application, then a homely illustration in everyday terms but not a parable – I should point to this fine composition.

89

Song of Songs Rabbah to Song of Songs 6:13

6:13 *Return, return, O Shulammite, return, return that we may look upon you. Why should you look upon the Shulammite, as upon a dance before two armies?*

LXXXIX:i

1. A. "Return, return, O Shulammite, return:"
   B. R. Samuel b. R. Hiyya b. R. Yudan in the name of R. Hanina, "In the present passage, the word 'return' is written four times.
   C. "These correspond to the four monarchies that have ruled over Israel, into the power of which, and out of the power of which, the Israelites entered and emerged whole."
2. A. "Shullamite:"
   B. the nation with whom the Eternal behaves in integrity [wholeness, a meaning imputed to the same letters as are used in the word for Shullamite].
   C. That is in line with this verse: "But I have walked in a tent and in a tabernacle" (2 Sam. 7:6).
3. A. Another explanation for the name Shullamite:
   B. it is the nation for whom, every day, peace is made:
   C. "And give you peace" (Num. 6:26).
4. A. Another explanation for the name Shullamite:
   B. it is the nation that I am going to seat in a peaceful dwelling:
   C. "And my people shall abide in a peaceful habitation" (Isa. 32:18).
5. A. Another explanation for the name Shullamite:
   B. a nation over whom I spread peace:
   C. "Lo, I will spread peace over her" (Isa. 56:12).
6. A. [Supply: Another explanation for the name Shullamite:]
   B. R. Eleazar b. R. Maron said, "It is a nation that complements this world and the world to come. [Simon, p. 275: the nation that completes the stability of the world, whether in this world or the world to come]."
7. A. [Supply: Another explanation for the name Shullamite:]

B.   R. Joshua of Sikhnin in the name of R. Levi said, "It is the nation solely on account of the merit of which all the good things in the world come about:

C.   "'So God give on your account of the dew of heaven and of the fat places of the earth' (Gen. 27:28).

D.   "The word for 'on your account' means, on account of your merit and on your account the matter depends.

E.   "That is the usage in the following: 'The Lord will open for your sake his good treasure' (Dt. 28:12),

F.   "on account of your merit and on you the matter depends."

8. A.   [Supply: Another explanation for the name Shullamite:]

B.   R. Samuel b. R. Tanhum and R. Hanan, son of R. Berekhiah of Bosrah in the name of R. Jeremiah: "[God says,] 'It is the nation that made peace between me and my world.

C.   "'For had they not accepted my Torah, I should have returned my world to formlessness and void.'"

D.   For Huna said in the name of R. Aha, "It is written, 'The earth and all its inhabitants are dissolved' (Ps. 75:4):

E.   "if the Israelites had not stood before Mount Sinai and said, 'Whatever the Lord has spoken we shall do and obey' (Ex. 24:7), the world would have by now dissolved.

F.   "And who is it who founded the world? It is 'I,' thus: 'I myself establish the pillars of it, *selah*' (Ps. 75:4), meaning, 'for the sake of their 'I am the Lord your God,' I have established its pillars."

9. A.   "Return that we may look upon you:"

B.   The nations of the world say to Israel, "How long are you going to die for your God and [Simon:] devote yourselves completely to him?"

C.   "For thus Scripture says, 'Therefore do they love you beyond death' (Song 1:3).

D.   "And how long will you be slaughtered on his account: 'No, but for your sake we are killed all day long' (Ps. 44:23)?

E.   "'How long are you going to do good deeds on his account, for him alone, while he pays you back with bad things?

F.   "Come over to us, and we shall make you governors, hyparchs, and generals,

G.   "'That we may look upon you:' and you will be [Simon:] the cynosure of the world: 'And you shall be the look out of all the people' (Ex. 18:21)."

H.   And the Israelites will answer, "'Why should you look upon the Shulammite, as upon a dance before two armies:'

I.   "In your entire lives, have you ever heard that Abraham, Isaac, and Jacob worshipped idols, that their children should do so after them? Our fathers did not worship idols, and we shall not worship idols after them.

J.   "But what can you do for us?

K.   "Can it be like the dance that was made for Jacob, our father, when he went forth from the house of Laban?"

10. A.   R. Berekhiah in the name of R. Levi said, "Sixty myriads of angels were dancing and carousing before our father Jacob when he went forth from the house of Laban."

B. And rabbis say, "It was one hundred and twenty myriads: 'And Jacob said when he saw them, This is God's camp' (Gen. 32:3), that is, sixty myriads; 'and he called the name of that place Two Camps' (Gen. 32:3), thus one hundred twenty."

11. A [Continuing 9.K:] "Or can you make a dance for us such as was made for our fathers at the sea? 'And the angel of God removed...' (Ex. 14:19).

B. "Or can you make a dance for us like the one that was made for Elisha: 'And when the servant of the man of God was risen early and gone forth, behold a host with horses and chariots was round about the city. And his servant said to him, Alas, my master, what shall we do? And he answered, Do not be afraid, for they who are with us are more than those who are with them. Forthwith Elisha prayed and said, Lord, I pray you, open his eyes that he may see. And the Lord opened the eyes of the young man, and he saw, and behold, the mountain was full of horses and chariots of fire around about Elisha' (2 Kgs. 6:15).

C. "Or can you make a dance for us like the one that the Holy One, blessed be He, will make for the righteous in the age to come?"

12. A R. Berekiah and R. Helbo and Ulla of Beri and R. Eleazar in the name of R. Hanina said, "The Holy One, blessed be He, is going to serve as the lord of the dance for the righteous in the age to come:

B. "'Mark well her ramparts' (Ps. 48:14) may be read, 'her dance.'

C. "And the righteous will celebrate him with their finger: 'For this is God, our God, forever and ever. He will guide us eternally' (Ps. 48:15).

D. "[The letters for the word 'eternally'] yield the meaning, 'like women,

E. "like the dance of the righteous."

The work on the several meanings that the letters of the word Shulammite contain is accomplished at No. 1, then in the matched sets of Nos. 2-5, then continued at the free-standing items, not matched with the foregoing but wholly harmonious with them, Nos. 6, 7, 8. No. 9, bearing with grace a variety of secondary expansions, makes its own point, which complements the foregoing. Israel is whole with God, but cannot make peace with the nations of the world. This is another particularly strong evocation, through the metaphor of the Song, of the condition of Israel.

Part Seven
PARASHAH SEVEN

Song of Songs - Chapter Seven

7:1   *How graceful are your feet in sandals,*
O queenly maiden!
Your rounded thighs are like jewels,
the work of a master hand.

7:2   *Your navel is a rounded bowl,*
that never lacks mixed wine.
Your belly is a heap of wheat,
encircled with lilies.

7:3   *Your two breasts are like two fawns,*
twins of a gazelle.

7:4   *Your neck is like an ivory tower.*
Your eyes are pools in Heshbon,
by the gate of Bath-rabbim.
Your nose is like a tower of Lebanon,
overlooking Damascus.

7:5   *Your head crowns you like Carmel,*
and your flowing locks are like purple;
a king is held captive in the tresses.

7:6   *How fair and pleasant you are,*
O loved one, delectable maiden.

7:7   *You are stately as a palm tree,*
and your breasts are like its clusters.

7:8   *I say I will climb the palm tree*
and lay hold of its branches.
O, may your breasts be like clusters of the vine,
and the scent of your breath like apples,

7:9   *and your kisses like the best wine*
that goes down smoothly,
gliding over lips and teeth.

7:10   *I am my beloved's,*
and his desire is for me.

7:11   *Come my beloved,*

169

let us go forth into the fields,
and lodge in the villages;

7:12   let us go out early to the vineyards,
and see whether the vines have budded,
whether the grape blossoms have opened
and the pomegranates are in bloom.
There I will give you my love.

7:13   The mandrakes give forth fragrance,
and over our doors are all choice fruits,
new as well as old,
which I have laid up for you, O my beloved.

90

Song of Songs Rabbah to Song of Songs 7:1

7:1   *How graceful are your feet in sandals, O queenly maiden! Your rounded thighs are like jewels, the work of a master hand.*

XC:I

1. A. "How graceful are your feet in sandals, O queenly maiden:"
   B. Said R. Yudan, "Even for an ordinary person praise in this vulgar language would be an offense, and yet you say, 'How graceful are your feet'!
   C. "But Scripture speaks only of the festival-pilgrims' footsteps."

2. A. [Supply: "How graceful are your feet in sandals, O queenly maiden:"]
   B. But is it not the fact that sometimes the feet are bare, sometimes covered?
   C. But the sense is, "How graceful are your feet when they are in shoes" [Simon, p. 277, n. 2: to perform the precept of the removal of the shoe and the like].

3. A. Said R. Berekhiah, "This is how the two pinnacles of the age, R. Eliezer and R. Joshua, have interpreted the verse, 'How graceful are your feet in sandals, O queenly maiden:'
   B. "'How beautiful were your festival pilgrims, who locked the door against all suffering [for the words for sandals and lock the door share the same consonants].'"

4. A. There was the case of someone who forgot to lock the doors of his house when he went up for the pilgrim festival.
   B. And when he came home, he found a snake wound around the rings of his door.

5. A. There was another case of someone who forgot and did not bring his chickens into his house when he went up for the pilgrim festival.
   B. When he came home, he found cats torn to pieces before them.

6. A. There was another case of someone who forgot and did not bring his pile of grain into the house when he went up for the pilgrim festival.

171

	B.	When he came home, he found lions surrounding the wheat.
7.	A.	Said R. Phineas, "There was the case of two rich brothers who were in Ashkelon, who had wicked gentile neighbors, who said, 'When these Jews go up to pray in Jerusalem, we shall go into their houses and clean them out.'
	B.	"The time came and they went up.
	C.	"The Holy One, blessed be He, set up for them angels in their likeness, and they would go in and come out of their houses.
	D.	"When they came home from Jerusalem, they divided up what they had brought with them among all their neighbors.
	E.	"They said to them, 'Where were you?'
	F.	"They said to them, 'In Jerusalem.'
	G.	"'When did you go up?'
	H.	"'On such-and-such a day.'
	I.	"They said, 'Blessed is the God of the Jews, whom you have not abandoned, and who has not abandoned you! We thought, "When these Jews go up to pray in Jerusalem, we shall go into their houses and clean them out." But your God has sent angels in your likeness, who came out and went into your houses because you had faith in him.'
	J.	"This fulfills the verse, 'How graceful are your feet in sandals, O queenly maiden.'"

The first reading of our base verse works on the words for footsteps and sandals, as indicated, thus presenting the message that God praises Israel for their faithfulness, expressed in the pilgrim festivals. The extension of course is to the cult and its signification of the loyalty of Israel to God.

XC:ii

1.	A.	Another explanation of the verse, "How graceful are your feet in sandals, O queenly maiden:"
	B.	[The word for sandals is so written that it can be read,] in two closings [or: completions, with reference to the concluding days of the festivals of Tabernacles and Passover, as will be spelled out presently].
2.	A.	Said R. Hama b. R. Hanina, "The matter may be compared to two peddlers who came to a town. One of them took up the matter with the other, saying to his fellow, 'If we both open our shops together in this town, we shall [Simon:] bring down the price. You open your stall in your week, and I shall do so in my week.'"
3.	A.	R. Hananiah b. R. Aibu said, "'How graceful are your feet in sandals, O queenly maiden:'
	B.	"[The word for sandals is so written that it can be read,] in two closings.
	C.	"The one is the concluding days of Passover, the other, the concluding days of the Festival [Tabernacles].
	D.	"Said the Holy One, blessed be He, to the Israelites, 'You conclude the celebration before me on the Festival, and I shall conclude the celebration before you on Passover.

E.   "'You conclude the celebration before me on the Festival: and I shall open and restore the wind and bring up the clouds and bring down rains and make the sun shine, and make the grasses to grow and fatten the fruit and set a table before each and every one of you, providing all his needs and what each and every body requires.

F.   "'and I shall conclude the celebration before you on Passover: so you will go out and reap, thresh, winnow, and do everything necessary in the field and find it full of blessings.'"

4. A. Said R. Joshua b. Levi, "The Concluding Day of the Festival [the Eighth Day of Solemn Assembly] was suitable to be distanced fifty days from the Festival, corresponding to the Conclusion of Passover [which is Pentecost, fifty days after Passover].

B.   "But as to the Concluding Day of the Festival, since it marks the passage from summer to winter, it is not a time for going and coming.

C.   "The matter may be compared to the case of a king who had many daughters, some of them married and living near by, some of them married and living far off.

D.   "One day all of them came to greet the king, their father.

E.   "Said the king, 'Those who are married and living nearby can go and come as they like, but those who are married and living at a distance cannot come and go anytime they like.

F.   "'So while they are all with me, come, let us celebrate a single banquet for them all and rejoice with them all.'

G.   "So as to the Concluding Day of Passover [Pentecost], since the season is passing from winter to summer, said the Holy One, blessed be He, 'These are days for going and coming.'

H.   "But as to the Concluding day of the Festival, since the days are passing from summer to winter, with the roads dusty and hard for walking, therefore the [Eighth Day of Solemn Assembly] is not distanced by fifty days, [for,] said the Holy One, blessed be He, 'These are not days for going and coming. But while they are here, let us celebrate a single banquet for them all and rejoice with them all.'

I.   "Therefore Moses admonishes the Israelites, saying to them, 'On the eighth day you shall have a solemn assembly' (Num. 29:35).

J.   "Thus: 'How graceful are your feet in sandals, O queenly maiden.'"

The second reading has its own interest, leading us far from the discourse of the Song of Songs; now our base verse is simply an occasion for making the point that is at the center of matters: explaining the difference between the timing of the Eighth Day of Solemn Assembly, after the Festival, and Pentecost, after Passover. To all of this our base verse is peripheral, merely an occasion for linking the message to a verse of Scripture. But the interest of the compiler still is well served, since, after all, what interests him is the connection between Israel's admirable love for God, expressed in the pilgrim festivals, and God's expressed love for Israel, which the Song sets forth.

XC:iii
1. A.   "O queenly maiden [prince's daughter]:"
   B.   Daughter of Abraham, who is called a prince: "The princes of the peoples are gathered together, the people of the God of Abraham" (Ps. 47:10).
2. A.   "Your rounded thighs are like jewels, the work of a master hand:"
   B.   Said R. Yohanan, "All of the [Simon:] luxuries and delicacies that the Israelites enjoy and in which they luxuriate in this world is on account of the merit of circumcision,
   C.   "which is located between the thighs."
3. A.   Said R. Hiyya, "How come sages set the blessing of God as healer in the eighth blessing of the eighteen?
   B.   "It corresponds to circumcision, which is done on the eighth day:
   C.   "'My covenant was with him of life and peace' (Ma. 2:5)."
4. A.   "Your rounded thighs are like jewels [the work of a master hand]:"
   B.   [Since the word for jewels and for illnesses share the same consonants, the sense is this:] how many illnesses are on its account,
   C.   how many circumcised babies die on its account!
5. A.   Said R. Nathan, "There was this case. I came to the town of Cappadocia, and there was a woman who produced male children. When they were circumcised, they died. The first was circumcised and died, so too the second, so too the third. The fourth she brought before me, and I examined its flesh and found it pale. I looked at it and I did not find in it blood of the circumcision. They asked me, 'Should we circumcise him?'
   B.   "I said to them, 'Wait and let him be, until the blood of circumcision is produced. For we have learned there: "As to the infant and the sick person, they are not to be circumcised until they get well."
   C.   "They let him be, then circumcised him and he turned out to live, and they produced as his name, 'Nathan,' after mine.
   D.   "That is in line with this verse: 'like jewels.'"
6. A.   Another explanation of the verse, "like jewels:"
   B.   To what jewels is [the place of circumcision] to be compared?
   C.   R. Hunia and rabbis:
   D.   R. Hunia said, "To [Simon:] the chaplet around a pillar [supporting Israel]."
   E.   Rabbis said, "To the hole in pearls."
7. A.   And who made it ["like jewels"]?
   B.   R. Menahema said, "'the work of a master hand:'
   C.   "the work of the master hand of the Holy One, blessed be He, in this world."
8. A.   Said R. Samuel, "The matter may be compared to the case of a king who had an orchard, planted row by row of nuts, apples, pomegranates, and he handed them over to his son, saying to him, 'My son, I ask of you only that when these plantings bring their first fruit, you present it to me and let me taste it, so that I may see the work of my hands and take pleasure in you.'

B. "So said the Holy One, blessed be He, to the Israelites, 'My children, I ask of you only that when a first son is born to any of you, he be sanctified to my name: "Sanctify to me all the firstborn" (Ex. 13:2).

C. "'And when you go up for the pilgrim festivals, you bring him up and all your males to appear before me.'

D. "Therefore Moses admonishes Israel: 'Three times...in the year' (Ex. 23:14)."

We move on to a more sustained interest in the base verse, though the results are not much richer than the foregoing. No. 1 is routine and philological. No. 2 works on the image of "thighs" yielding, now, the male, and, hence, circumcision. Nos. 3, 4, 5, 6, 7, 8, carry forward the same theme, reverting, rather surprisingly, to the play on the word for jewels/ailments. No. 8 rejoins our original reading at 8.C-D, which hardly fits in with what has gone before. The net effect of the whole is not very compelling.

91

Song of Songs Rabbah to Song of Songs 7:2

7:2   *Your navel is a rounded bowl, that never lacks mixed wine. Your belly is a heap of wheat, encircled with lilies.*

XCI:i

1. A. "Your navel is a rounded bowl:"
    B. "Your navel:"
    C. this refers to the Sanhedrin.
    D. Just as an embryo, so long as it is in its mother's belly, lives only from its umbilical cord,
    E. so Israel can act only with its Sanhedrin.

2. A. "is a rounded bowl:"
    B. [Simon:] the seat of admonishment.
    C. Abun b. R. Hisdai said, "There are places in which the moon is called by the same word as is used here for bowl." [The Sanhedrin forms a half moon in its sessions.]

3. A. "that never lacks mixed wine:"
    B. The Sanhedrin never lacks a complement of twenty-three members.

4. A. Another explanation concerning "that never lacks mixed wine:"
    B. The Sanhedrin is not to lack the distinguished member [who is head of it].

5. A. Another explanation concerning "that never lacks mixed wine:"
    B. the Sanhedrin is not to lack the one who is to mix [Simon: will duly temper] the law for it,
    C. in line with that which we have learned: A mixture of two parts of water to one of wine, in the wine of Sharon.

6. A. Another explanation concerning "that never lacks mixed wine:"
    B. the needs of the world are not to be lacking: "The Lord is my shepherd, I shall not want" (Ps. 23:1).

7. A. "Your belly is a heap of wheat:"
    B. this refers to the book of Leviticus.
    C. Just as in the case of the belly, the heart is above and the legs below and it is in the middle,

176

	D.	so with the book of Leviticus, there are two books before and two afterward and it is in the middle.
8.	A.	"Your belly is a heap of wheat:"
	B.	[These words may be read to yield,] a heap of sin-offerings [as specified in the book of Leviticus].
9.	A.	"encircled with lilies:"
	B.	this refers to words of the Torah which are as soft as lilies.
	C.	How many specifications of religious duties and details pertaining to them are in the book of Leviticus,
	D.	in the book of Leviticus there are how many arguments *a fortiori*, how many rules governing the rendering of an offering unacceptable by reason of the officiating priest's improper attitude or by reason of leaving over the meat beyond the time in which it is to be eaten!
10.	A.	Said R. Levi, "Under ordinary circumstances, if a man marries a woman at the age of thirty or forty, after he has laid out a good bit of money [on the marriage], he comes to have sexual relations with her,
	B.	"and she says to him, 'I have seen a speck of red [menstrual blood],' and she forthwith separates from him.
	C.	"Now what made him not draw near here? What wall of iron is there between them, one pillar of iron?
	D.	"What snake bit him? What scorpion nipped at him, that he should not draw near her?
	E.	"Words of Torah, which are as soft as a lily: 'And you shall not approach a woman...as long as she is impure by her uncleanness' (Lev. 18:19).
	F.	"And so, one to whom a dish of chopped meat is brought, and who is told, 'Milk dropped in there,' withdraws his hand and does not touch the meat.
	G.	"What has caused him not to taste it?
	H.	"What snake bit him that he should not taste it? What scorpion nipped at him, that he should not taste it?
	I.	"Words of Torah, which are as soft as a lily: 'You shall not eat fat or blood' (Lev. 3:17)."
11.	A.	Another explanation of the phrase, "Your belly is a heap of wheat:"
	B.	But is not one of cedar cones [Simon] prettier than one of wheat?
	C.	[Why then is wheat the metaphor?] But the world can be without cedar cones, but the world cannot do without wheat.
12.	A.	[Supply: Another explanation of the phrase, "Your belly is a heap of wheat:"]
	B.	Said R. Idi, "Just as wheat is split down the middle, so the circumcision of an Israelite marks a split on the penis."
	C.	R. Yosé b. R. Hanina said, "Just as wheat absorbs water, so Israel absorbs the possessions of the nations of the world: 'You shall eat all the peoples' (Dt. 7:16); 'You shall eat the wealth of the nations and in their splendor you shall revel' (Isa. 61:6)."
	D.	Said R. Simeon b. Levi, "Just as in the case of wheat, the chaff is measured with the wheat, so in the case of Israel: 'From the hewer of your wood to the drawer of your water' (Dt. 29:10)."

E.   Said R. Isaac, "Just as in the case of wheat, when people go out to sow it, they go out only having measured it, and when they come in from the threshing floor, they come in only have measured the crop,

F.   "so when the Israelites went down to Egypt, they went down only having been counted up: 'Your fathers went down into Egypt with seventy persons' (Dt. 10:22), and when they came up from Egypt, they came up only having been counted up: 'About six hundred thousand men on foot, besides the children' (Ex. 12:37)."

G.   R. Hunia commented on this statement of R. Isaac, "Just as the householder does not take heed of baskets of dung or baskets of straw or chaff or stubble – why not?   because they are not regarded as worth a thing,

H.   "so the Holy One, blessed be He, does not take heed of the nations of the world – why not? because they are not [regarded as worth] a thing: 'All the nations are as nothing before him' (Isa. 40:17).

I.   "And to whom does he pay heed? To Israel: 'When you take the sum of the children of Israel' (Ex. 30:12); 'Take the sum of all the congregation of the children of Israel' (Num. 1:2)."

13. A.   R. Nehemiah in the name of R. Abun says, "The nations of the world have no planting, nor sowing, nor root.

B.   "The three matters derive from a single verse of Scripture: 'They are scarcely planted, scarcely sown, scarcely has their stock taken root in the earth' (Isa. 40:24).

C.   "But the Israelites have a planting: 'And I will plant them in this land' (Jer. 32:41); they have a sowing: 'And I will sow her to me in the land' (Hos. 2:25); they have a root: 'In days to come Jacob shall take root' (Isa. 27:6).

14. A.   To what may the matter be compared?

B.   The straw, chaff, and stubble argued with one another.

C.   This one says, "On my account the field is sown," and that one says, "On my account the field is sown."

D.   The wheat said to them, "Wait for me until the threshing floor arrives, and we shall see for whom the field is sown."

E.   The threshing floor arrived, and when they were brought into the threshing floor, the household came out to winnow it.

F.   The chaff was gone with the wind.

G.   He took the straw and tossed it on the ground.

H.   He took the stubble and burned it up.

I.   He took the wheat and made it into a pile.

J.   Those who passed by, whoever saw it, kissed it: "Kiss the wheat" (Ps. 2:12).

K.   So it is with the nations of the world:

L.   These say, "We are Israel, and on our account the world has been made," and those say, "We are Israel, and on our account the world has been made,"

M.   so Israel says to them, "Wait until the day of the Holy One, blessed be He, comes, and we shall then know on whose account the world has been made: 'For behold the day comes, it burns as a

furnace' (Mal. 4:1); 'You shall fan them and the wind shall carry
them away' (Isa. 41:16).

N.   "But of Israel Scripture says, 'And you shall rejoice in the Lord,
you shall glory in the Holy One of Israel' (Isa. 41:16)."

The opening interpretation of the metaphor has God speak of
Israel, now of the Sanhedrin; that reading runs through Nos. 2, 3, 4, 5
(which I cannot explain). No. 6 is free-standing. Nos. 7-10 go on to
another matter, the book of Leviticus and the rules therein. No. 11
introduces an interest in the metaphor of the wheat, and at No. 12 this
is exploited with a variety of explanations of the metaphor. Because
of the contrast of Israel and the nations, No. 13 is tacked on; with No.
14 in its wake. There are, therefore, essentially three readings here:
institutional (Sanhedrin); personal (obedience to the religious duties);
and national-salvific (Israel and the nations).

92

Song of Songs Rabbah to Song of Songs 7:3

7:3   *Your two breasts are like two fawns, twins of a gazelle.*

Our compilation has nothing on this verse.

93

Song of Songs Rabbah to Song of Songs 7:4

7:4   *Your neck is like an ivory tower. Your eyes are pools in Heshbon,*
by the gate of Bath-rabbim. Your nose is like a tower of
Lebanon, overlooking Damascus.

XCIII:i
1. A.   "Your neck is like an ivory tower:"
    B.   It is written, [Genesis Rabbah LXXVIII: IX.1:] "But Esau ran to
          meet him and embraced him, and fell on his neck and kissed
          him, and they wept" (Gen. 33:4):
    C.   [In the received text,] there are dots written over the word, "And
          he kissed him." [The matter requires explanation.]
    D.   Said R. Simeon b. Eleazar, "In any passage in which you find that
          the letters written plain, without a dot on top, are more numerous
          in the word at hand than the letters written with a dot, you should
          base your interpretation on the plain letters. If the letters written
          with a dot in the word are more numerous than those written
          without, you should interpret the letters written with the dot on
          top.
    E.   "Here the letters written with the dots on top are no more
          numerous than the others, and vice versa, so you interpret the
          matter in line with the dotted letters. They then yield the fact that
          he kissed him in all sincerity."
    F.   [Genesis Rabbah adds: Said R. Yannai,] "If so, what is the point of
          putting dots on the word? Rather, it teaches that he wanted to
          bite him. [The words for bite and kiss share consonants in
          common.]
    G.   "But our father Jacob's neck became stone, and hurt the teeth of
          that wicked man [Esau] and melted like wax.
    H.   "Then why does Scripture say, 'And they wept'?
    I.   "This one wept for his neck, that one for his teeth."
    J.   R. Abbahu in the name of R. Eleazar derived proof for the same
          proposition from the following verse: "Your neck is like an ivory
          tower."

2. A.   "Now when Pharaoh heard this thing, he sought to slay Moses.
           But Moses fled" (Ex. 2:15).

    B.   Now is there anyone who can flee from the king?

    C.   This teaches that he was standing under judgment on that day
           and held guilty of death through decapitation.

    D.   Said R. Abiatar, "The sword slipped from Moses's neck and
           beheaded the executioner instead: 'For the God of my father was
           my help and he delivered me from the sword of Pharaoh' (Ex.
           18:4).

    E.   "'Me did he deliver from the sword of Pharaoh, but the
           executioner he did not deliver.'"

    F.   In this connection R. Bun cited this verse of Scripture: "The
           righteous is delivered out of trouble and the wicked takes his
           place" (Prov. 11:8).

    G.   In this connection R. Berekhiah cited this verse of Scripture: "The
           wicked is a ransom for the righteous" (Prov. 21:18).

    H.   Bar Qappara said, "It teaches that an angel came down in the
           likeness of Moses, and they seized him and let Moses go, so he
           fled."

3. A.   R. Abba b. R. Pappi and R. Joshua of Sikhnin in the name of R.
           Levi: "All of the advisers of Pharaoh at that time turned, some
           dumb, some deaf, some blind, some lame.

    B.   "So they said to the dumb, 'Where is Moses?' but they could not
           answer.

    C.   "...to the blind, but they did not see.

    D.   "...to the deaf, but they did not hear.

    E.   "...to the lame, but they could not go.

    F.   "Thus: 'And the Lord said to him, Who has made man's mouth?
           or who makes a man dumb or deaf or sighted or blind? Is it not I
           the Lord' (Ex. 4:11).

    G.   "'Did not I do all these things?'

    H.   "'Come now therefore and I will send you to Pharaoh' (Ex. 3:10)."

The entire composition is thrown together on the theme that Israel
has a tough neck. No. 1 is inserted because our base verse serves in a
subordinate role as a prooftext. No. 2 [+3] explains how Moses's neck
was so hard that the sword slipped from his neck and hit the
executioner. Nothing, therefore, has been worked out for the
requirement of our document; and nothing advances the clarification of
our base verse.

XCIII:ii

1. A.   "Your eyes are pools in Heshbon:"

    B.   "Your eyes" refer to the Sanhedrin,

    C.   which is the eyes of the congregation: "And it shall come to pass, if
           it be hidden from the eyes of the congregation" (Num. 15:24).

    D.   There are two hundred forty-eight limbs in a person, and all of
           them follow the eyes.

    E.   So it is with Israel: they can do nothing without their Sanhedrin.

2. A.   "pools in Heshbon:"

B.	this refers to matters that are settled by totting up the vote: thirty-six for acquittal, thirty-five for conviction.

3. A.   "by the gate of Bath-rabbim:"
    B.   This refers to the law which comes forth from the gate and is made public [the word for public and rabbim sharing the same consonants].
    C.   Judah b. Rabbi said, "'turn aside after a multitude' (Ex. 23:2) [meaning, follow the majority]."

The exposition is now within the established program of having God praise Israel's institutions of government and administration.

XCIII:iii

1. A.   "Your forehead [RSV: nose] is like a tower of Lebanon, overlooking Damascus:"
    B.   This refers to the house of the sanctuary.
    C.   Just as the forehead is situated at the highest part of a person, so the house of the sanctuary is situated in the highest spot in the world.
    D.   Just as the forehead bears most of one's ornaments, so the priesthood, the Levites, and the royal house come from Jacob.

2. A.   "like a tower of Lebanon:"
    B.   "That goodly hill country and Lebanon" (Dt. 3:25)."

3. A.   [Supply "like a tower of Lebanon:"]
    B.   ["The Temple is called Lebanon,"] said R. Tabiyomi, "For it whitens the transgressions of Israel like snow [and the words for Lebanon and whiten share the same consonants]: 'If your sins are as red as scarlet, they will be made white as snow' (Isa. 1:18)."
    C.   ["The Temple is called Lebanon,"] R. Simeon b. Yohai says, "for all hearts rejoice in it [and the words for Lebanon and hearts share the same consonants]: 'Fair in situation, the joy of the whole earth' (Ps. 48:3)."
    D.   ["The Temple is called Lebanon,"] Rabbis say, "on account of this verse: 'My eyes and my heart shall be there perpetually' (1 Kgs. 9:3) [and the words for Lebanon and hearts share the same consonants]."

4. A.   "overlooking Damascus:"
    B.   Said R. Yohanan, "Jerusalem is destined to reach the gates of Damascus: 'The burden of the word of the Lord. In the land of Hadrach [and in Damascus shall be his resting place]' (Zech. 9:1)."

5. A.   [Supply "The burden of the word of the Lord. In the land of Hadrach and in Damascus shall be his resting place" (Zech. 9:1):]
    B.   What is the meaning of Hadrach?
    C.   R. Judah and R. Nehemiah:
    D.   R. Judah said, "It is a place that is called Hadrach."
    E.   Said to him R. Yosé b. Durmasqit, "By the Temple worship! I come from Damascus, and there is a place there that is called Hadrach."
    F.   R. Nehemiah said, "This refers to the royal Messiah, who is both sharp and tender [the first syllable of Hadrach may be read as

sharp, the second as tender], sharp to the nations of the world and tender to Israel.

G.   "Another explanation [of Hadrach]: Hadrach refers to the royal Messiah, for he is destined to lead [a word that uses the same consonants as the word Hadrach] all the nations of the world in repentance before the Holy One, blessed be He."

6. A.   [Supply "The burden of the word of the Lord. In the land of Hadrach and in Damascus shall be his resting place" (Zech. 9:1):]

    B.   Is Damascus really his resting place?

    C.   Is his resting place not solely in the house of the sanctuary: "This is my resting place forever" (Ps. 132:14)?

    D.   He [Yohanan, resuming 4.B] said to him, "Jerusalem is destined to spread out in all directions until it reaches the gate of Damascus, and the exiles will come and take up resting places under it, so fulfilling the following verse of Scripture: 'And Damascus shall be his resting place,' that is, as far as Damascus shall be his resting place."

    E.   How does R. Yohanan deal with the verse, "And the city shall be built upon her own mound" (Jer. 30:18)?

    F.   [He replied,] "It is like a fig tree that is narrow below and broad above. So Jerusalem is destined to spread out in all directions until it reaches the gate of Damascus, and the exiles will come and take up resting places under it, so fulfilling the following verse of Scripture: 'For you shall spread abroad to the right and to the left' (Isa. 54:3)."

    G.   That serves for length, what about breadth?

    H.   "From the tower of Hananel to the king's winepresses" (Zech. 14:10).

    I.   R. Zakkai the Elder said, [Simon, verbatim:] "Up to the pits of Ripa,"

    J.   "up to the winepresses that the King of kings of kings, the Holy One, blessed be He, pressed."

    K.   That serves for length and breadth, what about height?

    L.   "And the side chambers were broader as they wound about higher and higher" (Ezek. 41:7).

7. A.   It has been taught on Tannaite authority:

    B.   Jerusalem is destined to expand and rise until it touches the throne of glory,

    C.   until it says, "The place is too narrow for me, give me a place that I may dwell" (Isa. 49:20).

8. A.   R. Yosé b. R. Jeremiah said, "Still we have not learned the glory of Jerusalem.

    B.   "Whence do you learn its glory?

    C.   "From its walls: 'For I, says the Lord, will be to her a wall of fire round about' (Zech. 2:9)."

The exposition is consistent in focusing upon Jerusalem; God's praise now expresses his love for the holy city and sanctuary. No. 1 somewhat obviously spells out the relevance of the metaphor. Nos. 2, 3 then explain why Lebanon refers to Jerusalem, a set-piece proof. Nos. 4ff. then work out the reference to Jerusalem, expressing the notion that

Jerusalem will reach Damascus, which the metaphor suggests. Once Zech. 9:1 is introduced, we work on that verse, so Nos. 5, 6; the remainder then expands on the theme.

94

Song of Songs Rabbah to Song of Songs 7:5

7:5   *Your head crowns you like Carmel, and your flowing locks are like purple; a king is held captive in the tresses.*

XCIV:i

1. A.   "Your head crowns you like Carmel:"
   B.   Said the Holy One, blessed be He, to Israel, "'Your head crowns you like Carmel:' the poor [a word that uses the same consonants as head] are as precious to me as Elijah, who went up on the Carmel: 'And Elijah went up to the top of Carmel...and put his face between his knees' (1 Kgs. 18:42)."

2. A.   [Supply "And Elijah went up to the top of Carmel...and put his face between his knees'"(1 Kgs. 18:42):"]
   B.   Why did he put his face between his knees?
   C.   He said before the Holy One, blessed be He, "We do not have the merit. So just look upon the circumcision."

3. A.   "and your flowing locks are like purple:"
   B.   Said the Holy One, blessed be He, "The impoverished [the words for flowing locks and for impoverished share the same consonants] and the poor who are in Israel are as precious to me as David."
   C.   Of him it is said, "And he who stumbles among them at that day shall be like David" (Zech. 12:8).
   D.   Some say [in line with the verse, "are like purple"], "...like Daniel."
   E.   Of him it is said, "They clothed Daniel with purple" (Dan. 5:29).

4. A.   "a king is held captive in the tresses:"
   B.   "A king:" this refers to the King of kings of kings, the Holy One, blessed be He,
   C.   of whom it is written, "The Lord reigns, he is clothed in majesty" (Ps. 93:1).

5. A.   "is held captive in the tresses:"
   B.   For he bound himself by an oath that he would bring his Presence to dwell within Israel,

C.   among the swift messengers [a word that shares the consonants of tresses] of our father, Jacob.

D.   On account of whose merit?

E.   R. Abba b. R. Kahana and R. Levi:

F.   One said, "On account of the merit of our father, Abraham: 'And Abraham ran to the herd' (Gen. 18:7)."

G.   The other said, "On account of the merit of our father, Jacob: 'And he set the rods...in the gutters' [the words for gutters and tresses share the same consonants] (Gen. 30:38)."

6. A.   [Supply: "a king is held captive in the tresses:"]

B.   Said R. Berekhiah, "'A king:' this refers to Moses: 'And he was king in Jeshurun' (Dt. 33:5)."

C.   "'is held captive in the tresses:' for the decree was made against him that he not enter the Land of Israel.

D.   "How come? Because of the streams [a word that shares the consonants of the word for tresses] of the waters of Meribah: 'These are the waters of Meribah' (Num. 20:13)."

7. A.   [Supply: "a king is held captive in the tresses:"

B.   Said R. Nehemiah, "'A king:' this refers to Moses: 'And he was king in Jeshurun' (Dt. 33:5)."

C.   "Said the Holy One, blessed be He, to Moses, 'I have appointed you king over Israel, and the policy of a king is to make decrees for others to carry out.

D.   "'So you will make decrees over Israel and they will carry out those decrees: 'Command the children of Israel' (Lev. 24:2)."

95

Song of Songs Rabbah to Song of Songs 7:6

7:6   *How fair and pleasant you are, O loved one, delectable maiden.*

1. A.   "How fair and pleasant you are:" [XV:i.1: "Behold, you are beautiful, my love; behold, you are beautiful]:"
    B.   "Behold you are beautiful" in religious deeds,
    C.   "Behold you are beautiful" in acts of grace,
    D.   "Behold you are beautiful" in carrying out religious obligations of commission,
    E.   "Behold you are beautiful" in carrying out religious obligations of omission,
    F.   "Behold you are beautiful" in carrying out the religious duties of the home, in separating priestly ration and tithes,
    G.   "Behold you are beautiful" in carrying out the religious duties of the field, gleanings, forgotten sheaves, the corner of the field, poor person's tithe, and declaring the field ownerless.
    H.   "Behold you are beautiful" in observing the taboo against mixed species.
    I.   "Behold you are beautiful" in providing a linen cloak with woolen show-fringes.
    J.   "Behold you are beautiful" in [keeping the rules governing] planting,
    K.   "Behold you are beautiful" in keeping the taboo on uncircumcised produce,
    L.   "Behold you are beautiful" in keeping the laws on produce in the fourth year after the planting of an orchard,
    M.   "Behold you are beautiful" in circumcision,
    N.   "Behold you are beautiful" in trimming the wound,
    O.   "Behold you are beautiful" in reciting the Prayer,
    P.   "Behold you are beautiful" in reciting the *Shema*,
    Q.   "Behold you are beautiful" in putting a *mezuzah* on the doorpost of your house,
    R.   "Behold you are beautiful" in wearing phylacteries,

S. "Behold you are beautiful" in building the tabernacle for the Festival of Tabernacles,

T. "Behold you are beautiful" in taking the palm branch and etrog on the Festival of Tabernacles,

U. "Behold you are beautiful" in repentance,

V. "Behold you are beautiful" in good deeds,

W. "Behold you are beautiful" in this world,

X. "Behold you are beautiful" in the world to come.

2. A. "O loved one, delectable maiden:"

B. This refers to the love of Abraham, who explained himself to the king of Sodom [for declining the kind of love offered to him by the king of Sodom]:

C. "And Abram said to the king of Sodom, I have lifted up my hand to the Lord God, Most High...that I will not take a thread nor a shoe latchet" (Gen. 14:22-23).

3. A. Another explanation of the verse, "O loved one, delectable maiden:"

B. This refers to the love of Daniel, who explained himself to Belshazzar:

C. "Let your gifts be for yourself and give your rewards to another" (Dan. 5:17).

4. A. [Supply: "Let your gifts be for yourself and give your rewards to another" (Dan. 5:17):]

B. [Since the words for rewards and head contain the same consonants,] R. Abba b. R. Kahana said, "It means 'head,' for there they call the governor by a word that contains the same letters as the word for rewards [Simon, p. 290, n. 4: so Daniel declined the offer of a governorship]."

C. [Since the words for rewards and robberies contain the same consonants,] R. Berekhiah said, "It means 'your robberies.'

D. "You are thieves, sons of thieves.

E. "There is a proverb that says, '[Take] from one who has received by inheritance, not from one who has received through theft.'"

No. 1 repeats the treatment of Song 1:15, and with good reason. Nos. 2, 3 then invoke the names of Abraham and Daniel as those who are particularly distinguished in their love for God and in being loved by God. The two are chosen because they stand for the same thing: declining gifts from pagan kings.

96

Song of Songs Rabbah to
Song of Songs 7:7

7:7   *You are stately as a palm tree, and your breasts are like its*
       clusters.

XCVI:i
1. A.   "You are stately as a palm tree:"
    B.   R. Hunia in the name of R. Dosa b. R. Tebet: "Two impulses to do
          evil did the Holy One, blessed be He, create in his world, the
          impulse to worship idols, and the impulse to fornicate. The
          impulse to worship idols has already been eliminated, but the
          impulse to fornicate still endures.
    C.   "Said the Holy One, blessed be He, 'Whoever can withstand the
          impulse to fornicate do I credit as though he had withstood them
          both.'"
    D.   Said R. Judah, "The matter may be compared to the case of a
          snake-charmer who had [two] snakes. He charmed the larger and
          left the smaller, saying, 'Whoever can withstand this one is
          certainly credited as though he had withstood them both.'
    E.   "So the Holy One, blessed be He, eliminated the impulse to
          worship idols but left the impulse to fornicate. He said, 'Whoever
          can withstand the impulse to fornicate do I credit as though he
          had withstood them both.'"
2. A.   When was the impulse to worship idols eliminated?
    B.   R. Benaiah said, "In the time of Mordecai and Esther."
    C.   Rabbis said, "It was in the time of Hananiah, Mishael, and
          Azariah."
    D.   Rabbis objected to the view of R. Benaiah, "And was it eliminated
          by the efforts of an individual?"
    E.   Objected R. Benaiah to rabbis, "And were Mordecai and Esther
          mere individuals?"
    F.   The following sustains the position of R. Benaiah:
    G.   Said R. Tanhuma, R. Miasha, and R. Jeremiah in the name of R.
          Samuel b. R. Kahana, "'Many lay in sackcloth and ashes' (Est. 4:3)
          – [so] the great majority of that generation were righteous."

H.   The following sustains the position of rabbis:

I.   R. Phineas and R. Hilqiah in the name of R. Samuel: "'And those of you who escape shall remember me among the nations where they were carried captives, how I broke their straying heart, which has departed from me' (Ex. 6:9).

J.   "'And those of you who escape:' this refers to Hananiah, Mishael, and Azariah, who were refugees from the fiery furnace.

K.   "What is written is not 'among the nations who carried captive there,' but 'among the nations where they were carried captive.' [Simon, p. 291, n. 4: so the passage refers to Hananiah. By saying 'they were carried captive,' the text implies that they were carried into captivity straight from Jerusalem, whereas if it referred to Mordecai and Esther, it would have to say, 'they carried them captive,' that is, from Babylon to Persia.]

L.   "Said the Holy One, blessed be He, to Israel, "'Ephraim shall say, What have I to do any more with idols" (Hos. 14:9). What have I to do any more with the inclination to worship idols. "As for me, I respond" (Hos. 14:9) – I lift up my voice to him. "And look on him" – have we not sung hymns before you?'

M.   "[God continues,] 'If so, you must conclude that I was the one who subdued the impulse to worship idols.'"

3. A.   [If there was no idolatry in the time of Mordecai and Esther,] then why did the Israelites fall into danger in the days of Haman?

B.   Rabbis and R. Simeon b. Yohai:

C.   Rabbis said, "It is because the Israelites [once again] were worshipping idols."

D.   R. Simeon said, "It is because they ate food cooked by gentiles."

E.   They said to him, "But is it not the fact that only the people of Susa, the capital, ate the banquet? That is in line with this verse: 'And when these days were fulfilled the king made a feast for all who were present in Susa' (Est. 1:5)."

F.   He said to them, "Are not all Israelites responsible for one another? 'And they shall stumble one upon the other' (Lev. 26:37) – each one for the sin of the other."

G.   He said to them, "If matters are in accord with your view, you have convicted all Israel of sin punishable by extermination: 'He who sacrifices to the gods shall be utterly destroyed' (Ex. 22:19)."

H.   They said to him, "Even so, they did not worship the idol sincerely: 'For he did not afflict from his heart' (Lam. 3:33) [Simon, p. 292, n. 4: he did not afflict them with all his heart because they had not engaged in idolatry wholeheartedly].

I.   "Nonetheless, 'he grieved the children of men' (Lam. 3:33) – he appointed in charge of them a harsh man, to try them, who is Nebuchadnezzar, and he went and added salt to their wound."

4. A.   R. Berekhiah in the name of R. Levi said, "In two passages the Israelites acted [inconsistently, and so dissimulated] with the Holy One, blessed be He.

B.   "At Sinai they acted with their mouths but did not act with their hearts [wholeheartedly]: 'But they beguiled him with their mouth and lied to him with their tongue. For their heart was not steadfast with him' (Ps. 78:36).

	C.	"In Babylon they acted with their hearts but not with their tongues: 'For he did not afflict from his heart.'
	D.	"Nonetheless, 'he grieved the children of men' (Lam. 3:33) – he appointed in charge of them a harsh man, 'an adversary, an enemy, even the wicked Haman' (Est. 7:5), and he went and added salt to their wound."
5.	A.	[Reverting to 3.Cff.:] In the view of rabbis, the Israelites worshipped idols in the time of Nebuchadnezzar, in the opinion of R. Simeon b. Yohai, the Israelites did not worship idols in the time of Nebuchadnezzar.
	B.	In the view of rabbis, the Israelites worshipped idols in the time of Nebuchadnezzar: how so?
	C.	He set up an idol and chose twenty-three from each nation, and twenty-three from the whole of Israel.
	D.	In the opinion of R. Simeon b. Yohai, the Israelites did not worship idols in the time of Nebuchadnezzar: how so?
	E.	He set up an idol and chose three from each nation, and three from the whole of Israel.
6.	A.	Hananiah, Mishael, and Azariah, who were the three from Israel, went and determined to resist and did not worship the idol.
	B.	They went to Daniel and said to him, "Our lord, Daniel, Nebuchadnezzar has set up an idol and chosen three from each nation, and we are the three chosen from the whole of Israel. What have you got to say to us? Shall we bow down to it or not?"
	C.	He said to them, "Lo, there is a prophet available to you. Go to him."
	D.	They went their way forthwith to Ezekiel. They spoke to him as they had spoken to Daniel: "Shall we bow down to it or not?"
	E.	He said to them, "I have indeed received the tradition from my lord, Isaiah: 'Hide yourself for a little moment, until the indignation is past' (Isa. 26:20). [Hide out.]"
	F.	They said to him "What do you want people to say, that all the nations bow down to this idol [since people will not realize that we did not participate and will assume that Israel too was represented]?"
	G.	He said to them, "What do you say?"
	H.	They said to him, "We want to give it an insult by being there and not bowing down to it. Then people will say, 'As to this idol, every nation bowed down to it except for Israel!'"
	I.	He said to them, "If matters are to be in accord with your view, wait until I take counsel with the Almighty: 'Certain of the elders of Israel came to inquire of the Lord and sat before me' (Ez. 20:1)."
	J.	Who were these? They were Hananiah, Mishael, and Azariah.
	K.	He said before the Holy One, blessed be He, "Lord of the world, Hananiah, Mishael, and Azariah seek to give their lives for the sanctification of your name. Will you stand by them or not?"
	L.	He said to him, "I shall not stand by them: 'Son of man, speak to the elders of Israel and say to them...have you come to inquire of me' (Ez. 20:3). You have come only after you have made me destroy my house and burn my temple and exile my children

	among the nations. And after that are you coming to seek me? 'As I live, I will not be sought out by you' (Ez. 20:3)."
M.	At that moment Ezekiel wept, lamenting and wailing, saying, "Is this the answer that is coming to them! Woe then for [the enemies of] Israel! The remnant of Judah has perished, for only these alone remain of Judah: 'Now among these were, of the children of Judah, Daniel, Hananiah, Mishael, and Azariah' (Dan. 1:6)!"
N.	And he went on weeping.
O.	When they came, they said to him, "What did the Holy One, blessed be He, say to you?"
P.	He said to them, "'I shall not stand by them.'"
Q.	They said to him, "Whether he stands by us or does not stand by us, we are going to give our lives for the sanctification of his name."
R.	You may know that that is the fact, for lo, before they had gone to see Ezekiel, what had they said to Nebuchadnezzar? "We have no need to answer you in this matter. There is our God whom we serve, who is able to deliver us" (Dan. 3:16).
S.	After they had gone to Ezekiel and had heard this reply, they said to Nebuchadnezzar, "But if not, be it known to you, O King" (Dan. 3:16), which is to say, "Whether he stands by us or does not stand by us, 'Be it known to you, O king, that we will not serve your gods nor worship the golden image which you have set up' (Dan. 3:16)."
T.	When they had departed from Ezekiel, the Holy One, blessed be He, appeared and said to him, "Ezekiel, do you really think that I am not going to stand by them? Of course I am going to stand by them: 'Thus says the Lord God, I will yet for this be inquired of by the house of Israel' (Ez. 36:37). But let them go along and don't say a thing to them. I will let them go on in their innocence: 'He who walks uprightly walks securely' (Prov. 10:9)."
U.	What did they do? They went and circulated among the crowds and said, "And if he does not deliver, be it known to you" (Dan. 3:17).
V.	That is in line with what people say in an oath: "By him who established the world on three pillars."
W.	Some say these are Abraham, Isaac, and Jacob, and some say, these are Hananiah, Mishael, and Azariah.
7. A.	"You are stately as a palm tree:"
B.	[Since the word for palm tree is the same as the name Tamar,] you are likened to Tamar:
C.	just as Tamar was condemned to death through burning but was not burned [Gen. 38:24], so these were condemned to death through burning but were not burned up.
8. A.	What shape did the fire take for them?
B.	R. Eleazar and R. Samuel b. R. Nehemiah:
C.	R. Eleazar said, "It became tent [round about them]."
D.	R. Samuel b. R. Nehemiah said, "It become like a blaze without heat."

What in the base verse triggers a reference to unchastity I do not know, but to the compilers, there must have been some provocation, since the entire autonomous composition, which is continuous on its theme and a strong, well-crafted assembly, spins out its tale from that one reference. But there is no reason to be mystified concerning why this material has been parachuted down here, since the concluding item – Nos. 7-8 – explains why the compilers inserted the entire composite. The continuous character of the composite shows, of course, that it was whole and complete prior to insertion in this passage; the (possibly relevant) part ends with the allusion to Hananiah, Mishael, and Azariah. The rest is simply tacked on. No. 8 follows Simon, and his note, p. 295, n. 2; the translations are mere guesses based on the information given there. It is hard for me to point to a less successful treatment of any verse in this ordinarily exquisite compilation.

97

Song of Songs Rabbah to Song of Songs 7:8

7:8   *I say I will climb the palm tree and lay hold of its branches.*
O, may your breasts be like clusters of the vine, and the scent of
your breath like apples.

XCVII:i

1. A.   "I say I will climb the palm tree:"
   B.   "I said that I will be exalted by every nation, but I am exalted only by you."
2. A.   "and lay hold of its branches:"
   B.   "by its shoots.
   C.   "When a palm tree produces nothing, it still produces no fewer than three shoots."
3. A.   [Supply: "and lay hold of its branches:"]
   B.   Abun b. Hasdai said, "In our locale people call shoots [by the same word as is used here]."
4. A.   [Continuing 1.B:] "The sense of the verse is in line with the usage in the following verse, 'Then these men were bound in their cloaks' (Dan. 3:21). [Israel is the only one prepared to exalt God.] [Simon, p. 295, n. 5: "These men" but no others were prepared to sanctify God's name at the risk of their lives.]
5. A.   [Supply: "Then these men were bound in their cloaks" (Dan. 3:21):]
   B.   [As to the meaning of the word for cloaks,] R. Yudan and R. Huna:
   C.   R. Yudan said, "It means, 'In their garments.'"
   D.   R. Huna said, "It means, 'in their royal garments.'"
6. A.   [Supply: "Then these men were bound in their cloaks" (Dan. 3:21):]
   B.   Said R. Abedimi of Haifa, "Three miracles were done on that day:
   C.   "The furnace [originally dug into the ground] rose to the surface; the furnace was split open; and the four monarchies were burned up."
   D.   [There were three further miracles:] Nebuchadnezzar was half-burned.
   E.   The wind blew down the idol.
   F.   Ezekiel resurrected the dead in the valley of Dura.

7. A.   How on the basis of Scripture do we know that the furnace rose to the surface?

    B.   Said R. Isaac, "On the basis of this verse: 'Then Nebuchadnezzar the king was alarmed and rose up in haste; he spoke and said, "Lo, I see four men loose, walking in the midst of the fire...and the appearance of the fourth is like a son of God"' (Dan. 3:24-5)." [Simon, p. 296, n. 1: This shows that the furnace was visible and must therefore have been on the level.]

8. A.   [Supply: "Then Nebuchadnezzar the king was alarmed and rose up in haste; he spoke and said, 'Lo, I see four men loose, walking in the midst of the fire...and the appearance of the fourth is like a son of God'" (Dan. 3:24-5):]

    B.   R. Phineas in the name of R. Reuben said, "At that moment the angel Michael came down and slapped his mouth.

    C.   "He said to him, 'Wicked man! foul mouth! does He have a son! Retract and take back your words.'

    D.   "'Nebuchadnezzar spoke and said, "Blessed be the God of Shadrach [who sent his angel and delivered his servants who trusted in him]"' (Dan. 3:28).

    E.   "What is written here is not 'who sent his son,' but 'who sent his angel and delivered his servants who trusted in him.' [That shows he retracted]."

    F.   Said R. Reuben, "The coins were his own [Simon, p. 296, n. 2: he had to eat his words]."

9. A.   How on the basis of Scripture do we know that the furnace was split open?

    B.   "Then Nebuchadnezzar came near to the mouth of the burning fiery furnace; he spoke and said, Shadrach, Meshach, and Abednego, you servants of God most high" (Dan. 3:26).

    C.   What follows is not, "break through and come out," but simply, "come out and come here."

    D.   That shows the furnace was split open.

10. A.   How do we know that the four monarchies were burned up?

    B.   Said R. Isaac, "For it is written, 'King Nebuchadnezzar then sent word to gather the satraps, prefects, governors, counselors, treasurers, judges, officers, and all the provincial officials to attend the dedication of the statue that King Nebuchadnezzar had set up' (Dan. 3:2).

    C.   "[The text proceeds to translate the Aramaic of each of these words. Following Simon verbatim:] the *adargazrayya* are governors, the *gedabrayya* are generals, the *detabrayya* are counsellors; they are called *detabrayya* because they pervert [a word that uses the same consonants] the law; *tiftaye* are pimps; why are they called *tiftaye*? Because they incite to lewdness [and the words for incite and pimp use the same consonants].

    D.   "I know only about these. On what basis shall I encompass also his captains, local authorities, and state officials? Scripture states, 'and all the provincial officials.'

    E.   "I know that these were present only when they went down into the furnace. How do I know the state of affairs when they came up out of it?

F.   "'The satraps, the prefects, the governors, and the royal companions gathered around to look at those men, on whose bodies the fire had had no effect, the hair of whose heads and not been singed, whose shirts looked no different, to whom not even the odor of fire clung' (Dan. 3:27)."

11. A.   [Supply: "The satraps, the prefects, the governors, and the royal companions gathered around:"]

B.   As to the word translated satraps,

C.   R. Aha and rabbis:

D.   R. Aha said, "This refers to the magistrates, who are called by that word because they are suspect of perverting judgment in any direction they choose [the words for suspect and pervert judgment in any direction sharing the consonants of the word for satraps]."

E.   Rabbis say, "It is because they [Simon:] are show respect to persons in perverting justice."

12. A.   [Supply: "The satraps, the prefects, the governors, and the royal companions gathered around:"]

B.   The word translated prefects means counsellors.

C.   The word translated governors means treasury officials.

D.   The royal companions are the elders and astrologers.

13. A.   [Resuming from 9.F:] "'[The satraps, the prefects, the governors, and the royal companions gathered around] to look at those men:'

B.   "[Thus (Simon, p. 297, n. 2) four of those mentioned in the earlier verse are absent in the later one; hence they were burned.]

14. A.   How on the basis of Scripture do we know that Nebuchadnezzar was half-burned?

B.   Said R. Isaac, "That is shown by the fact that it was with his own mouth that he said, 'It has seemed good to me to declare the signs and wonders that God Most High has done toward me' (Dan. 3:32).

C.   "'has done toward me:' that is, on my own body."

15. A.   How on the basis of Scripture do we know that the wind blew down the idol?

B.   Said R. Isaac, "It is on the basis of the following verse: 'Bel bows down, Nebo stooped' (Isa. 46:1)."

16. A.   How on the basis of Scripture do we know that Ezekiel resurrected the dead in the valley of Dura?

B.   Said R. Isaac, "'Come from the four winds, O breath' (Ez. 37:9)."

17. A.   Said R. Phineas, "That same wind that blew down the idol is the wind that resurrected the dead."

B.   Said R. Eleazar, "That day was the Sabbath that coincided with the Day of Atonement."

18. A.   [Supply: "Bel bows down, Nebo stoops; their idols are upon the beasts and upon the cattle" (Isa. 46:1):] And rabbis say, "Nebuchadnezzar was trying to inveigle Daniel, saying to him, 'Do you not have to bow down to the idol, which is strong and substantial?'

B.   "He [further] said to him, 'See what it can do, and you of your own volition will bow down to it.'

C.   "What did that wicked man do? He took the plate of the high priest [worn on the forehead, Ex. 28:36] and put it into its mouth, and he brought together a variety of musicians, who sang praises to it, and the idol responded, 'I am the Lord your God' (Ex. 20:1).

D.   "When Daniel saw this, he said to him, 'Won't you give me permission to go up and kiss this idol of yours on its mouth?'

E.   "He said to him, 'Why on the mouth?'

F.   "He said to him, 'Because it speaks so nicely.'

G.   "So he gave him permission and he went up.

H.   "As he went up, he imposed an oath on the plate, saying to it, 'I am a mortal and the messenger of the Holy One, blessed be He, am I. So be careful that the Name of Heaven not be profaned through you. I decree upon you that you will come after me.'

I.   "He came to kiss the idol on the mouth and removed what the idol had swallowed from the midst of the idol's mouth.

J.   "When he got down, the diverse musicians got together and sang the praises of the idol, but it did not respond.

K.   "At that moment the wind blew the statue down.

L.   "When the nations of the world saw the wonders and acts of might that the Holy One, blessed be He, had done with Hananiah and his companions, they took their idols and smashed them and turned them into bells, which they hung on their dogs and asses.

M.   "When they tinkled, they said, 'Do you now see what we used to worship?'

N.   "This serves to fulfil this verse: 'Bel bows down, Nebo stoops; their idols are upon the beasts and upon the cattle' (Isa. 46:1)."

19. A.   "O, may your breasts be like clusters of the vine:"

B.   This refers to Perez and Zerach [the sons of Tamar, born after their mother had been condemned to be burned].

C.   Just as a decree of burning was made against Perez and Zerach but they were not burned to death,

D.   so against these a decree of burning was issued but they were not burned.

20. A.   "and the scent of your breath like apples:"

B.   Said R. Eleazar, "Now it is said of them, 'to whom not even the odor of fire clung' (Dan. 3:27),

C.   "and now you say, 'and the scent of your breath like apples'?

D.   "What did their odor resemble? It was like apples."

The inclusion of this massive composition on the events in the time of Daniel is for the same reason as in the earlier chapter, namely, the comparison of Israel to the palm tree, hence Tamar; then the rest follows, now by the route of No. 19. No. 1 is a fine prologue, since it prepares us for an essay on how only Israel, among all the nations, exalted God, but through Israel, all the nations would come to do the same, which of course is the goal of the composite, even if not of all of the components thereof. The "three shoots" of course should be the patriarchs; this is not made explicit; perhaps now the intent is to the three who went down into the furnace. No. 3 is a minor gloss; No. 4

resumes where No. 2 has left off; No. 5 again glosses. No. 6 then prepares the way for everything to follow. 6.B should give us six, not three miracles, and that is how Simon renders it; but the printed text before me has a G, which can only give me three. The key components, bypassing the secondary clarifications, then are at Nos. 7, 9, 10, 14, 15, 16, then 19-20. Even though the composite looks somewhat prolix, a second glance shows that it is quite neatly constructed.

98

Song of Songs Rabbah to
Song of Songs 7:9

7:9   *and your kisses like the best wine that goes down smoothly,*
gliding over lips and teeth.

1. A.   "and your kisses like the best wine:"

     B.   Said R. Yohanan, "At that moment, the Holy One, blessed be He, summoned all of the ministering angels and said to them, 'Go down and kiss the lips of the fathers of these.

     C.   "'For just as the one had done mighty deeds before me through fire, so their children did mighty deeds before me through fire.'"

2   A.   [Supply: "that goes down smoothly, gliding over lips and teeth:"]

     B.   R. Azariah in the name of R. Judah b. R. Simon: "At that moment the Holy One, blessed be He, summoned all of the ministering angels and said to them, 'Go down and kiss the lips of these men.

     C.   "'For if these had not accepted my Torah and my dominion at Sinai, I should have been made into an adversary [the words for go down smoothly and adversary sharing the same consonants] with those who sleep in the cave of Machpelah [as it is said, 'that goes down smoothly, gliding over lips and teeth,'] (for the words for asleep and teeth share the same consonants)."

3. A.   "that goes down smoothly, gliding over lips and teeth:"

     B.   [Since the words for asleep and teeth share the same consonants,] said R. Yohanan b. Torta, "Even though one is dead, his lips murmur in the grave.

     C.   "On what basis in Scripture is that statement made? 'gliding over lips and teeth.'"

     D.   Samuel said, "They are like [Simon:] a mass of heated grapes which ooze of themselves."

     E.   R. Hanina b. R. Papa and R. Simon:

     F.   One said, "It is like drinking spiced wine."

     G.   The other said, "It is like drinking old wine; even after drinking, the taste and scent linger."

While Nos. 1, 2 match, since both of them work on the play between "sleeping" and "teeth," invoking, moreover, the now well-established metaphorization of Daniel and his companions by the Song's verse. The interest now is in regaining the patriarchs and Sinai, the principal goals of all discourse when God is speaking of Israel. No. 3 is tacked on because of its relevance to sleeping in the grave, though it would not have struck me as absolutely requiring inclusion here.

99

Song of Songs Rabbah to Song of Songs 7:10

7:10   *I am my beloved's, and his desire is for me.*

XCIX:i

1. A.   "I am my beloved's, and his desire is for me:"
    B.   There are three yearnings:
    C.   The yearning of Israel is only for their Father who is in heaven, as it is said, "I am my beloved's, and his desire is for me."
    D.   The yearning of a woman is only for her husband: "And your desire shall be for your husband" (Gen. 3:16).
    E.   The yearning of the Evil Impulse is only for Cain and his ilk: "To you is its desire" (Gen. 4:7).
    F.   R. Joshua in the name of R. Aha: "The yearning of rain is only for the earth: 'You have remembered the earth and made her desired, greatly enriching her' (Ps. 65:10).
    G.   "If you have merit, the rains will enrich it, but if not, they will tithe it [the words for enrich and tithe differ by a single letter], for it will produce for you one part for ten of seed."

2. A.   Another reading of "I am my beloved's, and his desire is for me:"
    B.   "We are faint. Even though we are faint, we look forward and hope for the salvation of the Holy One, blessed be He, every single day, and we declare the unity of his name two times a day, saying, 'Hear Israel, the Lord our God, the Lord is one' (Dt. 65:4)."

Simon explains No. 2 as a play on the word "his desire," the letters of which are made to yield "weak" and "hope." No. 1 is an autonomous composition, not made to serve our base verse; No. 2 is possible only as an amplification of the base verse.

100

Song of Songs Rabbah to Song of Songs 7:11

7:11   *Come my beloved, let us go forth into the fields, and lodge in the villages...*

C:i
1. A.   "Come my beloved, let us go forth into the fields:"
   - B.   The Holy Spirit cries out, saying, "Let us go forth and walk about in the courts of the world.
   - C.   "and lodge in the villages:"
   - D.   [Since the word for village and the word for deny share the same consonants, the meaning is,] "among those who deny him."
   - E.   This refers to the cities of the nations of the world who deny the Holy One, blessed be He.
   - F.   Said R. Abba b. R. Kahana, "Even so, it is only transient."

The Holy Spirit continues to address Israel, now moving forward with the theme of gentile infidelity and Israel's loyalty.

101

Song of Songs Rabbah to Song of Songs 7:12

7:12　　*let us go out early to the vineyards, and see whether the vines have budded, whether the grape blossoms have opened and the pomegranates are in bloom. There I will give you my love.*

C:i
1. A.　"let us go out early to the vineyards:"
   B.　This refers to Israel: "For the house of Israel is the vineyard of the Lord of hosts" (Isa. 5:7).
   C.　"and see whether the vines have budded:"
   D.　This refers to the recitation of the *Shema*.
   E.　"whether the grape blossoms have opened:"
   F.　This refers to synagogues and houses of study.
   G.　"and the pomegranates are in bloom:"
   H.　This refers to the children occupied in Torah study.
   I.　"There I will give you my love:"
   J.　"There I shall give righteous men and women, prophetic men and women, who have stood before me."

This is a fixed list, moving from Israel reciting the *Shema* to Israel studying the Torah to the result, which is righteousness and prophecy.

102

Song of Songs Rabbah to Song of Songs 7:13

7:13   *The mandrakes give forth fragrance, and over our doors are all choice fruits, new as well as old, which I have laid up for you, O my beloved.*

CII:i

1.   A.   "The mandrakes give forth fragrance:"
          B.   This speaks of the Israelite youths who have not yet tasted the flavor of sin.
2.   A.   "and over our doors are all choice fruits:"
          B.   This refers to the Israelite maidens who cleave to their husbands and know no other man.
3.   A.   Another matter: "The mandrakes give forth fragrance:"
          B.   R. Yudan and R. Levi:
          C.   [Genesis Rabbah LXXII:V.3:] R. Yudan said, "Come and take note of how precious are mandrakes before the One who spoke and brought the world into being,
          D.   "for it was on account of the mandrakes that two great tribes arose in Israel, Issachar and Zebulun.
          E.   "For it is said, 'And Jacob came from the field' (Gen. 30:16)."
4.   A.   [Genesis Rabbah LXXII:III. 3:] R. Berekhiah said R. Eleazar and R. Samuel bar Nahman [discussed matters as follows]:
          B.   R. Eleazar said, "This one lost out and that one lost out, this one profited and that one profited. Leah lost the mandrakes and profited by getting the tribes [that were born of the transaction to her] and lost the right of burial [with Jacob in Machpelah]. Rachel benefited by getting the mandrakes, and she lost out on the tribes and lost the right of burial."
          C.   R. Samuel bar Nahman said, "This one lost out and that one lost out, this one profited and that one profited. Leah lost out on the mandrakes and benefited by getting the tribes as well as burial with Jacob. Rachel gained the mandrakes but won the birthright, even while she lost out on the tribes [Gen. R.: as well as burial with Jacob]."

5. A.   [Reverting to 3A-E:] Said R. Levi, "'The Lord showed me, and behold two baskets of figs...one basket had very good figs' (Jer. 24:1) – this speaks of the captivity of Jeconiah.

    B.   "'The other basket had very bad figs' (Jer. 24:1) – this refers to the captivity of Zedekiah.

    C.   "Now [to explain the difference,] should you wish to maintain that the exile of Jeconiah repented its sins, while the exile of Zedekiah did not repent its sins, Scripture states, 'and over our doors are all choice fruits.'

    D.   "This means that both mandrakes, the good and the bad, gave forth fragrance."

6. A.   "and over our doors are all choice fruits [supply: new as well as old, which I have laid up for you, O my beloved]:"

    B.   Members of the household of R. Shila and rabbis:

    C.   Members of the household of R. Shila said, "The matter may be compared to the case of a virtuous woman, to whom her husband left sparse possessions and little money for expenses [when he went overseas]. When her husband came back, she said to him, 'Remember what you left me, and see what I have collected for you and what I have also added for you beyond that!'"

    D.   And rabbis say, "The matter may be compared to a king who had an orchard, which he gave to a tenant-farmer. What did the tenant-farmer do? He filled baskets of figs from the produce of the orchard and put them at the gate of the orchard. Now when the king passed by and saw all this increase, he said, 'All this increase is at the doorway of the orchard – then in the orchard how much the more so!'

    E.   "So take the case of the earlier generations, the men of the great assemble, Hillel and Shammai, and Rabban Gamaliel the Elder. Then the latter generations, R. Yohanan b. Zakkai, R. Eliezer and R. Joshua, R. Meir and R. Aqiba and their disciples – how much the more so!

    F.   "And in their regard Scripture says, 'new as well as old, which I have laid up for you, O my beloved.'"

7. A.   "new as well as old, which I have laid up for you, O my beloved:"

    B.   Said R. Abba b. R. Kahana, "Said the Holy One, blessed be He, to Israel, 'You save things up for me, and I save things up for me.

    C.   "'You save things up through religious duties and good deeds, and I save things up for you in treasuries overflowing with more than all the good things that are in the world.'"

    D.   Said R. Abba b. R. Kahana b. R. Yudan, "But his are much greater than ours: 'O how abundant is your goodness, which you have laid up for those who fear you, which you have wrought for those who take their refuge in you' (Ps. 31:20)."

The exposition still has God speaking of Israel, now praising the virtuous youth, Nos. 1, 2. No. 3 then focuses elsewhere and does not deal with our verse in its context; the theme of mandrakes takes over, through No. 4. No. 5 reverts to our verse, but again with an interest in its evidence for a proposition important elsewhere. My sense is that the materials of No. 6 serve not 6.A but the next clause, since I see no clear relevance between Shila's parable and the prooftext about choice fruits over the door, but the rabbis' entry does require the base verse. Then the joining of the two entries, C and D, seems to me rather odd, and I cannot say I have a clear notion of what prompted someone to link the two parables. If, however, we give C the second part of the verse, that is, "new as well as old," then the whole fits quite well. So the only confusion rests in not citing the whole of the verse at A, since the two parables treat the second clause. No. 7 seems to me routine. So only at the outset do we stand within the rhythm and flow of the Song itself.

Part Eight
PARASHAH EIGHT

Song of Songs - Chapter Eight

8:1   *O that you were like a brother to me,*
that nursed at my mother's breast!
If I met you outside, I would kiss you,
and none would despise me.

8:2   *I would lead you and bring you*
into the house of my mother,
and into the chamber of her that conceived me.
I would give you spiced wine to drink,
the juice of my pomegranates.

8:3   *O that his left hand were under my head,*
and that his right hand embraced me!

8:4   *I adjure you, O daughters of Jerusalem,*
that you not stir up nor awaken love
until it please.

8:5   *Who is that coming up from the wilderness,*
leaning upon her beloved?
Under the apple tree I awakened you.
There your mother was in travail with you,
there she who bore you was in travail.

8:6   *Set me as a seal upon your heart,*
as a seal upon your arm;
for love is strong as death,
jealousy is cruel as the grave.
Its flashes are flashes of fire,
a most vehement flame.

8:7   *Many waters cannot quench love,*
neither can floods drown it.
If a man offered for love
all the wealth of his house,
it would be utterly scorned.

8:8   *We have a little sister,*
and she has no breasts.

> *What shall we do for our sister,*
> *on the day when she is spoken for?*

8:9 *If she is a wall,*
> *we will build upon her a battlement of silver;*
> *but if she is a door,*
> *we will enclose her with boards of cedar.*

8:10 *I was a wall,*
> *and my breasts were like towers;*
> *then I was in his eyes*
> *as one who brings peace.*

8:11 *Solomon had a vineyard at Baal hamon;*
> *he let out the vineyard to keepers;*
> *each one was to bring for its fruit a thousand pieces of silver.*

8:12 *My vineyard, my very own, is for myself;*
> *you, O Solomon, may have the thousand,*
> *and the keepers of the fruit two hundred.*

8:13 *O you who dwell in the gardens,*
> *my companions are listening for your voice;*
> *let me hear it.*

8:14 *Make haste, my beloved,*
> *and be like a gazelle*
> *or a young stag*
> *upon the mountains of spices.*

103

Song of Songs Rabbah to Song of Songs 8:1

8:1   *O that you were like a brother to me, that nursed at my mother's breast! If I met you outside, I would kiss you, and none would despise me.*

CIII:i

1. A. "O that you were like a brother to me:"
   B. Like what sort of brother?
   C. Like Cain with Abel? Cain killed Abel: "Cain rose up against his brother Abel and slew him" (Gen. 4:8).
   D. Like Ishmael with Isaac? Ishmael hated Isaac.
   E. Like Esau and Jacob?
   F. Lo, it is said, "And Esau hated Jacob" (Gen. 27:41).
   G. Like the brothers of Joseph with Joseph? They hated him: "And his brothers envied him" (Gen. 37:11).
   H. Then like what brother? It is one "that nursed at my mother's breast," namely, Joseph with Benjamin, who loved him with all his heart" "And when Joseph saw Benjamin with them" (Gen. 43:16).

2. A. "If I met you outside, I would kiss you:"
   B. "outside:" this refers to the wilderness, which is outside the settled territory.
   C. "I would kiss you:"
   D. Through the two brothers who kissed one another, Moses and Aaron: "And he went and met him in the mountain of God and kissed him" (Ex. 4:27).

3. A. "and none would despise me:"
   B. Said R. Phineas, "There was the case of two brothers, one in Meron, the other in Gush Halab. A fire burned up the house of the one who was in Meron. His sister came from Gush Halab and began to hug and embrace and kiss him, saying to him, 'This [public embrace] does not make me despicable, because my brother was in great danger, from which he has been saved.'"

211

The comments now begin away from the Song as narrow-based exegesis: which brother is meant. But the reference point is consistent with the principal line of interpretation: Israel in the time of the patriarchs, Israel in Egypt, and that of course supplies the point of interest. The point of No. 3 is that the embrace of God and Israel – when God finds Israel in the wilderness – is not to be despised, because God will rejoice as a sister rejoices for her brother who has been saved from danger. Simon, p. 303, n. 1, has the emendation, "should this not make me glad," but then, in that context, I cannot say I understand the point of Phineas's parable. Such a proposed emendation is possible only if we read the parable out of the context of the base verse under discussion; but the reading in front of us uses the same image, namely, despise, for the same purpose, namely, under these conditions, public affection is praiseworthy; here is a case in which reading only line by line, as the received exegetes tend to do, makes it impossible to understand the point of the materials that are read line by line. Note that in the printed text, Parashah Eight begins with Song 8:2. I have kept to RSV's chapter divisions.

104

Song of Songs Rabbah to Song of Songs 8:2

8:2   *I would lead you and bring you into the house of my mother, and into the chamber of her that conceived me. I would give you spiced wine to drink, the juice of my pomegranates.*

CIV:I

1. A.   "I would lead you:"
   B.   "I would lead you from the creatures of the upper world to the creatures of the lower world."
   C.   "and bring you into the house of my mother:"
   D.   This refers to Sinai.
   E.   Said R. Berekhiah, "Then why call Sinai 'the house of my mother'? For from there the Israelites were transformed into a babe a day old [and utterly without sin]."

2. A.   "[reading the Hebrew for, 'and into the chamber of her that conceived me' as] 'that you might instruct me:'"
   B.   Religious obligations and good deeds.

3. A.   "I would give you spiced wine to drink:"
   B.   This refers to the major collections of Mishnah teachings, for instance, the Mishnah teachings attributed to R. Hiyya the Elder, and the Mishnah teachings attributed to R. Hoshaia, and those of Bar Qappara, and the Mishnah teachings of R. Aqiba.
   C.   "the juice of my pomegranates:"
   D.   This refers to the love, the taste of which is like a pomegranate's.'

4. A.   Another interpretation of the phrase, "I would give you spiced wine to drink:"
   B.   This refers to the Talmud, which is flavored with Mishnah teachings like spiced wine.
   C.   "the juice of my pomegranates:"
   D.   This refers to the priestly garments: "A golden bell and a pomegranate" (Ex. 28:34).

No. 1f. remains within the framework of the Song, identifying Sinai as the honeymoon of God and Israel. Nos. 3, 4 identify the life in

Torah study of the sages with the love that is expressed here, which also is consistent with the established motif.

105

Song of Songs Rabbah to Song of Songs 8:3

8:3   *O that his left hand were under my head, and that his right hand embraced me!*

Our compilation has nothing on this verse.

106

Song of Songs Rabbah to Song of Songs 8:4

8:4   *I adjure you, O daughters of Jerusalem, that you not stir up nor awaken love until it please.*

This verse is ignored, though its counterpart earlier is richly articulated.

107

Song of Songs Rabbah to Song of Songs 8:5

8:5   *Who is that coming up from the wilderness, leaning upon her beloved? Under the apple tree I awakened you. There your mother was in travail with you, there she who bore you was in travail.*

CVII:i

1.   A.   "Who is that coming up from the wilderness:"
     B.   Her ascent was from the wilderness,
     C.   Her descent was via the wilderness,
     D.   Her death was in the wilderness: "In this wilderness they shall be consumed and there shall they die" (Num. 14:35).
2.   A.   "leaning upon her beloved:"
     B.   Said R. Yohanan, "For she abandons chapters of the Torah and chapters of the law for the age to come."
3.   A.   "Under the apple tree I awakened you:"
     B.   Paltion of Rome interpreted and said, "Mount Sinai was uprooted and set in the highest point of heaven,
     C.   "and the Israelites were put underneath it:
     D.   "'And you came near and stood under the mountain' (Dt. 4:11).
     E.   "[In the printed text, this sentence follows 5.E, but clearly it belongs here:] "Said the Holy One, blessed be He, 'If you accept the authority of my Torah, well and good, and if not, lo, I shall dump this mountain on you and kill you.'"
4.   A.   Another interpretation of the statement, "Under the apple tree I awakened you:"
     B.   This refers to Sinai.
     C.   And why is Sinai compared to an apple tree?
     D.   For just as an apple tree produces fruit in the month of Sivan [May],
     E.   So the Torah was given in Sivan.
5.   A.   Another interpretation of the statement, "Under the apple tree I awakened you:"
     B.   Why not invoke the nut tree or any other tree?

217

C.   But in the case of all other trees, the usual way is to produce leaves first, then fruit.

D.   But the apple tree produces fruit first, then its leaves.

E.   So the Israelites gave priority to doing over hearing: "We shall do and we shall hear" (Ex. 24:7) [Simon, p. 304, n. 3: They promised unqualified obedience, even before they heard what God demanded of them].

6. A.   "There your mother was in travail with you, [there she who bore you was in travail]:"

B.   Did she really go into labor there?

C.   Said R. Berekhiah, "The matter may be compared to the case of someone who went into a dangerous place and was saved from the danger.

D.   "His friend met him and said to him, 'Did you go through that perilous passage? What perils you have escaped! Your mother really bore you there! How much anguish you have survived! It's as though you were reborn today!'"

7. A.   [Supply: "There your mother was in travail with you:"]

B.   Said R. Abba b. R. Kahana, "There she was in travail and there she was wounded [since the word for travail uses consonants that yield the word for wound].

C.   "She was in travail when she said, 'All that the Lord has spoken we will do and obey' (Ex. 24:7).

D.   "She was wounded when she said, 'These are your gods, O Israel' (Ex. 32:4)."

8. A.   [Supply: "There your mother was in travail with you:"]

B.   [There] her pledge was taken away [for the word for travail and the word for pledge use the same consonants].

C.   For R. Simeon b. Yohai taught on Tannaite authority, "The weapon that was given to the Israelites at Horeb had the Ineffable Name of God incised upon it. But when they sinned, it was taken away from them."

D.   R. Aibu and rabbis:

E.   R. Aibu said, "It peeled off on its own."

F.   And rabbis said, "An angel came down and peeled it off."

9. A.   [Reverting to 7.D:] Said R. Simeon b. Halafta, "Shame on the bride who is faithless even in her bridal bower."

B.   Said R. Yohanan, "They thereby lost the good counsel that had been given to them at Sinai: 'You have set at nought all my good counsel' (Prov. 12:5), and 'counsel' refers only to the Torah: 'Counsel is mine and sound wisdom' (Prov. 8:14)."

C.   R. Joshua of Sikhnin in the name of R. Levi: "Also in Horeb you made the Lord angry' (Dt. 9:8):

D.   "Said the Holy One, blessed be He, 'I came to give you a blessing and I found your [Simon:] palate hollow and unable to hold a blessing.'

E.   "For so Scripture says, 'And Moses saw that the people were licentious' (Ex. 32:25), and the Hebrew word for licentious yields the meaning of hollow, as in this usage: 'But you have hollowed out all my counsel' (Prov. 1:25)."

F.   [With reference to C:] R. Levi said, "You made the Holy One,
          blessed be He, as though he were mourning for you, for there are
          places where they call the house of mourning 'the house of anger'
          [and the words for 'anger' and 'house of anger' share the same
          consonants]."

The basic motif continues: God's and Israel's marriage in the
wilderness. No. 1 introduces the matter. The sense of No. 2 is hidden
from me; Simon, p. 304, n. 2, has "she leaves certain problems arising in
both to be cleared upon in the future. Possibly R. Yohanan meant that
the observance of certain sections, such as those on sacrifices, as well as
the institution of monarchy, had perforce to be left for the Messianic
era, when they would be restored." Nos. 3, 4 pose no problems, in line
with the familiar way of reading the metaphor. No. 5 moves to
another issue within the same metaphor: why this, not that? The
answer is successful. The sense of No. 6 is to enrich our grasp of what is
at stake. Nos. 7ff. then work on the word choice and its meaning for the
articulation of the metaphor. Nos. 7, 8 work well, but beyond that
point, the discussion tends to wander a bit.

108

Song of Songs Rabbah to Song of Songs 8:6

8:6   *Set me as a seal upon your heart, as a seal upon your arm; for love is strong as death, jealousy is cruel as the grave. Its flashes are flashes of fire, a most vehement flame.*

CVIII:i
1.   A.   "Set me as a seal [upon your heart]:"
       B.   Said R. Meir, "Said the Israelites before the Holy One, blessed be He, 'Lord of the world, what you have thought in your heart to do for us, do!'"
       C.   For said R. Yohanan in the name of R. Eliezer, son of R. Yosé the Galilean, "When the Israelites stood before Mount Sinai and said, 'We shall do and we shall obey' (Ex. 24:7), at that very moment the Holy One, blessed be He, summoned the angel of death and said to him, 'Even though I have appointed you as executioner and world-ruler over all my creations, you have no business to do with this nation in particular.'
       D.   "That is in line with this verse: 'And it came to pass, when you heard the voice out of the midst of the darkness' (Dt. 5: 20).
       E.   "But is there such a thing as darkness on high? And lo, it is written, 'And the light dwells with him' (Dan. 2:22).
       F.   "What then is the sense of 'out of the midst of the darkness' (Dt. 5: 20)?
       G.   "This refers to the angel of death, who is called darkness. [Simon, p. 306, n. 2: thus: 'and they heard the voice which was to free them from the darkness, from death'].
       H.   "And so Scripture states, 'And the tablets were the work of God and the writing was the writing of God, graven upon the tablets' (Ex. 32:16).
       I.   "Do not read the letters of the word as graven but as freedom [which uses the same consonants]."
2.   A.   [Supply: "And the tablets were the work of God and the writing was the writing of God, graven upon the tablets" (Ex. 32:16):]
       B.   R. Judah and R. Nehemiah and rabbis:

	C.	R. Judah says, "Freedom from the angel of death."
	D.	R. Nehemiah said, "Freedom from the kingdoms' [rule]."
	E.	Rabbis say, "Freedom from suffering."
3.	A.	Another interpretation of the phrase, "Set me as a seal upon your heart:"
	B.	R. Berekiah said, "This refers to the recitation of the *Shema:* 'And these things will be upon your heart' (Dt. 6:4).
	C.	"as a seal upon your arm:"
	D.	This refers to the phylacteries: "And you shall bind them for a sign upon your hand" (Dt. 6:8).
4.	A.	Said R. Meir, "'Set me as a seal upon your heart, as a seal upon your arm:'
	B.	"like Jehoichin."
5.	A.	For said R. Meir, "The Holy One, blessed be He, took an oath that he would take the kingdom of the house of David out of his hand: 'As I live, says the Lord, though Coniah son of Jehoiakim king of Judah were the signet upon my right hand, yet I would pluck you hence' (Jer. 22:24)."
	B.	Said R. Hanina b. R. Isaac, "'From there I should take away the dominion of the house of David.'"
6.	A.	Another explanation [of "yet I would pluck you hence" (Jer. 22:24)]:
	B.	What is written here is not "I will pluck you hence" but [Simon:] "I will repair you,"
	C.	meaning, "I will repair you through repentance."
	D.	"From the place from which I have taken you away, there will be your remedy."
7.	A.	Said R. Zeira, "I heard the report of R. Isaac's session, in which he expounded this matter [of repentance], but I do not know precisely what it is."
	B.	Said to him R. Aha Arikhah, "You may say, 'Write this man childless, a man who shall not prosper in his days' (Jer. 22:30),
	C.	"[meaning,] 'In his days he will not prosper, but in the days of his son he will prosper.'
	D.	"Thus: 'In that day says the Lord of hosts will I take you, O Zerubbabel, my servant, son of Shealtiel, says the Lord, and I will make you as a signet' (Hag. 2:23)."
8.	A.	R. Aha b. R. Abin b. R. Benjamin in the name of R. Aha b. R. Pappi said, "Great is the power of repentance, for it can annul a harsh decree and annul even the power of an oath.
	B.	"How do we know that it can annul a harsh decree?
	C.	"'Write this man childless, a man who shall not prosper in his days' (Jer. 22:30), and further, 'In that day says the Lord of hosts will I take you, O Zerubbabel, my servant, son of Shealtiel, says the Lord, and I will make you as a signet' (Hag. 2:23).
	D.	"How do we know that it can annul even the power of an oath?
	E.	"'As I live, says the Lord, though Coniah son of Jehoiakim king of Judah were the signet upon my right hand, yet I would pluck you hence' (Jer. 22:24), and yet, 'The sons of Jeconiah, the same is Assir Shealtiel, his son' (1 Chr. 3:17)."
9.	A.	[Supply: "The sons of Jeconiah, the same is Assir Shealtiel, his son" (1 Chr. 3:17):]

B. R. Tanhum b. R. Jeremiah said, "'Asir' [a word which uses the letters that yield imprisoned or enchained], because he was imprisoned in the jailhouse.

C. "'Shealtiel' [a word the letters of which can yield plant] for from him was [re]-planted the dominion of the house of David."

10. A. Another explanation of "Assir Shealtiel" (1 Chr. 3:17):

B. "Assir," for the Holy One bound [a word that uses the same letters] himself by an oath upon himself.

C. "Shealtiel," for he inquired [a word that uses the same letters] of the court that is on high and it released him from his vow.

11. A. Said R. Aibu, "Two matters did the Israelites ask from the Holy One, blessed be He, but they did not ask properly, so the prophets went and corrected them in their behalf.

B. "The Israelites said, 'And he shall come to us as the rain' (Hos. 6:3).

C. "Said the prophets to them, 'You did not ask properly. For rain may well be a mark of inconvenience for the world. Travelers are bothered by them, seafarers are bothered by them, roofers are bothered by them, vintners are bothered by them, porters at the threshing floor are bothered by them, someone who has a full cistern or a full vat is bothered by them, and yet you say, "he shall come to us as the rain" (Hos. 6:3)?'

D. "The prophets went and corrected what they had said in their behalf: 'I will be as the dew to Israel' (Hos. 14:6)."

E. "Furthermore, the Israelites said before the Holy One, blessed be He, 'Set me as a seal upon your heart, as a seal upon your arm.'"

F. "Said the prophets to them, 'You did not ask properly. For at times the heart is visible, and at times it is not visible, so then the seal will not be visible.'

G. "What then would be the proper way? "You shall also be a crown of beauty in the hand of the Lord"' (Isa. 62:3).

H. R. Simon b. Quzit said in the name of R. Levi, "Said to them the Holy One, blessed be He, 'Neither you nor your prophets have asked in a right and appropriate manner.

I. "'For, after all, a mortal king can go along and have the crown fall off his head, with the royal diadem upon it! What, then, would be the proper way? "Behold, I have graven you upon the palms of my hands, your walls are continually before me" (Isa. 49:16). Just as a man cannot forget the palms of his hands, so "These may forget, but I will not forget you" (Isa. 49:15).'"

The reference to "heart" proves a not-very-sturdy peg on which to hand C, God's promise that Israel will not suffer death. No. 2 pursues the same general theme. I cannot say I am so persuaded as the compiler that the bulk of No. 1 and all of No. 2 amplify Meir's statement; or that Meir's statement forms an appropriate point of departure for the extension of the base verse. No. 3 seems far more interested in the actualities of the metaphor. No. 4 provides yet another reference point for linking a sizable, already complete composition with our base verse. No. 5, bearing in its wake Nos. 6, 7, 8, 9, 10 – a pastiche of pertinent and merely agglutinated materials – then amplify this rather lame allusion. No. 11 then shows us another theory of compilation, and a more conventional one: we include a composition that has taken shape in its own terms and for its own interests, in which our base verse serves as a prooftext. It is not a brilliant conception of compilation, but it surely improves upon the mass that forms the middle of this rather run-on composite.

CVIII:ii

1. A. "for love is strong as death:"
   B. As strong as death is the love with which the Holy One, blessed be He, loves Israel: "I have loved you says the Lord" (Mal. 1:2).
   C. "jealousy is cruel as the grave:"
   D. That is when they make him jealous with their idolatry: "They roused him to jealousy with strange gods" (Dt. 32:16).
2. A. Another explanation of "for love is strong as death:"
   B. As strong as death is the love with which which Isaac loved Esau: "Now Isaac loved Esau" (Gen. 25:28).
   C. "jealousy is cruel as the grave:"
   D. The jealousy that Esau held against Jacob: "And Esau hated Jacob" (Gen. 27:41).
3. A. Another explanation of "for love is strong as death:"
   B. As strong as death is the love with which Jacob loved Joseph: "Now Israel loved Joseph more than all his children" (Gen. 37:3).
   C. "jealousy is cruel as the grave:"
   D. The jealousy that his brothers held against him: "And his brothers envied him" (Gen. 37:11).
4. A. Another explanation of "for love is strong as death:"
   B. As strong as death is the love with which Jonathan loved David: "And Jonathan loved him as his own soul" (1 Sam. 18:1).
   C. "jealousy is cruel as the grave:"
   D. The jealousy of Saul against David: "And Saul eyed David" (1 Sam. 18:9).
5. A. Another explanation of "for love is strong as death:"
   B. As strong as death is the love with which a man loves his wife: "Enjoy life with the wife whom you love" (Qoh. 9:9).
   C. "jealousy is cruel as the grave:"
   D. The jealousy that she causes in him and leads him to say to her, "Do not speak with such-and-so."
   E. If she goes and speaks with that man, forthwith: "The spirit of jealousy comes upon him and he is jealous on account of his wife" (Num. 5:14).
6. A. Another explanation of "for love is strong as death:"
   B. As strong as death is the love with which the generation that suffered the repression loved the Holy One, blessed be He: "No, but for your sake we are killed all day long" (Ps. 44:23).
   C. "jealousy is cruel as the grave:"
   D. The jealousy that the Holy One, blessed be He, will hold for Zion, that is a great zealousness: "Thus says the Lord, I am jealous for Zion with a great jealousy" (Zech. 1:14).

7. A.   "Its flashes are flashes of fire, a most vehement flame:"
    B.   R. Berekiah said, "Like the fire that is on high,
    C.   "that fire does not consume water, nor water, fire."

The exposition, Nos. 1-6, shows us a more satisfying way in which to put together and amplify a base verse. We are able to encompass a variety of topics, yet both formally and conceptually make a coherent statement. We contrast love and jealousy, favoring the one, denigrating the other. No. 1 does not prepare us for that contrast, since here God's love for Israel contrasts with the emotions that Israel provokes in God; yet the contrast is established, so the rest will follow. Nos. 2-5 (Isaac, Jacob, Esau; Jacob, Joseph, the brothers; Jonathan, David, Saul; man, wife, paramour), then, work in sets of three, and No. 6 reverts to No. 1's pattern. Aesthetically this must be deemed a perfect design, without a single false move. No. 7 is routine.

109

Song of Songs Rabbah to Song of Songs 8:7

8:7   *Many waters cannot quench love, neither can floods drown it. If a man offered for love all the wealth of his house, it would be utterly scorned.*

CIX:I

1. A.   "Many waters:"
    B.   This refers to the nations of the world: "Ah, the uproar of many peoples, that roar like the roaring of the seas" (Isa. 17:12).
    C.   "cannot quench love:"
    D.   The love with which the Holy One, blessed be He, loves Israel: "I have loved you, says the Lord" (Mal. 1:2).
    E.   "neither can floods drown it:"
    F.   This refers to the nations of the world: "In that day shall the Lord shave with a razor that is hired in the parts beyond the River...now therefore behold the Lord brings up upon them the waters of the River" (Isa. 7:20, 8:7).

2. A.   Another matter: "If a man offered for love all the wealth of his house:"
    B.   If all of the nations of the world should open their treasuries and give their money in exchange for a single item of the Torah,
    C.   it would not achieve atonement in their behalf ever.

3. A.   Another matter: "If a man offered for love all the wealth of his house:"
    B.   If all of the nations of the world should open their treasuries and give their money in exchange for the price of R. Aqiba and his fellows,
    C.   it would not achieve atonement in their behalf ever.

4. A.   "it would be utterly scorned:"
    B.   R. Yohanan was going up on foot from Tiberias to Sepphoris, and R. Hiyya b. R. Abba was attending to him. They came by a field. Said R. Yohanan, "That field belonged to me, but I sold it to pay the expenses of laboring in the Torah."

225

C.   They came by a vineyard. Said R. Yohanan, "That vineyard belonged to me, but I sold it to pay the expenses of laboring in the Torah."

D.   They came by an olive grove. Said R. Yohanan the same thing, ["That olive grove belonged to me, but I sold it to pay the expenses of laboring in the Torah."]

E.   Then R. Hiyya b. R. Abba began crying.

F.   He said to him, "How come you're crying?"

G.   He said to him, "I am crying because you have left nothing for your old age."

H.   He said to him, "Hiyya, my son, is what I have done such a light thing in your eyes? For I have sold something which is given for six days [of God's labor], for it is said, 'For in six days did the Lord make' (Ex. 20:11), while the Torah took forty days to be given: 'And he was there with the Lord for forty days' (Ex. 34:28); 'Then I abode in the mount forty days' (Dt. 9:9)."

I.   When R. Yohanan died, his generation recited in his regard this verse: "'If a man offered for love all the wealth of his house,' – that is, for the love with which R. Yohanan loved the Torah,

J.   "'it would be utterly scorned,' – [Simon, p. 310, n. 4: such love could not be assessed in money]."

5. A. When R. Oshaiah of Teriyyah died, they saw his bier floating upward in the air.

B.   His generation recited in his regard this verse: "'If a man offered for love all the wealth of his house,' – that is, for the love with which the Holy One, blessed be He, loved R. Oshaiah of Teriyyah,

C.   "'it would be utterly scorned.'"

The interpretation of our metaphor presents no surprises. We have God speaking of his love for Israel, Nos. 1, 2, 3ff. But the shift is at No. 3, where we move from Israel to sages, and then that accounts for the next initiative, the step from sages to sages' love for Torah, No. 4, with No. 5 the completion, God's love for the sage who loves the Torah. To see these five compositions as distinct from one another is easy; but to understand that the compiler has assembled them to make his point, which is the intense love that God has for Israel, through the Torah, realized in its sages, is to grasp how the compiler has expressed his deepest convictions through the words initially made up by others. I cannot find a better example of precisely what is accomplished by those who assembled Song of Songs Rabbah.

110

Song of Songs Rabbah to Song of Songs 8:8

8:8   *We have a little sister, and she has no breasts. What shall we do for our sister, on the day when she is spoken for?*

CX:i

1. A.   "We have a little sister:"

     B.   This refers to Israel.

     C.   R. Azariah in the name of R. Judah b. R. Simon: "All the angelic princes who watch over the nations of the world in the coming age are going to come and make the case against Israel before the Holy One, blessed be He, saying, 'Lord of the world, these have worshipped idols, and those have worshipped idols. These have fornicated and those have fornicated. These have shed blood and those have shed blood. How come these go down to Gehenna, while those do not go [to hell]?'

     D.   "The Holy One, blessed be He, will say to them, '"We have a little sister." Just as in the case of a child, whatever he does, people do not stop him – why? because he's a child, so in the case of however the Israelites soil themselves all the days of the year through their transgressions, when the Day of Atonement comes, it effects atonement in their behalf: "For on this day shall atonement be made for you" (Lev. 16:30).'"

2. A.   R. Berekhiah interpreted the verse to speak of our father, Abraham:

     B.   "'We have a little sister:' this refers to Abraham, as it is said, 'Abraham was one and he inherited the land' (Ezek. 33:24).

     C.   "[The sense is,] he stitched together all those who pass through the world before the Holy One, blessed be He [since the word for one and stitched together share the same consonants].'

     D.   Bar Qappara said, "He was like a man who stitches a tear."

     E.   [Continuing C:] "While he was still a child, he engaged in religious duties and good deeds.

F.   "'and she has no breasts:' he had not yet reached the age at which he was subject to the obligation of carrying out religious duties and good deeds.

G.   "'What shall we do for our sister, on the day when she is spoken for:' On the day on which the wicked Nimrod made a decree and told him to go down into the fiery furnace."

No. 1 prepares the way for No. 2. By itself it makes no sense to declare Israel exempt from punishment because it is immature. No. 2 then is continued in what follows. The entire treatment of Song of Songs 8:8 is continuous with 8:9, as we shall now see. Beyond Abraham, we shall have Sodom and Israel, Hananiah, Mishael, and Azariah, the exiles who returned from Babylon, and so on.

111

Song of Songs Rabbah to Song of Songs 8:9-8:10

[8:8   *We have a little sister, and she has no breasts. What shall we do for our sister, on the day when she is spoken for?] 8:9 If she is a wall, we will build upon her a battlement of silver; but if she is a door, we will enclose her with boards of cedar. 8:10 I was a wall, and my breasts were like towers; then I was in his eyes as one who brings peace.*

CXI:i
1. A.   [Continuing CX:i.2:] "If she is a wall, we will build upon her a battlement of silver:"
    B.   "If she is a wall:" this refers to Abraham.
    C.   Said the Holy One, blessed be He, "If he insists on his views like a firm wall,
    D.   "'we will build upon her a battlement of silver:' we shall save him and build him in the world.
    E.   "'but if she is a door:' if he is poor [a word that uses consonants that appear also in the word for door], impoverished of religious duties and [Simon:] sways to and fro in his conduct like a door,
    F.   "'we will enclose her with boards of cedar:' just as a drawing [a word that uses the same consonants as the word for enclose] lasts for only a brief hour, so I will stand over him for only a brief time. [Simon, p. 312, n. 2: In his own lifetime only, but his merit will not be so great that I should stand by his children for his sake.]"
    G.   Said Abraham before the Holy One, blessed be He, "'I was a wall:' and I shall be insistent upon my habit of doing good deeds like a firm wall.
    H.   "'and my breasts were like towers:' for I am destined to raise up parties and fellowships of righteous men in my model in your world."
    I.   "then I was in his eyes as one who brings peace:"
    J.   Said to him the Holy One, blessed be He, "Just as you descended into the fiery furnace, so I shall bring you out in peace: 'I am the

229

Lord who brought you out of the furnace of the Chaledeans' (Gen. 15:7)."

The first reading of the verse, which began in the preceding chapter, is fully worked out, with enormous care as to matching details, and the metaphor of the little sister has God praise Abraham. We proceed to a quite separate reading of the same metaphor. I see no interpolated material, only a sustained and well-crafted exposition of one thing in terms of something else, beautifully articulated.

CXI:ii

1. A. R. Yohanan interpreted the verses to speak of Sodom and of Israel:

    B. "'We have a little sister:' this refers to Sodom: 'And your elder sister is Samaria...and your younger sister...is Sodom' (Ez. 16:46).

    C. "'and she has no breasts:' for she has not sucked of the milk of religious duties and good deeds [by contrast to Abraham].

    D. "'What shall we do for our sister, on the day when she is spoken for:' on the day on which the heavenly court made the decree that she is to be burned in fire: 'Then the Lord caused to rain upon Sodom and upon Gomorrah brimstone and fire' (Gen. 19:24).

    E. "'If she is a wall, we will build upon her a battlement of silver:' this refers to Israel.

    F. "Said the Holy One, blessed be He, 'If they stand firm in their good deeds like a wall, "we will build upon them" and deliver them.'

    G. "'but if she is a door:' if they [Simon:] sway to and fro in their conduct like a door,

    H. "'we will enclose her with boards of cedar:' [God continues] 'just as a drawing lasts for only a brief hour, so I will stand over him for only a brief time.'

    I. "'I was a wall:' said the Israelites before the Holy One, blessed be He, 'Lord of the world, we are a wall, and we shall stand by the religious duties and good deeds [that we practice] as firm as a wall.'

    J. "'and my breasts were like towers:' 'for we are destined to raise up parties and fellowships of righteous men in my model in your world.'

    K. "'then I was in his eyes as one who brings peace:' why so? For all the nations of the world taunt Israel, saying to them, 'If so, why has he sent you into exile from his land, and why has he destroyed his sanctuary?'

    L. "And the Israelites reply to them, 'We are like a princess who went to celebrate in her father's house the [Simon:] first wedding anniversary after her marriage. [That is why we are in exile in Babylonia.]"

2. A. Another interpretation of "If she is a wall:"

    B. This refers to Hananiah, Mishael, and Azariah.

    C. Said the Holy One, blessed be He, "If they stand firm in their good deeds like a wall, 'we will build upon them' and deliver them.'

D.   "'but if she is a door:' if they sway to and fro in their conduct like a door,

E.   "'we will enclose her with boards of cedar:' [God continues] just as a drawing lasts for only a brief hour, so I will stand over them for only a brief time."

F.   "I was a wall:" said they before the Holy One, blessed be He, "[Lord of the world,] we are a wall, and we shall stand by the religious duties and good deeds [that we practice] as firm as a wall.

G.   "'and my breasts were like towers:' for we are destined to raise up parties and fellowships of righteous men in my model in your world."

H.   "then I was in his eyes as one who brings peace:"

I.   Said to them the Holy One, blessed be He, "Just as you have gone down into the fiery furnace in peace, so I shall bring you out of there in peace: 'Then Shadrach, Meshach, and Abednego came forth' (Dan. 3:26)."

We see now how carefully matched the treatments of the base verses are. The possibility of understanding 1.L, in particular, derives solely from the initial reading in terms of Abraham. And that seems to me the point of the exercise, thus far: to link Israel's exile to Babylonia to Abraham's initial origin. Not only so, but the link between Abraham in the fiery furnace and Shadrach, Meshach, and Abednego is explicit. That proves beyond a doubt the unity of the "another interpretation," and shows that the whole was planned as a single composition to express one fundamental and encompassing point. The third and final exposition, which completes the set, confirms that view.

CXI:iii

1. A.   Rabbis interpret the verses to speak of those who came up from the Exile:

B.   "'We have a little sister:' this refers to those who came up from the Exile.

C.   "'little:' because they were few in numbers.

D.   "'and she has no breasts:' this refers to the five matters in which the second house [Temple] was less than the first one:

E.   "[1] fire from above, [2] anointing oil, [3] the ark, [4] the Holy Spirit, and [5] access to the Urim and Thumim: 'And I will take pleasure in it and I will be glorified says the Lord' (Hag. 1:8), with the word for 'I will be glorified' written without the letter H, which stands for five.

F.   "'What shall we do for our sister, on the day when she is spoken for:' on the day on which Cyrus issues the decree, 'Whoever has crossed the Euphrates has crossed, but whoever has not crossed will not cross.'

G.   "'If she is a wall:' if the Israelites had gone up like a wall from Babylonia, the house of the sanctuary that they built at that time would not have been destroyed a second time [a sufficiently large population having been able to defend it]."

2. A.   R. Zeira went out to the market to buy things and said to the storekeeper, "Weigh carefully."

    B.   He said to him, "Why don't you get out of here, Babylonian, whose fathers destroyed the Temple!"

    C.   Then R. Zeira said, "Are my fathers not the same as that man's fathers?"

    D.   He went into the meeting house and heard R. Shila's voice in session, expounding, "'If she is a wall:' if the Israelites had gone up like a wall from Babylonia, the house of the sanctuary that they built at that time would not have been destroyed a second time."

    E.   He said, "Well did that ignoramus teach me."

3. A.   [Reverting to 1.G:] "'but if she is a door, we will enclose her with boards of cedar:' just as in the case of a drawing, if it is removed, still its traces are to be discerned,

    B.   "so even though the house of the sanctuary has been destroyed, the Israelites have not annulled their pilgrim festivals three times a year."

    C.   "I was a wall:"

    D.   Said R. Aibu, "Said the Holy One, blessed be He, 'I am going to make an advocate for Israel among the nations of the world.'

    E.   "And what is it? It is the echo: 'Except the Lord of hosts had left to us a very small remnant' (Isa. 1:9)."

4. A.   It has been taught on Tannaite authority:

    B.   Once the final prophets, Haggai, Zechariah, and Malachi had died, the Holy Spirit ceased from Israel.

    C.   Even so, they would make use of the echo.

5. A.   There was the case of sages voting in the upper room of the house of Gedia in Jericho. An echo came forth and said to them, "There is among you one man who is worthy of receiving the Holy Spirit, but his generation is not suitable for such to happen.

    B.   They set their eyes upon Hillel the Elder.

    C.   When he died, they said in his regard, "Woe for the modest one, woe for the pious one, the disciple of Ezra."

6. A.   There was another case, in which the Israelite sages took a vote, in the vineyard in Yavneh.

    B.   Now were they really *in* a vineyard! Rather, [they were like a vineyard, for] this was the Sanhedrin, that sat in rows and rows, lines and lines, like a well-ordered vineyard.

    C.   An echo came forth and said to them, "There is among you one man who is worthy of receiving the Holy Spirit, but his generation is not suitable for such to happen.

    D.   They set their eyes upon Samuel the Younger.

    E.   When he died, they said in his regard, "Woe for the modest one, woe for the pious one, the disciple of Hillel the Elder.

7. A.   Also: he said three things when he was dying: "Simeon and Ishmael are for the sword, the rest of his colleagues are destined to be killed, the rest of the people to be plundered, and great sufferings are going to come upon the world."

    B.   This he said in Aramaic.

8. A.   Also: for Judah b. Baba they ordained that when he died, they should say of him, "Woe for the modest one, woe for the pious one, the disciple of Samuel,"

B.   but the time was inappropriate, for people do not conduct public funeral services of mourning for those put to death by the government.

9. A.   There was the case in which Yohanan, the high priest, heard an echo come forth from the Most Holy Place, saying, "The young men who went out to war have won at Antioch."

B.   They wrote down that day and that hour, and that is how matters were: on that very day they had won their victory.

10. A.   There was the case in which Simeon the Righteous heard an echo come forth from the Most Holy Place, saying, "The action has been annulled that the enemy has planned to destroy the Temple, and Caius Caligula has been killed and his decrees annulled.

B.   This he heard in Aramaic.

11. A.   [Explaining the difference between the echo and the Holy Spirit or prophecy,] R. Hunia in the name of R. Reuben: "When the king is in town, people appeal to him and he acts.

B.   "If the king is not in town, his icon is there.

C.   "But the icon does not act in the way that the king can act."

12. A.   R. Yohanan and R. Samuel b. R. Nahman:

B.   R. Yohanan said, "'But the Lord will give you there a trembling heart' (Dt. 18:65):

C.   "When they went up from exile, trembling, having been given to them, went up with them."

D.   R. Samuel b. R. Nahman said, "There [in Babylonia] was trembling, but when they went up, they were healed."

13. A.   When R. Simeon b. Laqish saw them [Babylonians] swarming in the marketplace [in the Land of Israel], he would say to them, "Scatter yourselves."

B.   He would say to them, "When you went up, you did not come up as a wall [of people 1.G], now have you come to form a wall [of people]?"

14. A.   When R. Yohanan would see them, he would rebuke them, saying, "If a prophet can rebuke them, 'My God will cast them away, because they did not listen to him' (Hos. 9:17),

B.   "can I not rebuke them?"

15. A.   Said R. Abba b. R. Kahana, "If you have seen the benches in the Land of Israel filled with Babylonians, look forward for the coming of the Messiah.

B.   "How come? 'He has spread a net for my feet' (Lam. 1:13). [The word for net has consonants shared with the word for Persians, so, Simon, p. 317, n. 1, 'The presence of Babylonians (Persians) is a net to draw the Messiah.]"

16. A.   R. Simeon b. Yohai taught on Tannaite authority, "If you have seen a Persian horse tied up to gravestones in the Land of Israel, look forward to the footsteps of the Messiah.

B.   "How come? 'And this shall be peace: when the Assyrian shall come into our land, and when he shall tread in our palaces, then shall we raise against him seven shepherds and eight princes among men' (Mic. 5:4)."

17. A.   [Supply: "And this shall be peace: when the Assyrian shall come into our land, and when he shall tread in our palaces, then shall we raise against him seven shepherds:"]

B.   Who are the seven shepherds?

C.   David in the middle, to the right, Adam, Seth, and Methuselah; to the left, Abraham, Jacob, and Moses.

D.   Where is Isaac? He goes and takes a seat at the gate of Gehenna to deliver his descendants from the punishment of Gehenna.

E.   " and eight princes among men:"

F.   Who are the eight princes?

G.   Jesse, Saul, Samuel, Amos, Zephaniah, Hezekiah, Elijah, and the Messiah.

The final exposition reverts to the Exile in Babylonia, now with reference to the return to Zion, so Nos. 1, 3, with a minor interpolation at No. 2. The main point of the whole then cannot be missed. The history of Israel from Abraham to the Exile and back to the Land, encompassing also Israel in the Land after the destruction of the Second Temple, is brought into relationship, and, at the end, the resolution of the tension lies in Israel's access to continuing divine revelation through the echo. How this fits with the allegation that in the Second Temple there was no Holy Spirit is quite clear, and, in context, an effective statement: the Holy Spirit, Urim and Thummim, and other means of access to heaven have now been succeeded by the echo. That and one other consideration account, also, for tacking on the heavenly echo materials that follow. The other consideration is that Hillel came from Babylonia – so the materials available to our compilers believed – and, as is made explicit here, he was disciple of Ezra, in that he came from Babylonia to the Land of Israel and brought with him the Torah, just as Ezra had. So the inclusion is not an accident and not a mere secondary expansion for essentially agglutinative reasons; it is deliberate and further enriches the compilers' program and plan for this enormous and successful cogent statement of theirs.

112

Song of Songs Rabbah to Song of Songs 8:11

8:11   *Solomon had a vineyard at Baal hamon; he let out the vineyard to keepers; each one was to bring for its fruit a thousand pieces of silver.*

CXII:i

1. A.   "Solomon had a vineyard:"
    B.   This refers to Israel: "For the vineyard of the Lord of hosts is the house of Israel" (Isa. 5:7).
2. A.   "Solomon had:"
    B.   the king to whom peace belongs [the words for Solomon and peace sharing the same consonants].
3. A.   "at Baal hamon:"
    B.   The multitude of Baal [the word *hamon* means multitude, and Baal is the same],
    C.   for they swarmed after Baal: "And they served the Baalim and the Ashtarot" (Judges 10:6).
    D.   Therefore the swarms came against them.
4. A.   [Supply: "he let out the vineyard to keepers:"]
    B.   He appointed guards over them.
5. A.   "each one was to bring for its fruit a thousand pieces of silver:"
    B.   He brought a man against his fruit [Nebuchadnezzar],
    C.   and found therein a thousand righteous men, complete in their knowledge of Torah and good deeds.

The first reading applies the verse to Israel the people and the description of the verse as a metaphor for Israel's life. Now comes the Land.

CXII:ii

1. A.   Another interpretation of "Solomon had a vineyard:"
    B.   The vineyard is [the land of] Israel: "And I brought you into a land of fruitful fields" (Jer. 2:7), "a land which the Lord your God cares for" (Dt. 11:12).

C.   The king to whom peace belongs [the words for Solomon and peace sharing the same consonants].

2.   A.   "at Baal hamon:"

B.   For the multitudes of the kingdoms moaned for it [cf. Simon]: "I saw among the spoil a goodly Shinar mantle" (Josh. 7:21).

3.   A.   [Supply: ""I saw among the spoil a goodly Shinar mantle" (Josh. 7:21):]

B.   R. Hanin b. Isaac said, "It was Babylonian purple."

C.   And what was a Babylonian object doing there?

D.   R. Simeon b. Yohai taught on Tannaite authority, "He was king of Babylonia, and had bought in Jericho, and this one would send to that one dates, and that one would send to this one gifts."

E.   "That indicates that any king who did not have a captain [Simon: viceroy] in the Land of Israel did not regard himself as a king."

4.   A.   "he let out the vineyard to keepers:"

B.   This refers to Nebuchadnezzar.

5.   A.   "each one was to bring for its fruit a thousand pieces of silver:"

B.   He brought a man against his fruit and he picked from them a thousand righteous men, whole in the Torah and in good deeds: "And the craftsmen and the smiths a thousand" (2 Kgs. 24:16).

C.   A thousand of the one and a thousand of the other.

D.   But rabbis say, "This group and that group added up to a thousand."

The reading in terms of the land, not the people, of Israel, seems required by the prooftexts of No. 1, but, beyond that point, it is not entirely clear how the reading of the metaphor has changed very much on that account. The basic point seems firm, that the base verse refers to the disasters that came upon Israel in the time of the destruction of the first Temple.

CXII:iii

1.   A.   Another interpretation: "a vineyard:"

B.   This refers to the Sanhedrin.

2.   A.   For we have learned in the Mishnah:

B.   **Three matters did R. Ishmael state before sages in the vineyard in Yabneh and they accepted his view: [concerning a beaten-up egg which is put on top of vegetables which are in the status of heave offering, that it is deemed connected [to the vegetables]. But if it was set over them in the shape of a kind of a cap, it is not deemed connected. And concerning the tip of an ear of grain left standing after the reaping, with its head touching the standing grain – if it is reaped together with the standing grain, lo, it belongs to the householder. And if not, lo, it belongs to the poor. And concerning a small vegetable patch [surrounded by a wall] which is [made up] of trellised vines – if there is in the area a space sufficient for a grape gatherer with his basket on one side, and sufficient for a grape gatherer with his basket on the other side, it may be sown. And if not, it may not be sown] [M. Ed. 2:4].**

	C.	Now were they really in session in a vineyard!
	D.	But this refers to the Sanhedrin, which was arranged in rows like a vineyard.
3.	A.	"Solomon had:"
	B.	The king to whom peace belongs [the words for Solomon and peace sharing the same consonants].
4.	A.	"at Baal hamon:"
	B.	The multitude of Baal [the word *hamon* means multitude, and Baal is the same],
	C.	for they swarmed after Baal, therefore multitudes came against them, for multitudes of kings longed after them: "Kings of armies flee, they flee. [And the fair one in the house divides the spoil. Let them praise the name of the Lord, for his name alone is exalted; his glory is on earth and in heaven]" (Ps. 68:13).
5.	A.	[Supply: "Kings of armies flee, they flee" (Ps. 68:13):]
	B.	R. Yudan in the name of R. Oni: "What is written here is not 'angelic hosts' but 'kings' hosts,' meaning, the kings of the angels.
	C.	"[The sense then is, 'even Michael and even Gabriel fled, they fled.']"
6.	A.	[Supply: "Kings of armies flee, they flee" (Ps. 68:13):]
	B.	R. Yudan said, "The word 'they fled' means, they cast lots against them: 'And they have cast lots [a word that shares the same consonants] for my people' (Joel 3:3)."
7.	A.	[Supply: "Kings of armies flee, they flee" (Ps. 68:13):]
	B.	R. Judah b. R. Simon said, "They [Simon:] supported them when they went, and they supported them when they came back."
	C.	R. Ahvah son of R. Zeira said, "He made them race: 'Wherefore will you run, my son' (2 Sam. 18:22)."
8.	A.	[Supply: "And the fair one in the house divides the spoil" (Ps. 68:13):]
	B.	What is the meaning of the phrase, "And the fair one in the house divides the spoil"?
	C.	"the fair one in the house:" this is the Torah, "and you give it to him and he divides the spoil."
9.	A.	Another explanation of the phrase, "And the fair one in the house divides the spoil" (Ps. 68:13):
	B.	"You fairest in the house, you divide the spoil below."
	C.	"The fairest in the house" is Moses: "He is trusted in all my house" (Num. 12:7).
	D.	You give it to him and he divides it as spoil for all those who dwell below."
	E.	R. Phineas and R. Aha in the name of R. Alexander: "It is written, 'O Lord, our Lord, how glorious is your name in all the earth! whose majesty is rehearsed in the heavens' (Ps. 8:2)."
10.	A.	[Supply: "O Lord, our Lord, how glorious is your name in all the earth! whose majesty is rehearsed in the heavens" (Ps. 8:2):]
	B.	R. Joshua of Sikhnin in the name of R. Levi: "What is written here is not 'your majesty' but 'whose majesty is rehearsed,'
	C.	"your majesty is therein, your happiness is therein, it makes you happy that your Torah should be in heaven."

D.   "He said to them, 'No, the desire does not come from you [and it is none of your business].'"

11. A.   Said R. Yudan, "The matter may be compared to the case who had a son with stumped fingers. What did he do? He took him to a silkworker to teach him the craft. He began to look at his fingers. He said, 'The very essence of this craft is acquired only with the fingers. How is this one going to learn?'

B.   "Thus: 'No, the desire does not come from you [and it is none of your business].'

C.   "So when the Holy One, blessed be He, wanted to give the Torah to Israel, the ministering angels tried to intervene against Israel and to intervene before the Holy One, blessed be He, saying, 'Lord of the world, your majesty is therein, your happiness is therein, it makes you happy that your Torah should be in heaven.'

D.   "He said to them, 'No, the desire does not come from you [and it is none of your business].

E.   "'It is written therein, "And if a woman has an issue of her blood for many days" (Lev. 15:25). Now is there a woman in your midst? Thus: No, the desire does not come from you [and it is none of your business].

F.   "Further it is written therein, "When a man dies in a tent" (Num. 19:14). Now is there death among you? Thus: No, the desire does not come from you [and it is none of your business].'

G.   "That is why Scripture praises [Moses]: 'You have ascended on high, you have taken away your captive' (Ps. 68:19)."

12. A.   [Supply: "You have ascended on high, you have taken away your captive" (Ps. 68:19):]

B.   Said R. Aha, "This refers to the laws that apply to mortals,

C.   "for instance, the laws governing men and women who have suffered a flux, women in their menstrual period and after child birth.

D.   "Thus: 'No, the desire does not come from you [and it is none of your business].'"

13. A.   And rabbis say, "The matter may be compared to the case of a king who was marrying off his daughter outside of town.

B.   "The townsfolk said to him, 'Our lord, our king, it is praiseworthy and right that your daughter should be with you in town.'

C.   "He said to them, 'What difference does it make to you?'

D.   "They said to him, 'Perhaps tomorrow you may go to her and live with her and stay with her because of your love for her.'

E.   "He said to them, 'My daughter I shall marry off out of town, but I shall stay with you in town.'

F.   "Thus when the Holy One, blessed be He, was planning to give the Torah to the Israelites, the ministering angels said to the Holy One, blessed be He, 'Lord of the world, 'you are the one whose majesty is over heaven,' your happiness is therein, your glory and your praise is that your Torah should be in heaven.'

G.   "He said to them, 'What difference does it make to you?'

H.   "They said to him, "Perhaps tomorrow you will bring your Presence to rest among the creatures below.'

I.   "Said to them the Holy One, blessed be He, 'My Torah is what I am sending to the creatures below, but I shall continue to dwell among the creatures of the upper world.

J.   "'I shall give my daughter with her marriage settlement in another town, so she may be honored with her husband for her beauty and charm, for she is a princess, and they will honor her. But I shall dwell with you among the creatures of the upper world.'

K.   "And who made this matter explicit? It was Habakkuk: 'His glory covers the heavens and the earth is full of his praise' (Hab. 3:3)."

14. A.   R. Simon in the name of R. Joshua b. Levi said, "In every place in which the Holy One, blessed be He, brought his Torah to dwell, there he brought his Presence to dwell as well.

B.   "And who made this matter explicit? It was David: 'Let them praise the name of the Lord, for his name alone is exalted; his glory is on earth and in heaven' (Ps. 68:13) –

C.   "first 'on earth,' then 'in heaven.'"

Nos. 1-4 complete the exposition of the base verse, moving from the people to the Land to the Sanhedrin, a progression I have not seen before. The rather odd character of the whole is shown by the sustained exposition of the prooftext of No. 4. From that point forward, our problem of exposition of the base verse is simply forgotten. The reading that follows is not always clear, but the main point emerges without obscurity: the angels urged God not to give the Torah to Israel, but God gave it nonetheless. No. 5 then introduces the angels, and they are now the subject of the prooftext, Ps. 68:13. No. 5 identifies these as angels. I cannot say I grasp the point of Nos. 6-7, but No. 8 and No. 9 leave no doubt that under discussion is the angels' dealings concerning the Torah with Moses. No. 10 then makes the point that the angels argue God enjoys the presence of the Torah in heaven and should not give it up. Nos. 11 and 13 then spell out the message through parables, and these now are very effective in focusing the discussion on precisely what the authorship wishes to say. No. 14 then draws us back to our prooftext and brings the whole to a unifying conclusion. So while there are some passages that I cannot read in this context (or any other), the composite overall does hold together and register its point rather well, I would say because of the excellence of Nos. 11, 13, and 14. That the base verse has no clear relationship, thematic let alone propositional, to all of this hardly needs demonstration.

113

Song of Songs Rabbah to Song of Songs 8:12

8:12   *My vineyard, my very own, is for myself; you, O Solomon, may*
        have the thousand, and the keepers of the fruit two hundred.

CXIII:i

1.   A.   "My vineyard, my very own, is for myself:"

      B.   R. Hiyya taught on Tannaite authority, "The matter may be
            compared to the case of a king who was angry with his son and
            handed him over to his servant. What did he do? He began to
            beat him with a club. He said to him, 'Don't obey your father.'

      C.   "The son said to the servant, 'You big fool! The very reason that
            father handed me over to you was only because I was not listening
            to him, and you say, "Don't listen to father"!'

      D.   "So too, when sin had brought it about that the house of the
            sanctuary should be destroyed and Israel was sent into exile to
            Babylonia, Nebuchadnezzar said to them, 'Do not listen to the
            Torah of your father in heaven, but rather, "fall down and worship
            the image that I have made" (Dan. 3:15).'

      E.   "The Israelites said to him, 'You big fool! The very reason that the
            Holy One, blessed be He, has handed us over to you is because
            we were bowing down to an idol: "She saw...the images of the
            Chaldaeans portrayed with vermilion" (Ezek. 23:14), and yet you
            say to us, "fall down and worship the image that I have made"
            (Dan. 3:15). Woe to you!'

      F.   "It is at that moment that the Holy One, blessed be He, said, '"My
            vineyard, my very own, is for myself."'"

2.   A.   [Supply: "you, O Solomon, may have the thousand, and the
            keepers of the fruit two hundred:"]

      B.   Said before him that wicked man, "There were a thousand
            [righteous] and they are now cut down in numbers here and are
            only two hundred."

      C.   Said to him the Holy One, blessed be He, "Woe to that wicked
            man, rotten spit! There were a thousand and their numbers have
            increased here and they are now two thousand!"

3. A.   "you, O Solomon, may have the thousand:"

    B.   R. Hillel b. R. Samuel b. R. Nahman, "[If] the master takes a thousand, the disciple takes the fee for two hundred.

    C.   "How on the basis of Scripture do we know that fact? 'you, O Solomon, may have the thousand.'"

    D.   R. Alexandri said, "The master does not take a reward for his learning before he [Simon:] transmits it to others.

    E.   "How on the basis of Scripture do we know that fact? 'you, O Solomon, may have the thousand.'"

4. A.   R. Hiyya b. R. Ada of Jaffa said, "One who studies Torah with great difficulty takes a thousand, not with great difficulty takes two hundred as his reward. [If learning comes easily, the reward is less.]

    B.   "From whom do we know that fact? From the case of the tribe of Issachar and the tribe of Naphtali.

    C.   "The tribe of Naphtali, since they were engaged in studying the Torah with great difficulty, took as their reward a thousand: 'And of Naphtali a thousand captains' (1 Chr. 12:35).

    D.   "But the tribe of Issachar, because they learned the Torah not with great difficulty, took as their reward two hundred: 'The heads of them were two hundred, and all their brethren were at their command' (1 Chr. 12:33)."

    E.   R. Yudan in the name of R. Bun said, "One who studies Torah not in his own locale takes the reward of a thousand, but if it is in his own locale, he takes the reward of two hundred.

    F.   "From whom do we know that fact? From the case of the tribe of Issachar and the tribe of Naphtali.

    G.   "The tribe of Naphtali, since they were engaged in studying the Torah not in their own locale, took the reward of a thousand, 'And of Naphtali a thousand captains' (1 Chr. 12:35).

    H.   "But the tribe of Issachar, because they learned the Torah in their own locale, took as their reward two hundred: 'The heads of them were two hundred, and all their brethren were at their command' (1 Chr. 12:33)."

The parable reads "vineyard" to refer to Israel, God is the speaker, and the issue of the first clause is God's saying that the vineyard is God's, meaning, even though Israel has sinned, Israel remains loyal to God and learns obedience to God through its suffering. Then the parable bears the message, followed by the narrative restatement of the same proposition. Then God says our base verse, meaning, God knows now that his vineyard really does belong to him. That is a strong reading of our base verse and a fine articulation of the recurrent motif. No. 2 then continues No. 1. But of course No. 1 is complete without No. 2. Nos. 3-4 then leave the framework of the Song and read the verse quite autonomously, as a reference to Torah study in one way or another. This seems to me, of course, less successful and less important; in the present regard, our document serves as a compendium and a scrapbook, rather than as a coherent statement of a large-scale reading of the Song of Songs.

114

Song of Songs Rabbah to Song of Songs 8:13

8:13   *O you who dwell in the gardens, my companions are listening for your voice; let me hear it.*

CXIV:i

1. A. "O you who dwell in the gardens, my companions are listening for your voice; let me hear it:"

    B. R. Nathan in the name of R. Aha said, "The matter may be compared to the case of a king who got mad at his staff and imprisoned them. What did the king do? He took all his officers and staff and went to listen to what they were saying.

    C. "He heard that they were saying, 'Our lord, the king, is our praise, he is our life. May we never fail our lord, the king, forever.'

    D. "He said to them, 'My children, raise your voices so that the my companions who are near by you may hear.'

    E. "Thus even though the Israelites are occupied with their daily work all six days of creation, on the Sabbath day they get up early and come to the synagogue and recite the *Shema* and pass before the ark and proclaim the Torah and conclude with the words of the prophet.

    F. "And the Holy One, blessed be He, says to them, 'My children, raise your voices so that the my companions may hear.'

    G. "And companions can be only the ministering angels.

    H. "And pay heed that you not hate one another or envy one another or contend with one another or shame one another, so that the ministering angels may not say before me, 'Lord of the World, the Torah that you have given to the Israelites – they are not engaged by it, for lo, there are hatred, jealousy, enmity, and contentiousness among them.' But you keep it in peace."

    I. Bar Qappara said, "Why are the ministering angels called 'companions'?

    J. "It is because among them there are no traits of hatred, jealousy, enmity, or contentiousness, let alone strife and division."

2   A.   Another matter concerning the verse, "O you who dwell in the gardens, my companions are listening for your voice; let me hear it:"

     B.   When the Israelites go into the synagogues and recite the *Shema* with proper deliberation, in one voice, in one intention and thought, then the Holy One, blessed be He, says to them, "O you who dwell in the gardens, when you call my companions, I am listening for your voice; let me hear it."

     C.   But when the Israelites recite the *Shema* distractedly, this one hurrying it, the other dawdling, and are not one in intention and thought in reciting the Shema,

     D.   then the Holy Spirit cries aloud, saying, "'Make haste, my beloved, and be like a gazelle:' like the host on high [the words for host and gazelle share the same consonants], who [Simon:] pay homage to you with one voice and one chant,

     E.   "'upon the mountains of spices:' in the highest heavens above."

No. 1 continues working on the message that God delivers to Israel. The key now is "my companions," who are the angels. The angels then hear Israel praising God even while imprisoned, and the king tells them to pray in a loud voice. But at 1.Eff. the message broadens itself considerably, for the main point now is that the Israelites should attain social tranquillity. Still, the exposition remains quite close to the language at hand, as I-J indicate. No. 2 carries forward the same message in more or less the same way, except that now we move on to Song 8:14. Further readings of Song 8:13-14 are given in Chapter One Hundred and Fifteen.

115

Song of Songs Rabbah to Song of Songs 8:14

8:14 *Make haste, my beloved, and be like a gazelle or a young stag upon the mountains of spices.*

CXV:i

1. A. Another matter concerning the verse, "Make haste, my beloved, [and be like a gazelle or a young stag upon the mountains of spices]:"
   B. "Make haste my beloved:"
   C. From the exile in which we are located, soiled in sins.
2. A. "and be like a gazelle:"
   B. "make us clean like a gazelle."
3. A. "or a young stag:"
   B. "May you accept our prayer like an offering of kids and rams [the words for rams and stag using the same consonants].
4. A. "upon the mountains of spices:"
   B. "May a good fragrance [emanating from us] come to you by reason of the merit of our patriarchs, the fragrance of whom rises before you like spices."
5. A. [Supply: "upon the mountains of spices:"]
   B. This refers to the Garden of Eden, which is wholly made up of spices.
   C. Therefore it is said, "Upon mountains of spices."

The first reading of the verses of Song 8:13-14 dealt with Israel on the Sabbath. The second now carries us forward to the Temple cult, on the one side, and the counterpart in heaven, the Garden of Eden, on the other. We now proceed to a third reading of the whole.

CXV:ii

1. A. Another interpretation of the verses, "O you who dwell in the gardens, my companions [are listening for your voice; let me hear it. Make haste, my beloved, and be like a gazelle or a young stag upon the mountains of spices]:"

245

B.   R. Jeremiah in the name of R. Hiyya the Elder: "If two companions who are occupied with a matter of law and give way to one another in law, in their regard Scripture says, 'Then they who feared the Lord spoke with one another and the Lord hearkened and heard' (Ma. 3:16).

C.   "For the word 'spoke' bears the sense of concession: 'He subdues peoples under us' (Ps. 47:4).

D.   "Not only so, but if they should err [by excessive conciliation reaching the wrong decision,] the Holy One, blessed be He, makes up their error for them [and corrects it]: 'And the Lord hearkened and heard, and a book of remembrance was written before him, for those who feared the Lord and thought about his name' (Ma. 3:16).'

E.   "'...heard and a book of remembrance was written:' for he writes it on their heart, 'In their heart I will write it' (Jer. 31:33).

F.   "'...a book of remembrance...before him:' for he reminds them.

G.   "Whom? 'for those who feared the Lord and thought about his name.'"

2. A.   Said R. Yudan, "When the Israelites recite the Torah in groups, then, 'let me hear it.' But if not, then 'Make haste, my beloved.'"

B.   Said R. Zira, "When the Israelites recite the *Shema* in unison, in one voice, in one melody, then, 'let me hear it.' But if not, then 'Make haste, my beloved.'"

3. A.   "Make haste, my beloved:"

B.   Said R. Levi, "The matter may be compared to the case of a king who made a banquet and invited guests. Some of them ate and drank and said a blessing to the king, but some of them ate and drank and cursed the king.

C.   "The king realized it and considered making a public display at his banquet and disrupting it. But the matron [queen] came and defended them, saying to him, 'My lord, O king, instead of paying attention to those who ate and drank and cursed you, take note of those who ate and drank and blessed you and praised your name.'

D.   "So is the case with Israel: when they eat and drink and say a blessing and praise and adore the Holy One, blessed be He, he listens to their voice and is pleased. But when the nations of the world eat and drink and blaspheme and curse the Holy One, blessed be He, with their fornications of which they make mention, at that moment the Holy One, blessed be He, gives thought even to destroy his world.

E.   "But the Torah comes along and defends them, saying, 'Lord of the world, instead of taking note of these, who blaspheme and spite you, take note of Israel, your people, who bless and praise and adore your great name through the Torah and through song and praise.'

F.   "And the Holy Spirit cries out, '"Make haste, my beloved:" flee from the nations of the world and cleave to the Israelites.'"

4. A.   "and be like a gazelle:"

B.   Just as in the case of a gazelle, when it sleeps, it is with one eye open and one eye shut,

	C.	so when the Israelites carry out the will of the Holy One, blessed be He, he looks steadily upon them with both eyes open: "The eyes of the Lord are toward the righteous" (Ps. 34:16).
	D.	But when they do not carry out the will of the Holy One, blessed be He, he looks upon them with only one eye: "Behold the eye of the Lord is toward those who far him" (Ps. 33:18).
5.	A.	"upon the mountains of spices:"
	B.	Said R. Simon, "Said the Holy One, blessed be He, 'Wait for me until I sit in judgment on their mountains, who are their guardian angels, located with me in heaven: 'upon the mountains of spices.'"
	C.	Said R. Isaac, "The sense is [entirely literal, and not figurative,] in line with the following: 'Take you also the chief spices' (Ex. 30:23); 'with camels that bore spices and gold in quantity' (1 Kgs. 10:2)."
	D.	R. Hunia said in regard to that which R. Isaac [better: Simon] said [namely, that the reference of "spices" is to the nations of the world], "The Holy One, blessed be He, exacts a penalty from a nation below only after he casts down its guardian angels above.
	E.	"And he presents five verses of Scripture in support of that reading:
	F.	"'And it shall come to pass in that day that the Lord will punish the host of the high heaven on high' (Isa. 24:21) – first of all, and then, 'and the kings of the earth upon the earth' (Isa. 24:21).
	G.	"'How are you fallen from heaven, O day star, son of the morning' (Isa. 14:12), and then, 'how are you cut down to the ground' (Isa. 14:12).
	H.	"'For my sword has drunk its fill in heaven' (Isa. 34:5), and then, 'behold it shall come down upon Edom' (Isa. 34:5).
	I.	"'To bind their kings with chains' (Ps. 149:8), and then, 'and their nobles with fetters of iron' (Ps. 149:8), in which regard R. Tanhuma said, "'to bind their kings with chains" refers to the heavenly guardian angels.'
	J.	"'To execute upon them the judgment that is written' (Ps. 149:9), and then, 'he is the glory of all his saints, hallelujah' (Ps. 149:9)."
6.	A.	To four matters the redemption [reading *ge'ulatan* rather than *ge'utan*] of Israel is comparable:
	B.	harvest, vintaging, spices, and a woman in labor.
	C.	To a harvest, for if a field is harvested not at its right season, it does not produce even decent straw, but if it is harvested in its right season, then the entire crop is first class: "Put in the sickle, for the harvest is ripe" (Joel 3:13).
	D.	It is comparable to vintaging, for if the grapes of a vineyard are not harvested at the right time, they do not produce even good vinegar, but if it harvested at the right time, then even the vinegar is first rate: "Sing you of her, a vineyard of foaming wine" (Isa. 27:2), when it produces foaming wine, then pick the grapes.
	E.	It is comparable to spices, for when spices are picked when they are soft and moist, their fragrance does not give a scent, but when they are picked dry, then their fragrance gives a scent.
	F.	It is comparable to a woman in labor, for when a woman gives birth before term, the foetus cannot live, but when she gives birth

at term, the foetus can live: "Therefore he will give them up until the time that she who is in labor has brought forth" (Mic. 5:2).

7.   A.   R. Aha in the name of R. Joshua b. Levi said, "'I the Lord will hasten it in its time' (Isa. 60:22):

    B.   "if you have not attained merit, then 'in its time.'

    C.   "But if you have attained merit, then 'I will hasten it.'

    D.   "So may it be his will speedily in our days, Amen."

The final interpretation draws us to the importance of harmony within the community of Israel. The earlier readings have prepared us, of course, for this emphasis, and the whole then flows from the word "companions," which sets the key for the entire composite. No. 1 tells people not to argue too contentiously about right and wrong interpretations of the law, since God will correct the errors anyhow. No. 2 repeats the main point. No. 3 is parachuted down because of 3.F, that is, the citation of the base verse, but the cited passage is hardly critical to the composition, and the interest of the composite is not paramount here. This is simply available material. Nor do I see how Nos. 4, 5, 6 are compiled because of an interest in the cogent reading of the Song's verses at hand. They are tacked on not as "another matter," but simply as bearers of a proposition of an autonomous character, so it seems to me. The concluding entry, No. 7, provides an appropriate finish for the entire compilation.

Index

Brown Judaic Studies

Brown Studies on Jews and Their Societies

Brown Studies in Religion

DATE DUE

MAY 28 1994			
DEC 31 '98	OCT 27 200		
MAY 24 '00			
MAY 0 5 2006			

HIGHSMITH   #LO-45220